D0085860

JOHANNINE POLEMIC

SOCIETY
OF BIBLICAL
LITERATURE

DISSERTATION SERIES

William Baird, Editor

Number 67
JOHANNINE POLEMIC
The Role of Tradition and Theology

by
Rodney A. Whitacre

Rodney A. Whitacre

JOHANNINE POLEMIC
The Role of Tradition and Theology

Scholars Press
Chico, California

JOHANNINE POLEMIC
The Role of Tradition and Theology

Rodney A. Whitacre

Ph.D., 1980   Advisor:

University of Cambridge   M. D. Hooker

© 1982
Society of Biblical Literature

Library of Congress Cataloging in Publication Data
Whitacre, Rodney A.
  Johannine polemic.

  (Dissertation series / Society of Biblical Literature ; no.
67)(ISSN 0145-2770)
  Originally presented as the author's thesis (Ph.D.—
University of Cambridge, 1980)
        1. Bible. N.T. John—Criticism, interpretation, etc.
2. Bible. N.T. John, 1st—Criticism, interpretation, etc.
I. Title. II. Series: Dissertation series (Society of Biblical
Literature) ; no. 67.
BS2615.2.W48 1982   226'.506   82-5457
ISBN 0-89130-579-3   AACR2

Printed in the United States of America

LIBRARY
ALMA COLLEGE
ALMA, MICHIGAN

CONTENTS

PREFACE

This dissertation is the result of my own work and includes nothing which is the outcome of work done in collaboration. The Greek New Testament used is the 26th ed. of Nestle-Aland (Stuttgart: Deutsche Bibelstiftung, 1979) and the English translation used is the Revised Standard Version. After the first citation works are referred to by a short title, which is indicated by underlining in the first citation. Most subtitles and all bibliographical details except dates are included only in the bibliography.

I am very pleased to record my thanks to the Hort Fund in the University of Cambridge, to the Purvis Fund of Corpus Christi College, and to the Mullegan Memorial Fund of Westside United Protestant Church, Richland, Washington for generous financial help. I have benefited greatly from the resources of Tyndale House, Cambridge, both the works consulted there and the people met. I am very greatful to Mr. R. T. McClelland and Prof. J. Wilson for proofreading the body of the dissertation. I am greatly indebted to Dr. William Horbury, Dean of Chapel at Corpus Christi College, for his friendship, his example, his advice and his willingness to read the present study in its final stages. My debt is particularly great to my supervisor, Prof. M. D. Hooker, who by her direction, patience and encouragement has provided not only very valuable help during the writing of this dissertation but also an example to follow.

Without the help, financial and otherwise, of my parents, Mr. and Mrs. C. E. Whitacre and my parents-in-law, Prof. and Mrs. W. N. Kerr, this research would not have been possible; my gratitude is inexpressible. My wife, Margaret, and my children, Seth and Chad, have provided what one of my professors has called "islands of reality" amidst my theological studies; to them my debt and gratitude is greatest.

Finally, I wish to express my appreciation for the author(s) of these writings I have spent the last few years studying, known to the Church as St. John the Theologian. Before beginning the

ix

present study I had little appreciation for the johannine
writings, but during the course of my study my attitude changed
greatly.

Εὐαγγελιστὰ 'Ιωάννη, ἰσάγγελε Παρθένε, θεολόγε θεο-
δίδακτε, ὀρθοδόξως τῷ κόσμῳ, τὴν ἄχραντον πλευράν,
τὸ αἷμα καὶ τὸ ὕδωρ βλύζουσαν ἐκήρυξας, ἐν ᾧ τὴν
αἰώνιον ζωήν, ποριζόμεθα ταῖς ψυχαῖς ἡμῶν.

MHNAION ΣΕΠΤΕΜΒΡΙΟΣ ΚΣΤ'

Shed upon your Church, O Lord, the brightness of your
light, that we, being illumined by the teachings of
your apostle and evangelist John, may so walk in the
light of your truth, that at length we may attain to
the fullness of eternal life; through Jesus Christ our
Lord, who lives and reigns with you and the Holy
Spirit, one God, for ever and ever. *Amen.*

The Book of Common Prayer
(U.S.A.)

AB   Anchor Bible

AnBib   Analecta biblica

Antijudaismus   *Antijudaismus im Neuen Testament? Exegetische
                und systematische Beiträge*, eds. W. P. Eckert,
                N. P. Levinson, and M. Stöhr, Abhandlungen zum
                christlich-jüdischen Dialog 2 (Munich: Kaiser,
                1967).

APOT   *Apocrypha and Pseudepigrapha of the Old Testament*,
                ed. R. H. Charles

ATANT   Abhandlungen zur Theologie des Alten und Neuen
                Testaments

ATR   *Anglican Theological Review*

BAGD   W. Bauer, *A Greek-English Lexicon of the New
                Testament and Other Early Christian Literature*,
                tr. and adapt. W. F. Arndt, F. W. Gingrich, and
                F. W. Danker (Chicago: University of Chicago
                Press, 1979).

BBB   Bonner biblische Beiträge

BDF   F. Blass, A. Debrunner, *A Greek Grammar of the
                New Testament and Other Early Christian Litera-
                ture*, ed. and tr. R. W. Funk (Chicago: University
                of Chicago Press, 1961).

BETL   Bibliotheca Ephemeridum Theologicarum Lovaniensium

BETS   *Bulletin of the Evangelical Theological Society*

BEvT   Beiträge zur evangelischen Theologie

Bib   *Biblica*

BJRL   *Bulletin of the John Rylands Library*

BNTC   Black New Testament Commentary

BS   *Bibliotheca Sacra*

BSt   Biblische Studien

BT   *The Bible Translator*

BTB   *Biblical Theology Bulletin*

BVC	*Bible et vie chrétienne*
BZ	*Biblische Zeitschrift*
BZAW	Beihefte zur *Zeitschrift für die alttestamentliche Wissenschaft*
BZNW	Beihefte zur *Zeitschrift für die neutestamentliche Wissenschaft*
CBQ	*Catholic Biblical Quarterly*
CJG-RC	*Christianity, Judaism and Other Greco-Roman Cults. Studies for Morton Smith at Sixty,* ed. J. Neusner 4 Vols. (Leiden: Brill, 1977)
ComJn	*A Companion to John. Readings in Johannine Theology (John's Gospel and Epistles),* ed. M. J. Taylor, (New York: Alba House, 1977)
DNTT	*The New International Dictionary of New Testament Theology,* ed. C. Brown, 3 Vols. (Exeter: Paternoster, 1975-1978)
DowR	*Downside Review*
EBib	Études biblique
EstBib	*Estudios bíblicos*
EvJean	*L'Évangile de Jean. Sources, rédaction, théologie,* ed. M. de Jonge, BETL 44 (Gembloux: Duculot, 1977)
EvQ	*Evangelical Quarterly*
EvT	*Evangelische Theologie*
ExpT	*Expository Times*
HNT	Handbuch zum Neuen Testament
HTKNT	Herders theologischer Kommentar zum Neuen Testament
HTR	*Harvard Theological Review*
ICC	International Critical Commentary
IDB	*Interpreter's Dictionary of the Bible,* ed. G. A. Buttrick
Int	*Interpretation*
JAAR	*Journal of the American Academy of Religion*

JBL	*Journal of Biblical Literature*
JQ	*John and Qumran*, ed. J. H. Charlesworth (London: Chapman, 1972)
JR	*Journal of Religion*
JSJ	*Journal for the Study of Judaism*
JTS	*Journal of Theological Studies*
Jud	*Judaica*
MNTC	Moffatt New Testament Commentary
MTZ	*Münchener theologische Zeitschrift*
NICNT	New International Commentary on the New Testament
NovT	*Novum Testamentum*
NovTSup	*Novum Testamentum*, Supplements
NRT	*La nouvelle revue théologique*
NTAbh	Neutestamentliche Abhandlungen
NTS	*New Testament Studies*
NTSMS	*New Testament Studies* Monograph Series
RB	*Revue biblique*
RevExp	*Review and Expositor*
RGG	*Religion in Geschichte und Gegenwart*, 3d ed.
RQ	*Revue de Qumran*
RSR	*Recherches de science religieuse*
SBLDS	Society of Biblical Literature Dissertation Series
SBT	Studies in Biblical Theology
SE	*Studia evangelica*, ed. F. L. Cross, et al.
SJT	*Scottish Journal of Theology*
ST	*Studia theologica*
StANT	Studien zum Alten und Neuen Testament

StBib   *Studia Biblica 1978. II. Papers in the Gospels,*
ed. E. A. Livingstone, Journal for the Study of
the New Testament Supplement Series 2 (Sheffield:
JSOT, 1980)

St-B   H. Strack, P. Billerbeck, *Kommentar zum Neuen
Testament aus Talmud und Midrash,* 4 Vols. (Munich:
Beck, 1922-1928)

StJn   *Studies in John Presented to Professor Dr. J. N.
Sevenster on the Occasion of his Seventieth Birth-
day,* NovTSup 24 (Leiden: Brill, 1970)

TBT   *The Bible Today*

TDNT   *Theological Dictionary of the New Testament,* eds.
G. Kittel, G. Friedrich, 10 Vols. (Grand Rapids:
Eerdmans, 1964-1976)

Text   *Text and Interpretation. Studies in the New
Testament presented to Matthew Black,* eds. E.
Best, R. McL. Wilson (Cambridge: University Press,
1979)

TLZ   *Theologische Literaturzeitung*

TNTS   J. A. T. Robinson, *Twelve New Testament Studies,*
SBT 34 (London: SCM, 1962)

TS   *Theological Studies*

TZ   *Theologische Zeitschrift*

WMANT   Wissenschaftliche Monographien zum Alten und
Neuen Testament

ZKT   *Zeitschrift für katholische Theologie*

ZNW   *Zeitschrift für die neutestamentliche Wissenschaft*

ZRGG   *Zeitschrift für Religions- und Geistesgeschichte*

ZTK   *Zeitschrift für Theologie und Kirche*

ZWT   *Zeitschrift für wissenschaftliche Theologie*

1. INTRODUCTION

A. The Topic

The first Christian century may have been a period of relative peace and stability for the Roman Empire but it was certainly not such for the newborn Christian Church. Most documents
in the NT are explicitly concerned with controversy, or at least
reflect indirectly the existence of controversy. There are controversies both between Christians and those outside the Church
who reject the gospel, especially the Jews, as well as within the
Church among Christians themselves. From the evidence of the NT
it seems that the period in which the NT was written was marked
by great confusion, with conflicts both inside and outside the
Church between various individuals and groups who claimed to
speak for God.

Amidst such conflicting claims how was a person to know whom
to believe? Many of the writings in the NT stress the importance
of distinguishing truth from error, but what criteria are offered
for doing so? How did these authors of the NT go about convincing their readers that their views were right and those of
their opponents were wrong? These are the questions with which
the present study is concerned. It is impossible for present
purposes to examine the whole NT with these questions in mind,[1]
so I have chosen to limit the discussion to the polemic found
in the Gospel and First Letter of Saint John. A comparison
of the polemic of these two documents is particularly interesting
for they are universally recognized as being very closely related to one another; if they are not by the same person then
they are at least from the same school or milieu.[2] But while
their thought and language are so similar, it appears that the
controversies they address are very different. I will argue that
the Gospel is primarily concerned with the threat posed by Jewish
opponents outside the community while in the Letter the author
opposes former members of the community who consider themselves
to be Christians. Despite such differences in the opponents,

1

however, I will suggest that the arguments in the two documents
share certain fundamental features in common. In particular,
underlying the arguments in both documents there is an appeal to
the religious traditions held in common with the opponents. In
John this tradition consists in those sources that were authoritative for Hellenistic Judaism, especially the OT, and in 1
John the tradition is the teaching of the Johannine community as
it is represented in the Gospel. More significantly, it will be
suggested that this common principle of appeal to tradition is
used in both documents to refer to the same key criterion for
distinguishing truth from error, namely, an appeal to theology
proper, the understanding of God. The central argument in both
documents is theological and in both documents it is the same
view of God which is said to deny the opponents' positions, even
though these positions are so very different.

B. The Organization of the Study

     I will first study the documents separately and then com-
pare them. The first chapter is devoted to the Gospel and the
second to the Letter. In each of these chapters I will present
a hypothesis for the life-setting and purpose of the document,
and analyze the polemic on the basis of these hypotheses. In
the final chapter I will compare the two documents, first evaluating the differences scholars have noted between them and then
drawing attention to further differences highlighted by the present study. I will conclude by drawing attention to the fundamental similarity of the polemic in John and 1 John.

C. Major Assumptions

     In this study I am concerned with the two documents as we
have them and I am assuming that the Gospel as we have it was
written prior to the Letter as we have it. Such an approach is
taken by a recent major study of Johannine Christianity, and has
there proved its fruitfulness.[3] But objections to such a study
could be raised, especially by those who believe that certain
parts of the Gospel come from the same period as the Letter.
G. Richter, for example, holds that an anti-docetic element is
incorporated into the Gospel from the time of the Letter.[4]

Brown objects to Richter's reading into the Gospel a struggle
that is clearly present only in the Letters (*Community*, 176).
My own objection is even more fundamental for I will argue below
(pp. 126-130) that neither document is clearly concerned with
Docetism and thus Richter's position is without weight. As
Brown's objection suggests, such theories are not based on explicit concerns in the texts and thus are open to the charge of
being subjective and arbitrary. The same can be said of efforts
to distinguish redactional elements within the Letter itself.
As W. G. Kümmel has said after a review of such redactional
theories, "the distinction on the ground of stylistic peculiar-
ities cannot be convincingly presented."[5] The same is true of
matters of content as well (ibid. 439-440) so Kümmel can conclude, "It must be regarded as probable, therefore, that I John
in the form we have it is the work of a single author" (ibid.
440). Thus, both theories of redaction within the Letter and
theories of interpolation into the Gospel of elements from the
period of the Letter do not seem sufficiently reliable for use
in the interpretation of John and 1 John.

Another objection to my assumption would come from those
who believe that the Letter is prior to the Gospel. Few scholars, however, actually hold this view (see ibid. 445), and there
are many features of the texts which are difficult to reconcile
with this view. For example, the love command is called καινή
in the Gospel (13.34), but it is called both καινή and παλαιά
in the Letter (2.7-8). This introduction of παλαιά suggests
the Letter comes from some time after the Gospel.

My decision to study the documents as we have them is not
a denial that the process of composition of both John and 1 John
may well have been extremely complex. The present study, however, is not intended as a contribution to the on-going and perhaps ultimately impossible task of disentangling the various
sources and redactions.[6] Rather, I want to ask what meaning
the texts may have had when they finally attained the form in
which we have them. Such studies as the present one have some
indirect bearing on the source and redaction discussions in that
if sense can be made of the text as it stands then at least some
source and redaction studies are called into question. While it

is not my purpose to draw out such implications it might be noted
that to approach the material in the way in which I propose does
lead to a very different view of the author(s) and his purpose
than is usually the result of studies looking for sources and
redactions. Instead of assuming that in John and 1 John we have
a jumble of sources in conflict with one another, I am assuming
that the author(s) wanted all these supposedly disparate elements
in his Gospel and Letter because he believed that they were all
necessary for an adequate presentation of what he intended to
say. On this assumption there emerges the picture of an au-
thor(s) who can hold very diverse views together either without
tension or in tension. His thought is not so much contradictory
as it is ambiguous.[7] An important aspect of the hypothesis I
am following in this study is that it is precisely this ambiguous
diversity that causes trouble in his community and necessitates
the writing of the Letter, for there are some in the community
who seem to have taken the ambiguous Johannine traditions and
focused them in a gnostic direction.[8] The Letter is here viewed
as an attempt to refocus the tradition more in accord with the
Christianity of the apostolic churches. This general hypothesis
is becoming somewhat popular[9] and has recently had a very thorough presentation by Brown in *Community*. Concerning Brown's reconstruction of the life and thought of the community prior to
the Gospel I have a number of reservations,[10] but this general
view of the relationship between the Gospel and the Letter I
find most suggestive for the interpretation of both.

Thus, the following study tries to make sense of the polemic
in John and 1 John on the basis of a working hypothesis which
understands the primary conflict in the Gospel to be with those
outside the Christian community, the Jews, and in the Letter
with a problem that later arose from within the community.
Each of the next two chapters will present a more detailed description of the opposition reflected and provide an analysis of
the polemic against these opponents.

2. JOHANNINE POLEMIC: THE GOSPEL

A. Life-Setting and Purpose: The Context of the Polemic

1. *Introduction*

The central theme of John's Gospel is the presentation of Jesus as the revelation of God. Such a general statement could also be applied to 1 John, and I will develop this idea in the next chapter. But while both John and 1 John seek to present Jesus as the revelation of God, they do so in very different ways and for different purposes. They have different purposes because, as I will try to demonstrate in this chapter and the next, the Gospel and the Letter are addressed to two very different situations in the life of the Johannine community. That they develop their common theme in different ways is evident from their difference in genre. Whether 1 John be considered a letter, a sermon, or a tractate,[11] it is certainly very different from the Gospel, which is essentially a story.

The plot of this story centers on the conflict between Jesus and his Jewish opponents. This conflict is already suggested in the Prologue through the use of the abstract symbolism of light versus darkness (1.5). The opponents are mentioned immediately after the Prologue (1.19) and the first twelve chapters depict the growing tension as Jesus provokes his opponents and they in turn become increasingly hostile and violent. There is something of an interlude during the Farewell Discourse in chs. 13-17, though even in this section the conflict that Jesus experiences is brought into relation with that which his disciples will experience in the future (15.18-16.4). With chs. 18-19 there is a return to the story's plot. Here the conflict comes to a climax as the opponents finally bring about Jesus' death. Even after this climax, however, the conflict is not entirely left behind. Already in the story of the resurrection the persecution predicted in the Farewell Discourse is beginning to take place (20. 19). The prediction of Peter's martyrdom (21.18-19) also presupposes a conflict, though the author draws no connection

5

between Peter's martyrdom and the Jewish opposition described
in the rest of the Gospel.

This introductory survey indicates that conflict is an all-
pervasive theme in John's Gospel, but why is this so? The author
is ostensibly telling the story of Jesus, but he is not simply
trying to give an objective account of certain historical events;
he is writing for faith (20.31). Who, then, is he writing for
and how does he expect this story to meet their needs?

2. *Life-Setting*

It is the Farewell Discourse that gives the clearest hint
concerning the situation of the readers. In this section of the
Gospel Jesus is speaking to his disciples of their relationship
with him and the Father and of their relations with one another.
The keynote of these chapters is comfort and assurance. This
comfort is necessary in the face of two coming difficulties.
The first is that caused by Jesus' death. The disciples are
here prepared for the sorrow they will experience at Jesus' death
(14.1-3, 28-29; 16.16-22) and for the change which his death
will bring about in their relationship with him. To prepare
them for this change in their relationship is one of the functions of the material concerning the παράκλητος (14.15-26; 15.
26; 16.7-15). Jesus assures them that after his death they
will be related to him more closely than before, for they will
be ἐν him (14.20; 15.4-7; 17.23; cf. 6.56).

Comfort is necessary, secondly, because of the persecutions
the disciples themselves will later experience (15.18-16.4a).
For the present study it is of the greatest significance that we
here find a connection *explicitly* drawn between what Jesus suffered and what his disciples will suffer (15.18-21). The author
consciously intends that his readers find parallels between the
conflicts they are experiencing and those which Jesus experienced.[12] This explicit parallel legitimates the search for the
function which the polemic portrayed in the story may have
served for the author's audience.

But it is only possible to detect such a function if we
have a sufficiently clear idea of the nature of the conflict the
readers are experiencing. If there were no clear hints

concerning this conflict then we would be doomed to the subjective arbitrariness that mars so many hypotheses concerning the
situation and purpose of John.[13] I believe, however, that the
reference here in the Farewell Discourse to being put out of the
Synagogue (ἀποσυνάγωγον ποιεῖν) clearly indicates that the conflict is between Christians and their Jewish opponents. This
reference in 16.2 to ἀποσυνάγωγον ποιεῖν (cf. 9.22; 12.42) is the
clearest indication in John of the situation facing the author
and his readers, and as such it provides the best starting point
for constructing a working hypothesis of the Gospel's life-
setting.

The references to ἀποσυνάγωγον ποιεῖν points to a crisis in
the relationship between Christians and the Synagogue. Up to
this point Christians have been able to remain in the Synagogue,
but now they are forced to withdraw. There even seem to have
been some Christians who suffered death from their Jewish opponents (16.2). J. L. Martyn, among many others, has argued that
this crisis is to be identified with the institution of the
birkath ha-minim in about AD 85.[14] Working from this identification[15] he has developed a picture of the life-setting of John
that has been summarized as follows:

> What he unearths is the likelihood that the Christians
> of the evangelist's day of his locale were subjected
> to open conflict and continuing dialogue with the synagogue
> and that members of the synagogue(s) were required to
> undergo an examination of their faithfulness in the face
> of growing apostasy in the favor of [*sic*.] the Christian
> community. The critic finds reason to believe that
> these persons were required to recite the "Benediction
> Against Heretics" (the *Birkat-ha-minim*) which had been
> revised to encompass (perhaps only by implication) those
> who adhered to the Christian faith. Moreover, the ex-
> pression "excluded from the synagogue" (*aposynagōgos*,
> 9:22; 12:42; 16:2) refers to the experience of Jewish
> Christians being expelled from their synagogue home due
> to their alliance with the Christians (Kysar, *Evangelist*,
> 149-150).

While certain aspects of Martyn's work have been questioned, his
general hypothesis has found wide acceptance.[16] At least on
this question of the particular historical crisis behind John
his view does seem the most probable. A serious challenge, however, comes from those who question whether the *birkath ha-minim*
did indeed refer, during the first century, to Christians. For
some, such as S. Sandmel[17] and E. Schürer,[18] the textual problems

involved in the *birkath ha-minim* counsel caution in affirming
that it explicitly referred to Christians at the first.   Others,
such as P. Schäfer,[19] seem to have even stronger reservations.
After showing that the textual variations indicate that a variety of heretical groups were in view, Schäfer concludes:[20]

> *Eine* dieser Gruppen war, vielleicht schon in Jabne,
> vielleicht aber auch erst später (dies lässt sich
> kaum noch entscheiden), die Gruppe der *nôtzerîm*
> (Judenchristen). . . . . Mit Sicherheit richtete sich
> die *birkat ham-mînîm* jedenfalls nicht ausschliesslich
> gegen Judenchristen bzw. (später) Christen und war
> deswegen auch kein "Mittel zur völligen Scheidung der
> beiden Religionen." Eine solche Festlegung verkennt
> einmal, dass es sich bei der Einführung der *birkat
> ham-mînîm* zweifellos primär um einen innerjüdischen
> Vorgang handelt und überschätzt zum anderen die Bedeutung
> der christlichen Religion für das Judentum Palästinas
> um die Wende des 1. zum 2. nachchristlichen Jahr-
> hundert.

Schäfer may be correct in saying that the *birkath ha-minim* was
not aimed exclusively at Jewish Christians.[21] But it is difficult to see how this point indicates that it would not have
brought about a separation within the Synagogue between Jewish
Christians and other Jews. It seems, on the contrary, that the
polarization which this addition to the liturgy brought about
was a very significant step toward the creation of differences
large enough to enable one to speak of two separate religions.
Up to this point the problem would have been an intra-Jewish
problem, so that Schäfer's point that "es sich bei der Ein-
führung der *birkat ham-mînîm* zweifellos primär um einen inner-
jüdischen Vorgang handelt" can be accepted, but not the conclusion he draws from it. John is written to speak to the very
point of separation, the formation of two separate religions.
But both the Christians and their Jewish opponents still view
it as a Jewish problem.[22] Schäfer's other point, that the significance of Christianity for Palestinian Judaism is overstated,
is also unacceptable in the light of texts from the Tannaitic
period (e.g. *Sanhedrin* 43a) which clearly reflect Jewish hostility toward Jesus.[23] The Church Fathers also, beginning already with Justin Martyr (e.g. *Dialogue with Trypho* 16.4), not
only reflect hostility but even seem to refer to the *birkath
ha-minim* when they discuss Jewish persecution of Christians.[24]
Furthermore, the NT in general reflects the bitter conflict between Christians and their Jewish opponents, conflicts both

between Jews and Christians still within the Synagogue and
between the Church and Synagogue as two distinct communities.
So the Christian material definitely suggests that the *birkath
ha-minim* was directed against Christians, and the Jewish material
reflects hostility between the two groups. Along with the majority of scholars, therefore, I think it most likely that the
birkath ha-minim referred, at least in part, to Christians.

Another challenge to this identification of ἀποσυνάγωγον
ποιεῖν with the *birkath ha-minim* questions whether the conflict
reflected in John could not have occurred at some period before
the formulation of the *birkath ha-minim*.[25] As W. Doskocil has
noted, the reference in John may be to an earlier stage in the
hostilities which then later resulted in the excommunication.[26]
In agreement with Doskocil, I have found nothing in John that
unquestionably points to the *birkath ha-minim*. Presumably it is
possible that the conflict we find reflected in John is limited
to one particular community and, if so, there are no overwhelming
reasons why this conflict in a particular location could not
have arisen in the middle of the first century rather than at
its end.[27] However, while I do not think the majority view among
scholars is indisputable, I do think it the most probable.
There are two considerations in particular that make me think
the conflict reflected in John is probably not that of an isolated community near the middle of the century. First, it is
unlikely that the various Christian communities were so isolated
that such a conflict could be merely a local phenomenon.[28] It is
possible that there were some such isolated communities, but the
cosmopolitan nature of the author's thought does not make his
community a likely candidate.[29] Second, and more important, the
general character of the author's thought points to a later rather
than an earlier date. Not that any particular idea or image is
so "advanced" that it must reflect a later date.[30] Rather, the
variety of the images and the way they are so tightly interwoven
is evidence of a period of reflection. It is impossible to say
that it must have taken, say, sixty years rather than thirty for
the author's thought to develop as it has. But I think the later
date is more likely. So despite these difficulties I accept
that the most likely historical situation reflected in John is

the separation of Christians from the Synagogue at the institution of the *birkath ha-minim* late in the first Christian century.[31]

3. *Purpose*

From this working hypothesis concerning the life-setting
of the Gospel I draw certain conclusions about the purpose of
John. The Gospel is addressed to people experiencing persecution for their Christianity from Jewish opponents. They have
been forced to separate from the Synagogue. Since, according
to the author, they did not leave voluntarily, it seems that, up
to this crisis brought on by the *birkath ha-minim,* they have
viewed themselves as Jews. "It never occurred to those Jews
who joined the Jesus-movement that they must abandon the faith
of the fathers."[32] But now the mother community has rejected
them and thereby severely challenged their identity as Jewish
followers of the Jewish Messiah. The significance of this crisis lies in the fact that it has forced the Christians to change
both their self-understanding and their understanding of Judaism.
Therefore, I believe one of the author's primary purposes in
writing this Gospel is to interpret this division that has taken
place. He is concerned first and foremost with comforting and
assuring his Christian readers in their new identity, separated
from the Synagogue. He seeks to accomplish this task in two
interrelated ways. Positively, he assures his readers by establishing their identity as children of God. It is they who worship the Jewish God in spirit and truth for they have the
παράκλητος and they indwell Jesus, the Son who perfectly reveals
the Father. This establishing of their identity is particularly
evident in the Farewell Discourse, but is not lacking elsewhere,
as will be made evident below. But if Christians are worshiping
the Jewish God what does that say about the identity of their
Jewish opponents? The negative side of the author's presentation is his depiction of the Jewish opponents as children of the
devil. In rejecting Jesus, the Jewish opponents reject the God
of Judaism. The author, then, wants to "fortify" his Christian
readers "in their faith by showing them what they could reply
to objections raised by the Jews outside the Church."[33] This

denial of the opponents' claims is an aspect of his assurance of
his readers. How the author actually presents his case is the
subject of this chapter. But before turning to the story itself, a more detailed description must be given of the Johannine
Christians and their Jewish opponents, and some consideration
given to how these characters in the story are related to the
different groups caught up in the crisis in the author's own
day. In looking more closely at the depiction of the Christians
and their opponents I will give further details of how the author
attempts to achieve his purpose. In this way the scene will be
set for a study of the polemic itself.

4. The Johannine Christians and Their Opponents

a. The Johannine Christians

1) Jewish and Gentile

Since the Johannine Christians have been excommunicated from
the Synagogue it seems obvious that they are of Jewish origin.
More controversial is the assertion that some of them are also
of non-Jewish origin.[34] It is difficult to believe, however,
that any Jew would be in need of the "footnotes" the author provides when he translates ῥαββί (1.38) and Μεσσίας (1.41).[35]
Furthermore, the most natural interpretation of 7.35 and 12.20
is that Ἕλληνες refers to "Greeks who are interested in the
culture and religion of Judaism," i.e. proselytes (Barrett,
Judaism, 18). It is most likely that the Johannine Christians
were a mixed group of people from Jewish and non-Jewish backgrounds. But if one of the author's primary purposes in writing
is to interpret the Christians' expulsion from the Synagogue and
to forge an identity for them apart from the Synagogue, what
relevance would this have for non-Jews? It would seem that the
need for such a reworked identity would be as necessary for non-
Jewish Christians as it would for Jewish Christians. Christianity was obviously a form of Judaism. Judging from the importance
of antiquity in the Greco-Roman world,[36] Gentiles as well as
Jews would be interested in knowing what continuity Christianity
had with Judaism.[37] Proselytes may have been particularly concerned over the relation between Christianity and Judaism since

their adherence to Judaism had cost them dearly already. Sevenster says that to become a proselyte meant an isolation from
one's surroundings, a break with family and friends (*Roots,*
200): "they had to prepare themselves against the ridicule,
hatred and contempt aimed against the separateness of the Jews
that were now about to be turned equally against them, for now
they had become part of that *sceleratissima gens*" (ibid. 218).
Having paid dearly for their Judaism they would not be likely to
give it up easily. By the same token, the author's case in the
Gospel would be particularly attractive to them since they could
retain Judaism without its less attractive aspects, such as
circumcision. Thus, the author's assurance would be of value to
both the Jewish and the non-Jewish members of the community.

2) *Disciples at Second Hand*

Equally significant is another characteristic they seem to
share, whatever their background. A considerable portion of
the author's audience seems to be upset because they are, as
P. S. Minear says, "disciples at second hand."[38] That is,
Minear notes passages that "reflect a contrast between two
groups - those who had been present in the events narrated and
those who had not" ("Audience," 343). A clear reference to those
groups is found in 17.20, but the recognition of this distinction can be very helpful in the interpretation of more obscure
passages as well. For example, the "other sheep" of 10.16 could
refer to "the disciples at second hand, whose place in a united
flock is here assured to be the will and work of this self-
sacrificing shepherd" (ibid. 348). There is much discussion on
whether these "other sheep" are Gentiles or Jewish Christians
in synagogues in the Diaspora, but the text itself does not
speak explicitly in such terms. So it is possible that the
reference is more general,[39] i.e. that it speaks to a more general problem often encountered by second-generation believers
rather than to the question of Gentile converts or a mission to
the Diaspora. Minear argues convincingly that these disciples
at second hand were in need of "reassurance because their distance in time and space from Jesus created difficulties"
(ibid. 345). He offers a number of suggestions as to the nature

of these difficulties (ibid. 345-350), including the observation
that "it is almost certain that in John's day the hostility of
the synagogues was undermining the courage and poise of John's
readers" (ibid. 350). So the Johannine Christians have not only
experienced expulsion from the Synagogue, but also at least some
of them seem to feel separated from their own community's past
as well.

   To those who are experiencing such extreme isolation the
author speaks of the παράκλητος whom Jesus has sent. The author
shows his readers that Jesus has provided for them and even
prayed for them (17.20). As great as Jesus' works were, the
later disciples will experience even greater things (14.12). As
fortunate as the first followers of Jesus were, it is those who
have not seen and yet believe who are blessed (20.29). These
first followers are themselves mediators of Christ's presence
(13.20, cf. Minear, "Audience," 348-349), but their experience
of God is not qualitatively different from that of later disciples. While they were privileged to be with Jesus, nevertheless, before Jesus' death and resurrection and the giving of the
Spirit they were marked by weakness and lack of understanding
(cf. ibid. 350). But after the resurrection they understood
(cf. 2.22) and such understanding is promised to the later
disciples (14.26; 16.13-15). Thus the faith of the first followers was dependent on the Spirit in the same way as that of
all later disciples. And the quality of relationship is the
same because when the Spirit comes he indwells the believer (14.
17). The Spirit declares the things of Jesus to the disciples
and glorifies Jesus (16.13-15). Indeed the disciples experience
the glory of God as they indwell the Father and the Son (17.20-
26). This close relationship to God is what is significant, not
one's distance from the pre-resurrection Jesus. In this way,
then, the author seeks to assure his readers in their feeling of
isolation that they are actually intimately united to God and
one another. They are not forsaken in their suffering (cf. 15.
18). The παράκλητος plays an important role in assuring the
author's readers of their relationship with God.

   The Spirit's assurance comes not only by establishing the
Christians' identity as those who know God, but also through

judgment, the negative side of the argument. In ch. 16 the
Spirit is described as both comforting and judging (16.8-11).
The object of the judgment mentioned in these verses is the world
(16.8). The term ὁ κόσμος is used in John in negative, neutral,
and positive ways.[40] This pattern of usage is also found for
the term 'Ιουδαῖος (see Wiefel, "Die Scheidung," 223-224), to
be discussed later in this chapter. In the Farewell Discourse
there is an interesting fluctuation between the general term
ὁ κόσμος (e.g. 15.18; 16.8) and a reference specifically to
Jewish opponents (16.2). The possibility that different sources
are reflected in these different texts cannot be ruled out, but
as the text now stands they function together to depict the opposition. The reference to the Jewish opposition is the more
literal description while the reference to ὁ κόσμος sets the
conflict in the context of a dualistic struggle. Bultmann in
particular has not done justice to the relation of the κόσμος
motif to the life-setting of John.[41] He rightly draws attention
to the parallel between ὁ κόσμος in 1.10 and τὰ ἴδια, οἱ ἴδιοι
in 1.11, but his conclusion that τὰ ἴδια, οἱ ἴδιοι cannot refer
to Israel or the Jewish people is not acceptable (John, 56, 86-
87). His conclusion is based on his dehistoricizing of the
conflict in John, making the historical figures merely representative of a more mythological, cosmic conflict. There need be
no doubt that the author's use of his well known dualistic symbolism includes the notion of a cosmic conflict. But this cosmic aspect of the author's thought is his interpretation of specific historical conflicts in the life of Jesus and the Johannine
community.[42] It is these conflicts which, for the author, have
revealed the Jews as ὁ κόσμος in the negative sense, i.e. as
that "which stands over against God and confronts him with
hostility" (Bultmann, John, 54): "For the fourth gospel as we
know it in its final form, the Jewish opposition to Jesus does
not only represent the enmity of 'the world', it also symbolises
that the Jews as a group, that is the Synagogue, has, through
its denial, fallen into 'the world.'"[43] And it is the Jewish
opposition as ὁ κόσμος in this sense which is judged by the
Spirit in 16.8-11. "The judgment consists in the world's sinful
nature being exposed by the revelation that continues to take

place in the community" (Bultmann, *John*, 562). That is, in "the
Church's witness to Jesus. . . . shall all men discover who it
was that sinned, who is truly justified before God, and who it
is that was judged. In this spiritual sense the preaching of
the Church will always be directed against those who do not believe, and thus against the tenets of the Synagogue" (Baum, *Jews*,
130-131). This Gospel itself is an example of this work of the
Spirit, and the content of this "preaching" or "revelation" is
to be studied later in this chapter. The further question remains, however, of whether ὁ κόσμος refers also to opposition
other than that from the Jewish opponents. There are no explicit
references in John to other sources of opposition comparable to
the references to ἀποσυνάγωγον ποιεῖν, but this only makes the
matter obscure. It may well be that the use of ὁ κόσμος has a
wider reference because it was precisely the excommunication
from the Synagogue that took away Christianity's protective cov-
ering and opened it to harassment.[44] This wider opposition may
be in view in John but the term ὁ κόσμος does not indicate itself a wider reference, having as it did a negative use among
Christians before the separation of the Church and the Synagogue.[45] Since there are no clear references to opposition which
comes from anyone but the Jewish opponents, it is with this opposition that I concern myself in this dissertation, without thereby implying necessarily that other sources of opposition were
entirely lacking.

In summary, then, the Johannine Christians are second generation Christians from both Jewish and Gentile backgrounds.
The author is seeking to assure them of their knowledge of the
true God. He appeals in particular to their own experience of
the Spirit. This same appeal to the Spirit is also used as an
attack on the opponents; the Spirit judges the unbelieving world.

Before looking in more detail at the depiction of this unbelieving world it is worthwhile to examine the authority of the
author for making such claims. If these troubled Christians
who have been severed from the Synagogue and are perhaps feeling
isolated from their own Christian history are going to believe
the author's assessment of their identity and that of the Judaism
that has rejected them, he must have some authority in their

eyes to validate these proposed monumental changes in their
understanding.

3) The Author's Need of Legitimation

The author's authority, at least at some point in the community's life, must have been insecure because later disciples
add notes attesting to his trustworthiness (19.35; 21.24). There
is widespread recognition among scholars that there is concern
in John to defend the author's authority, but there is less
agreement on the identity of that which it is defended against.
The most popular theory is to find reflected in the Gospel a
conflict between Christians who consider Peter their leader and
those who look back to the Beloved Disciple. One of the more
significant representatives of this approach, R. E. Brown, finds
seven different groups of believers and non-believers in the
Gospel (*Community*, 59). One of these groups he labels "the
Christians of Apostolic Churches" (ibid. 81) and says that "they
are represented by Peter and other members of the Twelve"
(ibid.). Brown finds in John a "consistent and deliberate contrast between Peter and the Beloved Disciple" (*Community*, 82),
which means "the Johannine community is symbolically counter-
posing itself over against the kinds of churches that venerate
Peter and the Twelve" (ibid. 83). The Johannine community looks
upon these "Apostolic Christians" favorably but believes "they
do not reach the heights of the Johannine understanding of Jesus"
(ibid. 84), in particular, they are missing "the perception of
the pre-existence of Jesus and of his origins from above"
(ibid. 85). But even if, for the sake of argument, one accepts
that Peter and those of the Twelve mentioned in John represent
"Apostolic Christians," the point of difference between them and
the Johannine Christians cannot be christology, for John presents
one of the Twelve as making a confession of high christology.
Brown recognizes the difficulty raised by Thomas' confession,
but has an explanation: "In fact, Thomas' delayed confession of
Jesus as 'My Lord and my God' may be paradigmatic of the fuller
understanding of Jesus' divinity to which, John hopes, the
Apostolic Christians may ultimately be brought" (ibid.). But
the more natural reading would interpret this confession as an

acknowledgment by the Johannine Christians of the high christology which they already share with the Apostolic Christians. This
alternative interpretation to that of Brown would yield a picture
closer to that found by R. Schnackenburg. He has argued that
there is a contrast drawn between Peter and the Beloved Disciple,
but it does not involve rivalry or opposition ("Origin," 240).
Rather, in John "the leading role of Simon Peter was acknowledged
(cf. 1:42; 6:68f; 21:15ff), the traditions about Peter accepted
without polemic (cf. his attack with the sword, the denial), and
his martyr's death for Jesus highlighted (13:36; 21:18f)" (ibid.).
He finds instead of rivalry that "Peter's undisputed authority
served to enhance the reputation of this disciple" (ibid.).[46] I
find Schnackenburg's assessment more convincing than Brown's,
but I find less satisfactory his proposals for the purpose of
this motif. He posits that this association helped "to counter
among their own ranks the teachers of a false Christology and
overcome perhaps other ideologies too: so they were also struggling for their recognition within the Church at large" (Schnackenburg, "Origin," 240-241). There is no explicit reference in
the Gospel to such false christologies so it is questionable
whether there were such differences in view. Furthermore, while
such an attempt to seek recognition within the Church at large
is possible, this use of representative figures seems a very awk-
ward way to go about it. Unless, of course, the recognition to
be gained is not *in the eyes* of the larger Church but *through*
the larger Church, in the eyes of members of the Johannine community itself. While I do not rule out entirely these other
possible concerns, it is this last possibility that is of most
interest for my own working hypothesis. This possible attempt
at legitimation would correspond to the needs of the second generation Christians already mentioned.

     In John the Beloved Disciple is obviously the community's
teacher and authority (cf. 21.24), and it seems that this motif
of the Beloved Disciple itself may be a major means of legitimation. For the Beloved Disciple has special knowledge of those
points that it will be argued below are of crucial importance
in the author's argument. These crucial points have been well
summarized by de Jonge:[47]

As Jesus' most intimate disciple and eye-witness he is
allowed to know by whom Jesus will be betrayed
(xiii.13-21) and to understand the meaning of the empty
tomb (xx.2-10). He witnesses Jesus' suffering and death
and because he saw blood and water coming out of Jesus'
side he is able to state beyond doubt that Jesus died a
real death.

Thus the Beloved Disciple has insight into both Jesus and his
betrayer. His insight concerning Jesus centers on his knowledge
that Jesus really died and his understanding of the resurrection.
That is, in Johannine language, he understands Jesus' glorification through which the Father is revealed. It is this glorification and revelation that lies at the center of the truth of Jesus
over against the falsehood of those who reject him, and to demonstrate this aspect of Johannine thought is the principal concern later in this chapter. But note that the Beloved Disciple
also knows who will betray Jesus. This could imply special insight concerning Jesus' enemies. Thus the Beloved Disciple seems
to be credited with special knowledge that would enable him to
present both the positive and the negative sides of the case by
which the author wishes to reassure his readers, for he can both
testify to the truth and identify error. In this sense he shares
in the Holy Spirit's functions of comforting and judging. In
writing his Gospel he is himself the prime example of the Spirit
leading into all truth, teaching all things and bringing to
remembrance what Jesus said (cf. 14.26).[48]

The anonymity of the Beloved Disciple may also contribute
to his authority. For in John "Jesus does not belong to that
class of people who advertise themselves as such, . . . but
others discover his exceptional quality."[49] Perhaps this humility, because he shares it with Jesus, may function to legitimate
the author's authority. The nature of the evidence for this view,
as for that mentioned above that the Beloved Disciple's relation
to Peter serves to legitimate the author's authority, allows
these interpretations to be nothing more than interesting specu-
lations that fit within the larger picture. However, on the
general point that the teaching regarding the Holy Spirit and
the motif of the Beloved Disciple serve to legitimate the author's
authority in the eyes of his Christian readers, there should be
less doubt. On the basis of this authority he seeks to assure

his readers by identifying who is of God and who is not. Before examining the polemic I will describe more of the other two
groups involved along with the Christians.

b. *Jewish Christians*

The primary audience of the Gospel is an ethnically mixed
group of second generation Christians who have been excommunicated
from the Synagogue. In addition to these Christians who have
been excommunicated many scholars find reference to Jewish Christians who have not been excommunicated and who have "conservative
attachment to the Jewish national tradition."[50] "John 12:42-43
supplies the clearest reference to a group of Jews who were attracted to Jesus so they could be said to believe in him, but
were afraid to confess their faith publicly lest they be expelled
from the synagogue" (Brown, *Community*, 71). The story of the
blind man (Jn. 9) tells of one who is willing to be excommunicated for Jesus' sake (9.22,34), in contrast to these others who,
"like 'the Jews,' . . . had chosen to be known as disciples of
Moses rather than as disciples of 'that fellow' (9.28)" (ibid.
72). Such Jewish Christians may also be referred to at 8.31
where there is mentioned "the Jews who had believed in him."[51]
They believed in him but then sought to kill him because his
word found no place in them (8.37). For such people the author's
defense of Christianity would be an encouragement to leave the
Synagogue (Brown, *John*, lxxv). It is not impossible that some
of them had already left the Synagogue and then returned again.[52]
In speaking comfort and judgment the author seems concerned to
prevent such a return (cf. 16.1).[53] So, whether the author is
seeking to encourage Christians to leave the Synagogue and/or
not return, "seen from the standpoint of the Johannine group
and its theology there is no real difference between sympathizing
Jews and Jewish Christians if the latter are still thinking along
what the Fourth Gospel considers to be purely Jewish lines"
(de Jonge, "Expectations," 266). Perhaps this explains why he
refers to these Christians as οἱ Ἰουδαῖοι, the term he most often uses to refer to the Jewish opponents. By referring to
these Christians in this way the author would be showing them
the significance of their position. They think they are

Christians but they show themselves to be siding with those who
reject Jesus and his disciples.

c. *The Opponents*

The author's depiction of the Jewish opponents presents
fascinating problems. It has just been noted that the term most
often used for these opponents, οἱ 'Ιουδαῖοι, can sometimes refer to Christians. Actually, there are a number of ways in which
'Ιουδαῖος is used in John. It is an equivocal term, designating
"1) the opponents of Jesus; 2) the 'common' people or 'crowd'
(ὁ ὄχλος); 3) the Jewish people as opposed to the Gentiles;
4) the contemporaries of Jesus with their customs and practices;
5) Judeans."[54] This imprecision is found also in the author's
description of the Jewish opposition generally. The other terms
used for the opponents are οἱ Φαρισαῖοι, οἱ ἀρχιερεῖς, and οἱ
ἄρχοντες. Of these terms, οἱ ἄρχοντες is the most imprecise.
Apart from the phrase ὁ ἄρχων τοῦ κόσμου (τούτου) (12.31; 14.30;
16.11), it is used four times. In 7.26 οἱ ἄρχοντες is used in
a very general sense and seems equivalent to οἱ 'Ιουδαῖοι, which
occurs in the same context (7.1-25). They may be distinguished
here from οἱ Φαρισαῖοι (cf. 7.32) and, in any case, such a distinction is explicit in 7.48 when the Pharisees say "Have any
of the authorities or of the Pharisees believed in him?" The
answer implied is, of course, negative, but later it is said
"Nevertheless many even of the authorities believed in him, but
for fear of the Pharisees they did not confess it, lest they
should be put out of the synagogue" (12.42). This implies that
the Pharisees are at the core of the opposition. But once again
the author does not present a simple blanket accusation, for the
Pharisee Nicodemus, called an ἄρχων τῶν 'Ιουδαίων (3.2), is
anything but hostile towards Jesus. The Pharisees themselves
are later said to be divided over Jesus (9.16).

So it seems the Pharisees are the key element in the opposition, but they are joined by other leaders as well. This
group of other leaders is composed, at least in part, of οἱ
ἀρχιερεῖς. This identification is confirmed by the frequent
description of οἱ Φαρισαῖοι and οἱ ἀρχιερεῖς working together
(7.32,45; 11.47,57; 18.3), although the final condemnation of

Jesus was accomplished by the chief priests alone (18.35; 19.6,
15,21). This combination of terms is confusing in that, histor-
ically, one could be both a Pharisee and a chief priest (see
Martyn, *History*, 84, cf. Bowman, *Jews*, 41). So it seems that
the term οἱ Φαρισαῖοι is particularly important for the author,
which is not surprising if it is they who are behind the excommunication of Christians from the Synagogue.

This central place of the Pharisees in the author's portrayal
of the opposition to Jesus may also explain in part why οἱ
Φαρισαῖοι is sometimes used interchangeably with the more frequent general term οἱ Ἰουδαῖοι. That is, οἱ Ἰουδαῖοι is often
a general term for the opposition, but the Pharisees are at the
center of it. This interchanging of terms, evident especially
in 1.19-28 and 9.13-23, adds to the imprecision of the author's
depiction.[55]

From a comparison with the Synoptic Gospels it is apparent
that the author's description is not only imprecise but also
rather simplified. He makes no reference to the scribes, the
elders, the Sadducees or the Herodians; he seems willing to represent the complex reactions to Jesus with a few general terms.
But such an impression on the basis of the terms used could be
misleading. Despite the evident simplification in John and the
author's well known dualism, nevertheless he describes at least
as fully as the Synoptics the divisions caused by Jesus (cf. 6.
52; 7.12,43; 9.16; 10.19). So the simplification of terms does
not indicate a reduction of the various responses to stark dualistic contrasts. That is, while his imprecision and simplification give the impression that "the only division among the
Jews that John recognizes is that between those who believed in
Jesus and those who reject him" (Rivkin, *Revolution*, 100), nevertheless, this division cuts across all groups within Judaism as
the author depicts it.

But what is the significance of this imprecision and simplification? Brown seems to be on the right track when he suggests that

> the evangelist . . . never goes into detail about the
> various groups in Palestine (even the tax collectors
> and the Herodians have disappeared in John) because,
> by the time this Gospel was written, these groups were

no longer so meaningful. The Judaism that survived
the destruction of the Temple was of strongly Pharisaic
persuasion, and for a Gospel written with this situation
in mind 'Pharisees' and 'Jews' would be the most
meaningful titles for the Jewish authorities (*John*, 44,
cf. Barrett, *John*, 174).

The simplification of terms may well reflect the polemical situation.[56] With the destruction of the Temple, Judaism had to
modify its self-understanding. There were military and political
threats, but "more was at stake than military success and political independence. The latter was actually lost, but Judaism
lived on. The real danger lay in the loss of religious independence, the possibility that Judaism would simply assimilate itself to other religions; in this regard Christianity posed the
gravest threat."[57] Christianity seems to have had some attrac-
tion to Hellenistic Jews (see Barrett, "Judaizers," 241-242; Kysar, *Evangelist*, 150) and this called forth a tightening of the
boundaries, the best example of which was the institution of the
birkath ha-minim. Such a defense seemed necessary because important elements in the Jewish community's identity and its continuity with the past, such as the recognition of the Torah as
the revelation of God, the Sabbath, and circumcision (see Wiefel,
"Die Scheidung," 215), appeared to be threatened by Christianity.
Above all it was the Jewish view of God that seemed threatened.
For, though the Jews knew that God was revealed in the world,
nevertheless, "no nation, person, or event could provide anything
more than a partial and imperfect revelation of God" (Lowry,
"Syndrome," 225). But Christianity "held nothing less than that
God *had been* fully and perfectly revealed, in the person of Jesus
the Christ." Indeed, "Christianity considered that Jesus *was*
God, the Deity incarnate, the Word made flesh. A more un-Judaic
conception of the One God could hardly be conceived" (ibid.).
Lowry's formulation of the problem can be very misleading. If
he means full and perfect knowledge of God in his essence, then
Lowry misrepresents Christianity. If he means a full and perfect
revelation of God, then this is what Christians do believe of
Jesus, but it is also what Jews believe of the Torah. Indeed,
full knowledge of God was expected in the Messianic Age,[58] a
hope Christians find fulfilled in Jesus. While Lowry's description of the problem is unsatisfactory he has, nevertheless,

pinpointed the central issue at stake in the Johannine polemic
with the Jewish opponents. It will become evident below that
the key point at issue is indeed the nature and revelation of
God.

Thus, the Synagogue had come to the conclusion that Christianity had developed into something that was incompatible with
Judaism (see Lowry, "Syndrome," 224). But the same was true from
the other side as well. Judaism was also developing, making new
claims for the Law and its authority (see Bowman, *Jews*, 31) and
in the process it was rejecting Jesus and his followers.[59]

> In the eyes of John, then, a radical change had taken
> place. While Jewish religion once knew and loved the
> true God, the Synagogue had turned into a school of
> ignorance. They no longer held the truth, they gave
> voice to falsehood. In the words of Jesus, the
> evangelist tells the men of the Synagogue: you no
> longer know God (cf 7:28, 8:19). Since they have re-
> jected him who was sent, they do not love or honour the
> Father now (cf 5:23,42). The Jews have become part of
> 'the world'. They have never heard the voice nor seen
> the face of the God of the covenant (5:37).

So the author believes it is Judaism that is at fault due to this
change. In his eyes it is also the Jewish opponents who force
an either-or, that is, it is they who draw sharp boundaries between Judaism and Christianity. The author then repays in kind
with a different either-or: one is either from above/ἐκ τοῦ
θεοῦ or from below/ἐκ τοῦ διαβόλου (see Martyn, "Glimpses," 169).
But the author is involved in polemic and obviously does not present an objective picture. It is clear that developments in
both Judaism and Christianity contributed to the crisis:

> The choice, at a certain stage in the development of the
> Johannine groups, has been forced: in or out [of the
> Synagogue]. It has, moreover, been forced from both
> sides. From the Jewish side, the Christian development
> of the 'envoy of God' notion has reached the point of
> blasphemy, and anyone who makes that kind of claim
> about Jesus has to be expelled. From the Christian side,
> to remain in the synagogue now means to remain 'in the
> world,' in its hostility toward God and his messenger
> (Meeks, "Agent," 59).

The crisis comes when the traditional Jewish exclusivism comes
in conflict with the exclusivism of Christianity:[60]

> The exclusivist claims of the two groups are the nub of
> the controversies of the New Testament age. If one of
> the two was the only true religion, then the other was
> necessarily false. . . . The controversy was not genteel,
> and the partisans were not generous or sympathetic. This
> was the case whether the differences embroiled Jew
> against Jew, or Christian against Christian. How much
> the more when Jew and Christian were pitted against each
> other (Sandmel, *Anti-Semitism*, 127).

It is this context of jealousy, resentment, bitterness and frus-
tration which best explains the negative use of the term οἱ
'Ιουδαῖοι in John (cf. Lowry, "Syndrome," 221-223; Sandmel, *Anti-
Semitism*, 119). It may well be an example of the sort of name-
calling that mocks that which the opponent holds dearest.[61] It
is "Judaism" that is most important to these opponents and causes
them to reject Jesus, so the author uses the term 'Ιουδαῖος
tauntingly. But as already noted, he also uses the term in a
variety of other ways as well. The significance of this variety
is well expressed by Pancaro:

> Jn naturally tends to respect the distinction 'orthodox'
> Jews make between themselves and Jewish-Christians,
> especially since this very circumstance has forced him
> and his community to take the opposite stand and to
> affirm that they are the true heirs of the Mosaic
> tradition. Jn respects the distinction *as a fact*,
> but *in principle* he is not ready to concede that only
> 'orthodox' Jews can be called Jews. This determines
> the ambiguous usage of 'Ιουδαῖος in the Fourth Gospel.
> The term is used in a 'neutral' or 'positive' sense
> to designate the ethnic group to whom Jn and his com-
> munity still feel bound. On the other hand, 'Ιουδαῖος
> *tends* to become identified with the religious-national
> community constituted by 'normative' Judaism (the
> Synagogue) and is therefore also used in a 'negative'
> sense which is specifically Johannine (*Law*, 295).

The author's exclusivism was such that it did not mean a rejection of Judaism until after official Judaism had closed the door
on the Christians. The Gospel comes from the period in which
polarization had reached the point where confession of Jesus en-
tailed denial of official Judaism.

5. *The Crisis*

Thus the very imprecision in the terms used to describe the
opponents indicates something of the nature of the crisis. It
was a time of great confusion with different voices speaking

for God and yet disowning one another. For official Judaism,
Christianity had gone beyond the pale and had to be recognized
as having done so, while "for Christianity, anti-Judaism was not
merely a defense against attack, but an intrinsic need of Christian self-affirmation. Anti-Judaism is a part of Christian exegesis."[62] I believe one of the primary purposes of the author
of the Gospel is to provide such an exegesis. He does so by
telling the story of Jesus, showing how he also was accused by
Jewish opponents of rejecting the Jewish religion. The author
uses the traditions he holds in common with his Jewish opponents
to argue that, far from denying Judaism, Jesus is actually the
revelation par excellence of the Jewish God. As will emerge
from the study that follows, in the author's eyes the difference
between Christians and their Jewish opponents is that they worship different Gods, for in rejecting Jesus the Jews have rejected their own God.

B. The Polemic

1. *Introduction*

Faced with the need to reassure his Christian readers that
they are the children of God, the author presents a two-sided
defense, both attacking his opponents' self-understanding and
seeking to establish that of his readers. As the author presents it, his opponents' self-understanding has two foci:
loyalty to Moses and the Torah, and the view that they are children of Abraham and children of God. These two elements are so
interrelated as to be inseparable, but for the sake of analysis
it is helpful to distinguish them. I will look first at the issue of loyalty to Moses and the Torah. The author both denies
their claim that they are loyal to Moses and also shows how Moses
and the Scripture actually testify to Jesus.

2. *Polemic Against the Opponents' Claim to Be Loyal to Moses and the Torah*

a. *The Opponents' Claim*

1) *Explicit Texts*

In the first direct confrontation in the Gospel the opponents condemn Jesus for breaking the Sabbath (5.16) and blaspheming (5.18). Implicit in these charges is an appeal to the Torah. This concern for the Torah is explicitly stated in the ensuing controversy: "You search the scriptures, because you think that in them you have eternal life; and it is they that bear witness to me" (5.39).[63] Later it is said that Moses, on whom they set their hopes, wrote about Jesus (5.45-47). Thus, these texts in this first controversy state explicitly that the opponents consider themselves to be loyal to Moses and the Torah. Already it is evident that their condemnation of Jesus is based on this loyalty.[64]

In the other explicit assertion of loyalty, the Torah is not actually mentioned but it seems at least included in the opponents' description of Moses as one to whom God has spoken (9.29).[65] Furthermore, as in ch. 5, once again the context is a conflict over breaking the Sabbath (9.14,16) and the attendant issue of Jesus' identity, now expressed in terms of whether he is from God or is a sinner (9.24-34). This story depicts the sharp break between the disciples of Jesus and their Jewish opponents who identify themselves as "disciples of Moses" (9.28) (cf. Barrett, *John*, 362-363). The opponents' boast is in their certainty. They are sure that God spoke to Moses, but they do not even know where Jesus is from. This matter of Jesus' origin will be looked at more closely below (pp. 31-32). For now the important point is their appeal to Moses as a way of rejecting Jesus. They believe that in order to be loyal to Moses and the Scriptures they must oppose Jesus, for in their eyes he clearly stands condemned by the Law. The nature of the opponents' identity explicitly stated in these texts can be described in more detail by noting how they put into practice their claim of loyalty to the Torah and the implicit claim to religious authority this entails.

2) Passages Illustrating the Opponents' Claim

The hostility between Jesus and his opponents does not emerge
until ch. 5, but already in the opening chapters the self-understanding of the opponents which underlies the later controversy
is evident. Starting with various hints it gradually becomes
clear that the opponents view themselves as having the means
and the authority for evaluating religious activity, in particular, messianic claims.

In Jn. 1.19-28 the Jewish opponents question John the Baptist concerning his own identity and authority for baptizing.
Since those who question the Baptist are functionaries sent from
Jerusalem (Barrett, *John*, 172), the impression is given of the
central authorities investigating certain questionable activity.
The implication, in the light of texts such as Dt. 13 (discussed
below p. 30), is that the Jewish opponents consider themselves
in possession of some sort of authority. This authority may ex-
tend to matters of purification, as is mentioned later in 3.25.
But whether or not this is the case, the primary concern is obviously with the messianic overtones of the Baptist's activity.
In the eyes of the opponents, the Baptist's baptism implies
that he is an eschatological figure (1.25). Whatever notions of
authority on the part of the opponents are implied in this story,
it at least shows that the author depicts them as considering
themselves capable of determining the validity of messianic
claims.

Something of the same attitude seems present in the next
appearance of the opponents (2.13-22). As the Baptist's activity
implies that he has a certain identity, so Jesus' clearing of
the Temple also has such an implication in that it probably has
messianic overtones (Brown, *John*, 123). Many scholars view the
clearing of the Temple as a controversy between Jesus and the
Jews. For example, Gutbrod says that in "their eyes He seems
to reject the temple. For them the temple is the place of
God's presence. Hence their opposition arises from their essential Jewishness, from their attachment to the temple, 2:18,20"
("'Ισραήλ," 378). This incident indicates that the cult has an
important place in the opponents' self-understanding, but there
is no evidence that "in their eyes He seemed to reject the

temple." Their response to his action is a question, "What sign
have you to show us for doing this?" (2.18). They do not challenge the action itself, charging him with seeking to destroy
the Temple, since there is, after all, OT precedent for what he
did (see Brown, *John*, 121-122). Rather, they questioned *his*
authority for performing this action, since it had messianic
overtones. It is not the opponents but rather Jesus who mentions
destroying the Temple: "Destroy this temple, and in three days
I will raise it up" (2.19). This verse functions on two levels.
Brown suggests that it was "originally an eschatological proclamation referring to the Jerusalem Temple and would have been un-
derstandable as such to those who knew the OT background" (*John*,
123). In the context the opponents do take it as a reference to
the Jerusalem Temple (2.20), but the reference is said to be
actually to Jesus' body (2.21). Thus, Jesus' body is seen as
the Temple, the locus of true worship; he purifies the worship
(cf. 4.21-24). On neither level, however, is Jesus claiming to
destroy the Temple, nor is he charged with doing so. There is
no opposition in this passage, only questioning. In the author's
thought, Jesus has replaced the Temple, but this is not the same
as rejecting it. On the contrary, Jesus' statement that it is
"my Father's house" (2.16) and the quote from Ps. 69.9 (Jn. 2.
17) imply a positive view of the Temple; it is God's house and
Jesus is zealous for it. The idea of Jesus' *replacement* of the
Temple is raised in 2.19, but the opponents do not understand.
So while Jesus and his opponents are not yet in open conflict,
nevertheless the stage is being prepared for it. The opponents'
question in 2.18 implies that they think they are capable of
evaluating such claims to authority.

     This attitude, more or less implied in these first two
stories, becomes more explicit in the next section, the visit of
Nicodemus (3.1-21). He is introduced as a representative of the
Jews (3.1). Up to this point they have been depicted as questioning John the Baptist and Jesus concerning their authority
and thus Nicodemus seems to give their verdict on Jesus when he
says, "Rabbi, we know that you are a teacher come from God; for
no one can do these signs that you do, unless God is with him"
(3.2). So the "teacher of Israel" (3.10), who represents the

Jews, assumes the authority to grant recognition to others as
teachers "come from God" (3.2). Once again we have a hint of
the opponents' claim to religious authority. In this way we
are introduced in these early chapters to a major element in the
portrait of the opponents painted by the author of the Gospel.
This claim to authority comes to the fore later in their confrontation with Jesus. It becomes evident from their accusations
against Jesus that they believe they can judge religious claims
because they possess the Torah. So we come to an examination of
their exercise of this presumed authority.[66]

With ch. 5 there comes a shift in the opponents' attitude
toward Jesus. Instead of simple questioning, and even a favorable
opinion (3.2), there is now antagonism. They persecute Jesus
because he has broken the Sabbath (5.10,16) and blasphemes, making
himself equal with God (5.18). As we have seen, in this first
confrontation the rejection of Jesus is based on an understanding
of the Law. These same two charges occur elsewhere in the Gospel (Sabbath-breaking: 7.21-23; 9.16, blasphemy: 10.33; 19.7) and
to these is added the accusation that Jesus bears witness to himself (8.13).[67] Thus, every explicit dispute in John makes reference to Moses and/or the Law.[68] These three charges are all
based on particular laws in the Torah. To these charges are
added further charges that are not based on particular laws but
are, nevertheless, based on the Torah.

The first of these charges is that of being a deceiver (7.
12,47). This charge is presented as a general opinion of some
of the crowd and is not attached to any particular aspect of
Jesus' activity or teaching. From the context, the most likely
source of such a charge is Jesus' healing on the Sabbath (7.21-
23), which, in turn, involves the question of his identity (7.
26).[69] In this charge of being a deceiver the issue of the Law
is raised, for the word group πλανᾶν, κτλ. in the Jewish context
signifies departure from the revealed will of God, the Law.[70]
Indeed, this charge is latent in their observation that Jesus
never studied (7.15) (cf. Bultmann, *John*, 273 n.3).

In particular, this charge seems to represent an accusation
of being a false prophet.[71] The charge of being a false prophet
could rest on two possible accusations. According to Dt. 18.22

a prophet is false if his prophecies do not come true. This
charge against Jesus is not made explicitly in John, although
the emphasis on Jesus' words being fulfilled (e.g. 18.9,32, ἵνα
πληρωθῇ) may reflect such a charge. However, the other possible
accusation, based on Dt. 13, is more significant. Already in
the Tannaitic period (cf. e.g. *Sanhedrin* 43a) Dt. 13 is applied
to Christ in connection with a technical charge of being a deceiver,[72] and such a technical charge may well be in view in
John also.[73] According to Dt. 13.1-11 a prophet who teaches the
worship of false gods is to be stoned. In the Jewish setting,
to make oneself equal with God may well mean to make oneself in-
dependent of God.[74] Jesus' defense would seem to corroborate
such an interpretation of the charge for he stresses his dependence upon the Father (5.19). Thus, it seems likely that in the
eyes of the Jewish opponents Jesus is calling for the worship of
a false god, namely, himself.[75] The question at issue, then, is
whether Dt. 13 or Dt. 18 applies to Jesus:[76]

> The whole argument of 7.15-24 turns on the question
> whether Jesus is the true prophet like Moses or whether
> he is the false prophet. As the true prophet, Jesus
> insists that his teaching is not his own. He speaks the
> words God has commanded him, not "from himself." He
> does not "seek his own glory," that is, he does not
> speak "presumptuously" like the prophet described in
> Deuteronomy 18.20.

Thus, Jesus here defends himself "as if he were a prophet, de-
fending himself against the accusation of being a false prophet
whose teaching is not God's" (7.16-18).[77] He must do so because
his teaching and activity have gone counter to the Jewish interpretation of the Law (7.48-49),[78] and have raised the question
of his identity (7.52). The central issue at the heart of the
controversy is Jesus' identity. "The teaching of Jesus is his
self-revelation and he reveals himself as the Son of God. . . .
Such teaching, in the eyes of the Jews, cannot be reconciled with
the teaching of Moses. Jesus is a πλάνος, who leads astray from
Orthodoxy."[79] Thus the self-understanding of the opponents
clashes with the self-understanding of Jesus. Because of this
clash they charge him with deceiving the people and condemn him
to death. But this judgment of Jesus is really, in the author's
eyes, their judgment of themselves. They who charge Jesus with

deception are seen in John to be self-deceived, they who condemn
thereby stand (self-) condemned.

The second accusation, related to the Torah in that it concerns an interpretation of Scripture, revolves around the issue
of Jesus' origin. This charge, like the others that have been
mentioned, grows out of Jesus' claims for himself. However,
while the issues just mentioned all relate to Jesus' identity,
they could be raised against anyone who went contrary to the Law
as interpreted by the opponents. But Jesus' origin is an issue
only because he is understood to be making messianic claims.

This question of his origin moves, as it were, in two direc-
tions. First, it is said that it is known where Jesus is from
and it is this that disqualifies him as Messiah: "Yet we know
where this man comes from; and when the Christ appears, no one
will know where he comes from" (7.27). This view of the people
is modified later in the same chapter: "Others said, 'This is
the Christ,' But some said, 'Is the Christ to come from Galilee?
Has not the scripture said that the Christ is descended from
David, and comes from Bethlehem, the village where David was?'"
(7.41-42).[80] In this second form the objection moves in the
same direction as that in 7.27, i.e. Jesus' origin *is* known and
it is this that disqualifies him as Messiah. Here, however, the
problem is the specific place of origin.[81] The people are thus
represented as divided over this matter, which seems to be basically a problem of interpretation of Scripture. The authorities,
however, are not so divided here: "Search and you will see that
no prophet is to rise from Galilee" (7.52).

To this first kind of charge based on Jesus' known origin
is added a second which accuses him because his origin is not
known: "We know that God has spoken to Moses, but as for this
man, we do not know where he comes from" (9.29). It seems clear
that both varieties of this objection concern Jesus' authority,
but the first type of objection is in terms of geography while
the second refers directly to his relationship with God, contrasting it with that of Moses. "Here the Pharisees seem to be
questioning his claim to be from God, since they contrast it with
the known relation between Moses and God" (Brown, *John*, 374).
For the author, Jesus' origin is the Father and thus the

accusation of the opponents is an example of Johannine irony.
By admitting that they do not know where Jesus is from they are,
in his eyes, condemned out of their own mouths.[82]

Not only is Jesus' origin questioned on the basis of Scripture, but also, thirdly, his departure: "We have heard from the
law that the Christ remains for ever. How can you say that the
Son of man must be lifted up?" (12.34). This comment by the
crowd may refer to teaching concerning the eternal role of the
Davidic line or king, or that of a/the Son of Man (see Brown,
John, 469). In the context of the Gospel it may also be significant that "there is no text that says that the Messiah *remains*
forever. In fact, 'remains forever' is an expression that the
OT applies to Yahweh, His justice, truth, praise, etc." (Brown,
John, 469). Jesus, for the author, is the manifestation of divine life and so this could be a veiled reference to Jesus' identity in that he 'abides' because he shares this divine life.
Be this as it may, the more obvious reference is to the irony of
Jesus' dying in order to abide. Jesus does fulfill the OT reference to abiding, but he does so through death. The final question of the crowd, "Who is this Son of man?" (12.34), is the
last statement made to Jesus in the controversies in John. Unlike their question about his origin, their question here is not
an accusation but rather evidences an attitude of openness. But
Jesus' public teaching has come to an end. He has revealed already who this Son of Man is, so now he warns of the imminence
of the judgment (12.35-36, cf. 12.31). As in the question of
Jesus' origin, his departure can only be understood when his
relation to the Father is understood. As the reference to lifting
up indicates, his relation to the Father can only become known
through his death. In this final appeal to Scripture the people
are not so much hostile as puzzled. If Jesus' own disciples
could not understand Scripture until after the glorification
(cf. 2.22; 12.16), how much less the crowds. As for the opponents, they have already passed judgment on Jesus and thus, in
the author's eyes, stand self-condemned.

Thus the opponents' view that they are loyal to Moses and
the Law, which is explicitly stated in 5.36, 45-47 and 9.28-29,
is implied in the various charges they bring against Jesus and

their questioning of him. They believe that the Torah condemns
Jesus. Presumably it is a similar judgment by the leaders in
the author's own day that is causing distress for his readers.
For the sake of his Christian readers he must counter this appeal
to the Torah. In his own claim of loyalty to the Torah is evident his attempt to wrest the Torah from the hands of his opponents and claim it for his own side. This is one of the two
major parts of the polemic in the Gospel in that it counters the
first of the two foci of the opponents' identity which we are
considering, their loyalty to Moses and the Torah. We now come
to a consideration of this first half of his polemic.

b. *The Polemic Against the Opponents' Claim*

     The attack on this claim of the opponents has two sides,
one negative and the other positive. On the negative side, the
author both attacks their claim by saying that they themselves
do not keep the Law, and he also attacks their use of the OT
by countering each of their arguments with his own arguments from
the OT. On the positive side, he seeks to defend his own coun-
ter-claim of loyalty to Scripture by showing that the OT actually
witnesses to Jesus, rather than against him. I will examine in
some detail first the negative side and then the positive.

1) *Negative Side: Attack on Their Claim*

a) *They Themselves Do Not Keep the Law*

     The irony can escape no one that those who charge Jesus
with deception are themselves the ones who are deceived. But
this irony goes very deep indeed, for the author portrays those
who condemn Jesus on the basis of the Law as themselves condemned
by this same Law; for all their pride in Moses and the Law, they
do not keep the Law. Furthermore, this disloyalty to the Law
is even indicated by one of the Pharisees themselves, Nicodemus.
In upbraiding the officers who have failed to arrest Jesus, the
Pharisees say

> "Are you led astray, you also? Have any of the author-
> ities or of the Pharisees believed in him? But this
> crowd, who do not know the law, are accursed." Nicodemus,
> who had gone to him before, and who was one of them,

said to them, "Does our law judge a man without first
giving him a hearing and learning what he does?" They
replied, "Are you from Galilee too? Search and you will
see that no prophet is to rise from Galilee" (7.47-52).

So they who condemn Jesus for breaking the Law and condemn the
people for not knowing the Law go counter to the Law themselves.
The irony is strong at this point and recurs in the trial scene.
The Jewish opponents tell Pilate: "We have a law, and by that
law he ought to die, because he has made himself the Son of God"
(19.7). This concern for the Law, however, is shown a few verses
later to be hypocritical: "Pilate said to them, 'Shall I crucify
your King?' The chief priests answered, 'We have no king but
Caesar'" (19.15). This affirmation of allegiance to Caesar goes
counter to the teaching of the OT (e.g. Jud. 8.23; 1 Sam. 8.7).

This charge that the opponents do not keep the Law is stated
explicitly: "Did not Moses give you the law? Yet none of you
keeps the law. Why do you seek to kill me?" (7.19). Their
relation to the Law and their relation to Jesus are here juxtaposed. In saying that they do not keep the Law, Jesus seems to
refer to their opposition to the spirit of the Sabbath law (7.
21-23). Some scholars, however, suggest the reference is to
the Decalogue; in desiring to kill Jesus they desire something
contrary to the Law (Ex. 20.13).[83] But this interpretation is
unsatisfactory since, according to the Law, Jesus *does* deserve
death if he is breaking the Sabbath (cf. Ex. 31.14; Num. 15.32-
36) or blaspheming (cf. Lev. 24.16). Thus it is unlikely that
the command "You shall not kill" (Ex. 20.13) is in mind. Rather,
we seem to have here a repetition of what is said explicitly in
5.37-47, namely, their desire to kill him is evidence that they
have not received him to whom the Law testifies (cf. Pancaro,
Law, 130-138). They do not keep the Law in that they do not receive Jesus. "The Law should lead to the recognition of Jesus"
(ibid. 508-509).

It is this rejection of Jesus that is at the root of their
charges against him based on the Law. If they received him then
they would accept his interpretation of Sabbath observance and
his self-revelation.[84] He *did* teach that he is the Son of God
(e.g. 10.36) and there *is* a law against blasphemy, but obviously
Jesus only broke this law if he was not what he claimed to be.

It is because they consider him a deceiver that they think he
is breaking the Law. Because they possess the Law they think
they can rightly evaluate matters of religion, in particular,
whether messianic claims are valid or not. This self-understanding is considered by the author to be totally deluded, for
the opponents have misjudged Jesus and thereby have condemned
themselves.

b) Their Accusations and Questions Overturned

The opponents' own use of the Torah to accuse Jesus is
countered by appealing to passages from the OT for each of the
charges of law-breaking.

First, to the charge that Jesus is bearing witness to himself (8.13), Jesus begins by saying that if he did do so his
testimony would be true since he knows his origin and destination (8.14).[85] To this justification on the basis of knowledge
he then adds that if he were to judge he would do so together
with the one who sent him, and thus there would be two witnesses.
He secures this point by appealing to the Law: "In your law it
is written that the testimony of two men is true; I bear witness
to myself, and the Father who sent me bears witness to me" (8.
17-18). But how can Jesus' appeal to the Law be valid since it
requires two witnesses other than the person himself, and one's
own witness is invalid? It seems here "we are in the presence
of a valid juridical argument which does not have any validity
at all (cannot have any validity at all) for the Pharisees. Only faith can perceive the way in which the Law is fulfilled in
the testimony of the Father and the Son" (Pancaro, *Law*, 277).
A correct understanding of Jesus' identity and his relation to
the Father is necessary for an appreciation of this use of this
legal principle.

> Jn clearly distinguishes between the Father and the Son,
> even though the activity of the Father is that of the
> Son. Inasmuch as Jesus does not act or speak of him-
> self, his works and words are *his* and, at the same
> time, the works and words *of the Father*. Inasmuch as he
> does nothing on his own authority and seeks not his own
> will but the will of the Father (5,30), Jesus does not
> bear witness to himself in the ordinary sense of the
> expression (5,31) but in unity with the Father. His μαρτυρία
> is therefore not only truthful, it is his μαρτυρία and the

μαρτυρία of the Father. *There is one* μαρτυρία *but
there are two* μαρτυροῦντες, *two persons who testify to
the truthfulness of what Jesus says: Jesus and the
Father* (ibid. 276-277).

Thus the author turns the opponents' appeal to the Law back upon
themselves. If they understood Jesus they would understand the
Law which testifies to him.[86]

He makes this same point with regard to their charge of
Sabbath-breaking. As we have seen (above p. 34), Jesus accuses
them of not keeping the Law (7.19). This charge seems to be
based on their accusation that he has broken the Sabbath, since
in 7.12-22 there is an argument from the Law against their use
of the Law in condemning Jesus' Sabbath activity. According to
Lev. 12.3 a child is to be circumcised on the eighth day and
this is done even if that day is a Sabbath (cf. St-B 2:487).
This practice is used by Jesus in an *a fortiori* argument: "If
on the sabbath a man receives circumcision, so that the law of
Moses may not be broken, are you angry with me because on the
sabbath I made a man's whole body well?" (7.23). In this way
the Law is made to support Jesus rather than his opponents. As
necessary as it is for circumcision to take place on the Sabbath
in order that the Law not be broken, it is even more necessary
for Jesus to heal on the Sabbath in order that the Law not be
broken. But once again this argument only makes sense to one
who appreciates Jesus' identity. It is because Jesus is the
Son revealing the Father that he must heal on the Sabbath, for,
as he says when this controversy first arises, "My Father is
working still, and I am working" (5.17). Jesus' work on the
Sabbath is his Father's work in that it reveals the Father's
gracious love. "Jesus' action was not a transgression of the
word of God in the Old Testament but a fulfilment of it" in that
it is "the accomplishment of the redemptive purpose of God towards which the Law had pointed" (Barrett, *John*, 320, 321).
Circumcision was viewed in Judaism as a gift of God's graciousness,[87] and in this sense it is a reflection of God's love. It
is because the opponents do not recognize this same gracious
God at work in Jesus that they misuse the Law to condemn him.
They judge by appearances and not with right judgment (δίκαια
κρίσις, 7.24).

In the two charges noted thus far, concerning Jesus' witness to himself and his activity on the Sabbath, I have noted
that the author's use of the Torah to vindicate Jesus has been
dependent on a correct appreciation of Jesus' identity, his union
with the Father. Jesus' union with the Father is itself the
subject of the third counter-argument from Scripture (10.34-36).
This appeal to Scripture occurs within a passage that "represents
the climax of Jesus' self-revelation to the Jews" in that here
"Jesus declares more openly than ever before, that he is one with
God" (Pancaro, *Law*, 175, cf. 63-76). Here we find the author
using the tradition that he holds in common with his opponents
to support Jesus' claim and thereby counter their accusation.
There are two parts to the argument in 10.34-36 (see Brown, *John*,
409-410). First, the Scripture itself uses the word θεός of
someone other than God so the term itself need not indicate
blasphemy. This point then provides the point of reference for
the second part, an *a fortiori* argument: if Scripture itself
can use the term θεός of someone besides God himself, how much
more appropriate is the use of this term for Jesus.[88] This is
a very important argument from Scripture for the author, as is
implied by the parenthetical remark concerning Scripture in 10.
35. The Scripture witnesses to Jesus, καὶ οὐ δύναται λυθῆναι,
that is, it cannot be kept from fulfillment, it cannot be nul-
lified or rendered futile.[89] This parenthetical remark makes
something of the same point as 5.39, 45-47, namely, the Scripture witnesses to Jesus, and this witness can be neither avoided
nor negated. The Jewish opponents appeal to the Scripture
against Jesus but the author counters the very points they raise.
"The Jews are not to be allowed to escape the consequences of
their own canonical literature" (Barrett, *John*, 385). The Scripture uses θεός of certain people and the author believes Jesus,
"whom the Father consecrated and sent into the world" (10.36),
deserves this title par excellence. But once again, as in the
case of Sabbath-breaking and bearing witness to oneself, this
appeal to Scripture is only compelling for those who recognize
Jesus' identity. If one does not have faith in Jesus then this
witness of the Law will mean nothing. But for those who do have
such faith the author attempts to assure them in their faith by

showing them that the Law itself witnesses to Jesus. He appeals
to specific texts to counter the three specific charges brought
against Jesus on the basis of Scripture. He counters the remaining three charges somewhat differently since they are not
based on particular laws of the Torah.

The first of these other charges is that Jesus' origin disqualifies him from being the Messiah. The author seems to deal
with this accusation not by appealing to other passages from
Scripture to form a counter-argument but by placing side by side
the very different forms this expectation takes. By showing that
opinion is divided over the matter of the Messiah's origin (see
above pp. 31-32) he undercuts the appeal to Scripture on this
point. As we have seen, Jesus' origin according to the Gospel
is the Father. While the presentation of the variety of expectations concerning the Messiah's origin undercuts this accusation,
it is ultimately the author's view that Jesus' origin is the
Father which is most decisive (see Barrett, *John*, 330-331).

The crowd's question concerning Jesus' being lifted up
rather than remaining (12.34) is a contrast between what Jesus
says and what the Law says (see Lindars, *John*, 435). As we have
already noted (above p. 32) the author counters this alleged
contrast by showing that Jesus does μένειν precisely through
ὑψωθῆναι; "Der Evangelist hält es seinen Lesern gegenüber . . .
nicht für nötig, den Einwand zu widerlegen . . . . Sie wissen
ohnedies, dass ihr Christus 'in Ewigkeit bleibt', und die Juden
bezeugen es gegen ihren Willen (joh. Ironie)" (Schnackenburg,
Johannes 2:496).

The final charge is that of being a deceiver. As has been
noted (above pp. 29-30), this charge is based on no particular
text of Scripture. The author, in turn, does not counter with
any particular passage of Scripture. Rather, it is his entire
effort to show that Scripture witnesses to Jesus that counters
this charge; if the Scripture witnesses to Jesus then he is not
a deceiver.

So we see that the author responds to each of his opponents'
accusations or questions by appealing to Scripture either directly
or indirectly. Along with his refutation of their charges he also
levels his own accusation that they themselves do not keep the

Law. These are the two main elements in the negative side of his polemic in which he refutes his opponents' claims. In a sense the use of Scripture to refute the opponents' charges is an example of its witness to Jesus. But in these passages we have examined the agenda has been set by the opponents. We now turn to the author's own use of Scripture. Here the opponents' claims are refuted implicitly through his use of Scripture as a witness, the positive side of his polemic.

2) Positive Side: The Author's Appeal to Scripture

The author uses Scripture as a witness in two main ways. On the one hand he appeals to Scripture as a witness to the opponents' unbelief, and on the other as a witness to Jesus.

a) Scripture Witnesses to the Opponents' Unbelief

Scripture is appealed to directly for testimony concerning unbelief at the end of the first half of the Gospel (12.37-43), three times in the Farewell Discourse (13.18; 15.25; 17.12), and somewhat more indirectly in 6.45.[90]

The first of these passages, 12.37-38, is a part of the epilogue to the first twelve chapters (12.37-50). Here "the evangelist, speaking in his own person, comments upon the story he has told."[91] From this epilogue it is clear that the theme of the author's story has been the revelation of God in Jesus, and the response to this revelation. In 12.37-43 the author reflects on the rejection which Jesus has met. Various features of this text are relevant for a study of polemic so I will return to these verses again. Of interest now is 12.37-38 which "foretells the *fact* of unbelief" (Lindars, *John,* 437). This lack of faith is first stated (12.37), and then said to be a fulfillment (ἵνα πληρωθῇ) of Is. 53.1 (12.38). This verse seems to have a "general application to the whole of Jesus' ministry" (Lindars, *John,* 438), so the rejection of Jesus here picks up the note sounded in the Prologue (1.11). But if Jesus was really the Son of God, the Messiah, why was he rejected? This question was raised from the earliest days of Christianity, as soon as it became evident that Israel was not going to welcome her Messiah. At the point of separation between the Church and Synagogue,

which I am assuming lies behind John, this question would have
particular importance. With some of his readers tempted to return to Judaism and others tempted not to depart from it, the
author seeks to strengthen his case against his Jewish opponents
by showing that even their rejection is, in fact, "an element in
God's eternal purpose, and as such had been written in the Old
Testament" (Barrett, *John*, 430). That is, "the rejection of the
Messiah by His own people ought not to surprise those familiar
with the Old Testament Scriptures."[92]   Indeed, according to 12.
39 this rejection had to take place, since it was written in
Scripture. In the context of the polemic, διὰ τοῦτο οὐκ ἠδύναντο
(12.39) is closely related to the parenthesis in 10.35b: καὶ
οὐ δύναται λυθῆναι ἡ γραφή. This rejection is in the OT and
therefore it must occur.

     Jn. 12.41 says that Isaiah actually saw Jesus' glory in
his vision in the Temple (Is. 6). "The words which the prophet
spoke concerning the unbelief of the people of God therefore
refer to the mission of Jesus, for *He spake of him*" (Hoskyns,
Gospel, 501). Thus, the author is not simply drawing upon convenient striking phrases in the OT. Rather, he is drawing upon
the significance this passage has in its context in Isaiah, for
Isaiah is describing the rejection of the messenger of YHWH.
But the author finds here not merely a correspondence between
what Isaiah experienced and what Jesus experienced. There is
a correspondence because Is. 53.1 was written about Jesus. The
nature of this vision will be considered below (pp. 46-48).

     It is noteworthy that this section of Jn. 12 is the closest
the author comes to appealing to OT figures representing unbelief. According to M. Wiles such a use of negative characters
was common in the polemic of the first Christian centuries:[93]

> If Jesus be the true Messiah, rejected by the Jews but
> accepted by the Christians, then the Christians are by
> that fact constituted the true Israel of God. It is from
> there but a small step to regard the Christian church as
> the heirs of all who have played a creditable part in the
> history of the preparation for the coming of the Messiah,
> and the Jews as the heirs of all those who have opposed
> that preparation at any stage. This process is thrown
> back as far as Cain and Abel; the traditional motif of the
> goodness of the younger son in contrast to the elder lent
> itself easily to interpretation in terms of the superiority
> of the 'younger' religion of Christianity as against
> Judaism.

The author's practice is strikingly different. In the Gospel
where his opponents are Jews loyal to the OT, the chief character
representing unbelief is Judas, one of the Twelve. But in 1
John, where the conflict is with those who consider themselves
to be Christians, an OT figure is referred to, Cain (3.12).
Both Judas and Cain represent betrayal by one who is close to
the betrayed. Judas is the subject of the next two references
to Scripture to be considered.

The next appeal to Scripture (13.18), to Ps. 41.9, describes
betrayal by a close friend and thus provides not only the needed
phrases, but also a deeper correspondence. "This psalm--one of
many which could be applied to Jesus as the righteous sufferer
(cf. 12.27)--was especially valuable for the problem of Judas,
because it stresses the enormity of the breach of table fellowship on the part of the psalmist's enemy" (Lindars, *John*, 454).
The fact that the author explicitly appeals to Scripture at this
point (ἵνα πληρωθῇ) indicates something of the importance of
Judas' betrayal for him. This betrayal raises two issues for
the author. The first is the question of why Jesus chose one
who would betray him, given that he "knew what was in man"
(2.25). He makes it clear that Jesus was not ignorant of Judas'
character (6.64; 13.11); this betrayal was necessary because it
was present in Scripture. Thus the betrayal does not cast doubt
on Jesus' identity. Indeed, the author makes use of the coming
betrayal to further highlight Jesus' identity. The quote from
Ps. 41.9 is given by Jesus in the form of a prophecy. In the
author's account, the beginning of the betrayal does not occur
until 13.27. Jesus' foreknowledge of this event is emphasized
(cf. 14.28,31), and is even given as evidence by Jesus that ἐγώ
εἰμι (13.19). As elsewhere in the Gospel, the author here appeals to the common theme in the OT that God and true prophets
are known by the ability to foretell events (e.g. Is. 48.5)
(see Brown, *John*, 554). One of his concerns is to guard against
Judas' betrayal endangering the readers' view of Jesus' identity.

A second concern becomes evident when we consider the figure
of Judas in the Gospel. He is mentioned many times and it is
"redundant to note at every mention of Judas that he was the betrayer" (6.71; 12.4; 13.2,21; 18.2,5; cf. 6.64; 17.12) (Shepherd,

"Jews," 102). But this redundancy highlights the function Judas
plays in John as representative of those who oppose Jesus. Thus,
given my working hypothesis for the situation and purpose of
John, in this figure of Judas the author may indicate to those
in the community who are tempted to side with the Jewish opponents the implications of their action. Similarly, those who
remain loyal to Jesus could see that, just as Scripture shows
that Jesus' betrayal was inevitable, so they should not be surprised by those in their midst who abandon Jesus and his community (16.4).

This concern to assure the readers is the main point of
17.12, another text mentioning the necessity of Judas' betrayal
ἵνα ἡ γραφὴ πληρωθῇ. Here Jesus is emphasizing the security of
his own followers. But if Judas could be lost, how could they
be secure? The author singles out Judas as an exceptional case,
which occurred as predicted. No particular passage of Scripture
is mentioned, though most commentators suggest Ps. 41.9, already
used for the betrayal in 13.18. A different approach is offered
by E. D. Freed who suggests 17.12 may refer to Jesus' own words
at 6.70-71, which are in the process of being fulfilled in 17.12
and 18.9.[94] The strength of this suggestion lies in the two instances when the author does seem to refer to Jesus' words as
being fulfilled later in the Gospel (18.9,32; cf. Brown, *John*,
811). However, the use of ἡ γραφή in 17.12 makes this proposal
unacceptable. Rather, as at 13.18, the author is drawing upon
the tradition he holds in common with his opponents, the OT, as
a witness against them. The irony of this point, and the relation between Jesus' rejection and that of the community, is
stated explicitly in the next use of Scripture concerning the
opposition.

Jn. 15.18-16.4 correlates Jesus' rejection and that of his
disciples. This rejection is said to fulfill (ἵνα πληρωθῇ) the
text, "They hated me without a cause" (15.25). The passage referred to is most likely Ps. 69.5, though it could be Ps. 35.19
(see Barrett, *John*, 482). In either case the innocent Psalmist
is complaining to God about his persecutors, and thus again there
is a correspondence between the Scripture and its application
that is more than merely verbal. The author is saying that his

readers should not be surprised by the opposition Jesus and they
experience; it is there in Scripture. In this way he seeks to
assure his readers. But the negative side of his argument is
also evident. "There is a touch of irony here, that the Jews'
rejection of the one sent from God is foretold in their own
sacred scriptures" (Lindars, *John*, 495).

One final text (6.45) to be included here goes deeper than
these first four in that it appeals to the Scripture not only
for the fact of unbelief but also for its cause. The author's
analysis of the cause of unbelief will be examined later, in the
second half of this chapter. For the present topic of the use
of the OT, note that the phrase "And they shall all be taught
of God" (Is. 54.13) is used as a contrast to the opponents. They
think they possess knowledge of God but their rejection of Jesus
belies this claim, since "Every one who has heard and learned
from the Father comes to me" (6.45). The author has modified the
OT text by leaving out בניך/τοὺς υἱούς σου, thereby emphasizing
the πάντες (Freed, *Quotations*, 19-20). This change has the effect
of making God's teaching virtually universal, but the opponents'
lack of faith excludes them from this "all." Thus the author
is here using the OT to refer to the Father's activity in bringing people to faith in Jesus and thereby presents the opponents
as separated from God.

The author, then, uses the Scripture to testify both against
the opponents and of them. The Scripture testifies of them in
its prediction of their unbelief and opposition, and it testifies
against them in its witness to Jesus. The basic elements of
this use of the OT to witness to Jesus will now be considered.

b) Scripture Witnesses to Jesus

The use of the OT as a witness to Jesus in John is an enormous topic and one about which a great deal has been written.
It is generally agreed that the author's use of the OT is exten-
sive; it has even been called "the most *alttestamentlich* of
New Testament books."[95] J. Luzarraga has claimed, "El reconocimi-
ento del hecho de la meditación del A.T. por parte del evangelista
es clave para comprender la innegable profundidad a la que Juan
ha llegado en su presentación del Misterio de Cristo."[96] The

language and imagery of the OT affects the very diction of the
Gospel,[97] and allusions can be found in virtually every passage,
though some of the allusions are clearer than others.[98] For
the present study of Johannine polemic, a survey of the dominant
features of the author's use suffices. So I limit myself, for
the most part, to a consideration of the more explicit material,
namely, most of the citations[99] and the explicit references to
OT characters.[100] In this explicit use of the OT the author argues that, great as the OT worthies were, Jesus is greater.
Furthermore, the OT feasts and the symbols such as the serpent
in the wilderness and the manna were revelations of God and as
such have now been fulfilled in Jesus, the ultimate revelation of
the Father. This revelation of the Father occurs above all in
the death of Jesus, hence in the account of the Passion the author
cites a number of texts which interpret the Passion as God's
will. These are the chief points in the use of the OT as a witness to Jesus. The details behind this summary will now be considered.

α. *The Use of OT Characters to Witness to Jesus*

Jacob and Joseph are referred to in the story of Jesus'
conversation with the woman of Samaria. Joseph is only mentioned
as the one who was given the well by his father Jacob, and he
plays no further role in the Gospel. The story is full of patri-
archal allusions (see Lindars, *John*, 180), but the author's
use of Jacob as a witness to Jesus is straightforward. In response to Jesus' claim that he could give her ὕδωρ ζῶν (4.10),
the woman says "Are you greater than our father Jacob, who gave
us the well, and drank from it himself, and his sons, and his
cattle?" (4.12). The point the author is making is obviously
that Jesus is indeed greater than Jacob. The significance of
this claim becomes clear when the role Jacob played in Samaritan
thought is considered. First, there was his role in covenant
history:[101]

> Abraham was the progenitor of Israel and other nations
> too, and so Isaac alone of Abraham's offspring was chosen
> to be the 'father' of a particular family of tribes from
> whom would arise the true elect. Ishmael was rejected
> and Israel chosen. Thus Jacob Israel, son of Isaac,
> became the actual progenitor of the elect, the Hebrew
> tribes.

By the same fact "Jacob Israel represents the last of a line,
the line of the Patriarchs, and the beginning of a new line, the
line of the elect" (ibid. 448). These covenants with Abraham,
Isaac, and Jacob were of prime importance for the Samaritans'
identity as the elect of God (ibid. 242-243). The reason God
chose these patriarchs was "because of the way they lived, or,
as the philosopher puts it, because of the degree of manifestation of the divine light in their experience on earth" (ibid.
277, cf. 297). Since these "righteous three" were chosen on account of their virtue, it is not surprising that they are taken
as examples of how one is to live (ibid. 244-245), and how one
is to pray (ibid. 273). These features are paralleled in the
Jewish evaluation of Jacob.[102] Crucial for both Samaritan and
Jew is the fact that "it is the name of Jacob which defines the
people of the covenant" (Odeberg, "'Ιακώβ," 191-192). Thus a
claim to be greater than Jacob suggests a superiority to the
covenant, which is central to the identity of both Jew and
Samaritan. Such a notion of superiority is evident when Jesus
speaks of a change in the religion of both Jew and Samaritan:
"Woman, believe me, the hour is coming when neither on this
mountain nor in Jerusalem will you worship the Father" (4.21).
What is necessary for worship is πνεῦμα καὶ ἀλήθεια (4.23-24)
and these have come in Jesus (e.g. 14.6; 20.22). Both Judaism
and Samaritanism have been superseded in Jesus; such is the implication of Jesus' superiority to Jacob. Thus, in this passage
Jacob serves to represent these religions. He is not said to
have personally in his own day known Jesus, as will be claimed
for others. Rather, the contrast is drawn between Jacob's gift
and that of Jesus. Jacob gave a well which provides water,
whereas Jesus is the giver of a greater gift, ὕδωρ ζῶν (4.10).
The significance of the contrast between Jacob and Jesus is evident in the deeper meaning of ὕδωρ ζῶν in John. Given the
Samaritan (see MacDonald, *Theology*, 276, 425) and Jewish[103] use
of ὕδωρ for God's revelation, Torah and the Spirit (cf. Brown,
John, 178-179) it is most likely that the ὕδωρ ζῶν is either
Jesus' own teaching/revelation or the Holy Spirit. The author
clearly identifies the ὕδωρ ζῶν with the Holy Spirit (7.38-39),
but in the light of 6.63, where he describes the Spirit as

ζωοποιοῦν and in the next phrase says Jesus' words are spirit
and life, it seems best not to separate Jesus' revelation and
his gift of the Spirit. By this use of the figure of Jacob,
therefore, the author is saying that in Jesus there is a revelation greater than the old covenant, for Jesus not only brings
revelation of God but gives the Spirit by which this revelation
is internalized in believers.[104]

Whereas the author seems to use Jacob as a representative
figure who witnesses to Jesus by way of contrast, Isaiah appears
to be used more as a direct witness to Jesus (12.41). Here the
author asserts that Isaiah's vision of the Lord (Is. 6.1-13) was
a vision of Jesus' δόξα. Some scholars disagree over whether
he means that Isaiah saw into the future and beheld Jesus'
ministry, the δόξα revealed in his works (1.14; 2.11; 11.40), or
whether Isaiah saw the pre-existent Christ. In favor of the first
interpretation Hoskyns says:

> The prophet Isaiah saw the Lord (Isa. vi. 1-3). To
> the Evangelist this vision of the prophet was not a
> naked vision of God (i. 18), but a vision of the future
> glory of Jesus the Messiah (cf. viii. 56) and of His
> earthly mission to His own people. The words which the
> prophet spoke concerning the unbelief of the people of
> God therefore refer to the mission of Jesus, for *He spake
> of him* (*Gospel*, 501).

Lindars appeals to Sir. 48.24f. for the opinion that Isaiah "saw
the last things . . . and revealed what was to occur in the end
of time" (*John*, 439). J. Dupont appeals to Jn. 8.56, where it
is said Abraham rejoiced ἵνα ἴδη τὴν ἡμέραν τὴν ἐμήν.[105]

On the other hand, Schnackenburg argues that the first person singular, ἰάσομαι, in 12.40 indicates that the author believed Isaiah saw the pre-existent Christ: "Nur auf diese Weise
findet die Wendung in der ersten Person ihre volle Erklärung.
Die Herrlichkeit Gottes, die Jesaja geschaut hat, und das Reden
Gottes, von dem der Prophet gesprochen hat, sind auf den präexistenten Christus übertragen."[106] Hanson notes that "neither
in 12.41 nor in 8.56 is it said that Isaiah or Abraham 'foresaw'
Christ,"[107] and he implies from Jn. 1.18 that the author regarded
the theophanies in the OT as manifestations of Jesus, the pre-
existent λόγος (ibid. 105-107). W. Thüsing adds that the author
clearly refers elsewhere to Jesus' pre-existent δόξα (17.5,
24).[108]

For my own part, I am closer to Bultmann, who considers the distinction to be ill-conceived: "to the Evangelist both fall together: that which Isaiah beheld in the Temple at that time was the future δόξα of Jesus which would be given him through his work" (*John*, 452 n.4).[109] The key to understanding this use of Isaiah as a witness to Jesus is found in the word δόξα. This term refers to that which the Son and the Father share in common (17.5) and which the Son gives to believers (17.22). It is used to describe that which Jesus reveals (1.14; 2.11; 11.4,40). It "means throughout the Gospel the manifestation of God's or Christ's true nature" (Hanson, *Jesus*, 106) and, as will become evident as this study progresses, that which Jesus reveals par excellence is the Father's gracious love. Such a reference seems present in the use of δόξα in 12.41. This δόξα is said to be expressed in the quotation in 12.40 (whether ὅτι or ὅτε is read). How then does 12.40 express God's character as the author understands it? The reference to divine graciousness is found in the very last phrase: καὶ ἰάσομαι αὐτούς. This phrase stands out for it is identical to the LXX, in contrast to the rest of the quotation from Is. 6.10 (Freed, *Quotations*, 85). Furthermore, this final clause is emphasized through the sudden shift from a third person singular to this first person singular. But how does this final emphatic phrase referring to divine graciousness relate to the references to divine hardening and blinding? It should be noted that the author's form of the text differs from both MT and LXX (see Lindars, *John*, 438), with the effect of heightening the divine initiative. Now an indicative is used rather than an imperative (Hebrew) and its subject is God rather than the people (Greek). This stress on both the divine love and the divine hardening is typical of Johannine thought and is more clearly expressed in 9.39: "Jesus said, 'For judgment I came into this world, that those who do not see may see, and that those who see may become blind.'" God's character is gracious love, but there is also judgment. He has blinded and hardened by the very revelation in Jesus of his graciousness. Schnackenburg is close to agreement with such an interpretation when he says: "Er sprach über Jesus und seine Tätigkeit des 'Heilens'. Der Prophet, der die Herrlichkeit Jesu sah und um

seine Heilssendung wusste, musste dennoch bezeugen, dass eine
Heilung der ungläubig-verstockten Menschen durch Jesus nach dem
Willen Gottes ausgeschlossen ist" (*Johannes* 2:520). In this
testimony of Isaiah is summed up the theme of the first twelve
chapters of the Gospel: God's graciousness has been revealed
and rejected. This rejection is underlined by the verses that
follow (12.42-43). Here this divine δόξα, to which Isaiah has
borne witness, and the human δόξα that people have preferred,
are contrasted. Thus, as noted above on 12.37-38, the author is
concerned, in part, to undercut any derrogation of Jesus due to
his rejection. "Der hartnäckige Unglaube wird im Licht der
Schrift kein Gegenargument gegen Jesus und sein Wirken, vielmehr
eine Bestätigung seines Auftretens" (Schnackenburg, "Joh 12,39-
41," 175).

But Isaiah's testimony not only puts the rejection of Jesus
in perspective, it also points to Jesus' own identity with the
Father. Behind the witness of Is. 6.10 to Jesus' revelation of
divine graciousness and judgment lies the graphic witness to
Jesus' identity with the Father. "In the vision of Isa. 6, the
prophet contemplates the awful glory of the invisible God; but
the evangelist, in affirming that he spoke of the glory of
Christ, identifies Christ with the Yahweh of Israel" (Bernard,
John, 452). The author here uses the Scripture to prepare for
Jesus' later explicit statement, "he who has seen me has seen
the Father" (14.9). It seems, then, that Isaiah is used to witness to Jesus' identity with the Father, the δόξα he had with
the Father πρὸ τοῦ τὸν κόσμον εἶναι (17.5) and to Jesus' revelation in history of the Father's δόξα, his character of gracious
love that judges. Because δόξα has these connotations, it is
possible that the author believed that Isaiah saw the pre-existent Christ, but saw him as rejected. "Isaiah could report on
Christ's saying concerning the predestined unbelief of the Jews
because he had in his vision seen the glory of the crucified
Son of God."[110] Thus, both the historical aspect and the pre-
existent may here be combined. In this climactic passage at the
end of the first half of the Gospel the author uses Isaiah to
bear witness to Jesus in a way that draws together a number of
major themes in the first twelve chapters relating to Jesus'
revelation and rejection.[111]

The witness to Jesus of the next OT figure has certain
similarities with what has been found for Isaiah and Jacob.
Like Jacob, Abraham serves as a representative of God's covenant
with Israel, and like Isaiah he himself is said to have had
knowledge of Jesus. The passage containing both of these functions, 8.31-59, is the theological climax of the polemic against
the Jewish opponents.

As noted already (p. 25), the opponents' self-understanding
has two basic elements, their loyalty to Moses and the Law and
their identity as children of Abraham and children of God. This
second deeper aspect of their identity is presented in 8.31-59
through the use of Abraham as the representative of the covenant.
Since this is the subject of the next section of the present
study, Abraham's role representing the covenant will not be
discussed now. That leaves Abraham's own personal witness to
Christ mentioned in 8.56: Ἀβραὰμ ὁ πατὴρ ὑμῶν ἠγαλλιάσατο ἵνα
ἴδῃ τὴν ἡμέραν τὴν ἐμήν, καὶ εἶδεν καὶ ἐχάρη.

Lindars interprets this verse in the light of the belief,
current in the first century, that Abraham is alive in Paradise
(cf. Lk. 16.19-31) (*John*, 334-335). The first reference to
Abraham's joy is taken as that which he experienced at the birth
of Isaac, which "is the fulfilment of God's promise, and is the
beginning of the whole process of promise and fulfilment which
is consummated in the Incarnation of Jesus" (ibid. 334). Perhaps there is also reference here to a vision Abraham had of the
advent of Jesus, like Isaiah's vision of the future. The second
reference to his rejoicing is the joy Abraham has in Paradise
as he now sees "the fulfilment of that vision in the coming of
Jesus" (ibid.). A different interpretation, and the one held by
the majority of scholars, takes both references to joy as referring to the experience Abraham had in a vision, either of the
future coming of Jesus (Brown, *John*, 367), or of the pre-existent
Jesus (Schnackenburg, *Johannes* 2:299), or both.[112] Much is made
by these scholars of the view in Jewish literature of Abraham
having had a vision (e.g. *Apocalypse of Abraham* 9-32; *Gen. R.*
44.21-22).[113] If John is saying that Abraham had a vision of
the future then he is most likely drawing upon such reflection
in Jewish circles since no such vision is recorded in the OT.

But it seems possible that he does not have any such vision of
the future in mind at all. It is clear from the context that
the Jewish opponents in the story do not think Jesus is referring
to a vision Abraham had of the future, but rather that Jesus is
asserting his own existence at the time of Abraham. This emphasis is especially evident in the preferred reading ἐώρακας,[114]
and their reference to his age (8.57). Thus, the reference is
probably not to a vision of the future to be inferred from Gen.
15, but a vision of God such as that mentioned in Gen. 17.1, or
the visit of the three angels in Gen. 18 and the appearance of
YHWH attached to it (Gen. 18.22).

The main difficulty with this interpretation is the reference to ἡμέρα in 8.56, since this seems to refer to a vision of
the future. It is possible, however, to take this term as referring to "the definitive revelation of His glory,"[115] or, more
generally, the eschatological day of salvation (Bultmann, *John*,
326 n.2; Barrett, *John*, 352). To draw upon the notion of the
eschatological ἡμέρα, as Lindars well expresses it, "in John's
terminology could only mean the exaltation of Jesus after his
Passion (cf. 14.20, and the frequent use of 'the last day'),
which is still future at the time of speaking" (*John*, 335).[116]
So the author may be saying that Abraham has seen the salvation
which Jesus is bringing, which in Johannine language is the
revelation by the Son (particularly in his death) of the Father
as love. Abraham has seen this salvation in that he has seen
Jesus himself. To the opponents' objection to this claim, Jesus
responds: ἀμὴν ἀμὴν λέγω ὑμῖν, πρὶν 'Αβραὰμ γενέσθαι ἐγὼ εἰμί
(8.58).

> The implication is that Jesus does not stand within the
> temporal series of great men, beginning with Abraham
> and continuing through the succession of the prophets,
> so as to be compared with them. His claim is not that
> He is the greatest of the prophets, or even greater than
> Abraham himself. He belongs to a different order of being.
> The verb γένεσθαι is not applicable to the Son of God
> at all. He stands outside the range of temporal relations.
> He can say ἐγὼ εἰμί. . . . That which is from all eternity
> is the unity of Father and Son, in a mutual 'knowledge',
> an 'indwelling', of which the real character is ἀγάπη.
> This is the ultimate mystery of Godhead which Jesus
> revealed to the world--ἐγνώρισα αὐτοῖς τὸ ὄνομά σου καὶ
> γνωρίσω ἵνα ἡ ἀγάπη ἣν ἠγάπησάς με ἐν αὐτοῖς ᾖ (xvii. 26)
> (Dodd, *Interpretation*, 261-262).

So the author may draw upon Jewish conceptions of Abraham as a
visionary, but the vision attributed to him goes far beyond
Jewish views (cf. Schnackenburg, "Joh 12,39-41," 176; *Johannes*
2:298). For our present purpose the main point is that the one
the Jewish opponents appeal to as an authority, Abraham, is
claimed by the author as a witness to Jesus. It has already been
noted how Moses in his relation to the Scriptures is used by the
author in this same way (p. 26). It now remains to return to
Moses to see other ways in which he is used as a witness.

Moses is the OT character most often mentioned in John (12x)
and yet, in contrast to Abraham who is mentioned almost as often
(11x), any personal role of Moses himself is consistently played
down in favor of his role in the giving of Scripture and in connection with the signs of the serpent (3.14) and the manna
(6.32).

As already noted (p. 26), 5.45-47 clearly presents Moses
in his capacity as author of Scripture. Some interpreters have
found in 5.45 a reference also to another role of Moses. Moses
is depicted in Jewish tradition as a defender of the Jews before
God (e.g. *Ex. R.* 18.3; 43; Josephus, *Jewish Antiquities* 4.194).[117]
It may well be that in describing Moses as their κατηγορῶν the
author is denying this expectation. Pancaro, in particular,
argues for such an interpretation of 5.45, and concludes that
this verse is an attack on the Jewish opponents' opinion and
hope:

> Their opinion is false: Jesus is not their accuser,
> Moses is; Moses is not their advocate, Jesus is the new
> advocate. Their hope is vain: it is directed towards
> Moses as their advocate, the one who will save them
> from "judgment"; in reality it is only faith in Christ
> which can accomplish this (*Law*, 258).

It seems quite possible that the author may have had some such
view of Moses as intercessor in mind. However, Pancaro's position is too extreme in that he wants to separate Moses from the
Scriptures. He argues that Moses does not simply stand for the
Law or the Scriptures, but also in 5.45-47 functions as an individual apart from his role as Law-giver (Pancaro, *Law*, 255).
But the emphasis in 5.39,45-47 is on his identity as the one
who witnessed to Jesus in the Scriptures. Furthermore, as we

have seen (pp. 39-43), the author presents the Law itself as
condemning the Jewish opponents, so even this role of accuser
could be a reference to the Law. It also might be significant
that eight of the twelve references to Moses concern his relation to the Law (1.17,45; 5.45,46; 7.19,22 (twice), 23). So,
while I do not deny that certain opinions about Moses may be in
view apart from his role in relation to the Law, it does seem
clear that in 5.45-47 the emphasis is on the possession of the
Scriptures.

The reference to the serpent comes in a very significant
passage in which Jesus' advent and death are connected with the
revelation of God's love for the world. Jesus' testimony is
mentioned in 3.11-12, ending with a reference to τὰ ἐπουράνια,
which shifts the focus to Jesus' identity as ὁ ἐκ τοῦ οὐρανοῦ
καταβάς (3.13). But why is this affirmation concerning Jesus
connected with the denial, οὐδεὶς ἀναβέβηκεν εἰς τὸν οὐρανόν?
Within Judaism there was speculation concerning the ascension of
various figures, including Moses.[118] It is possible that an
element of the Jewish opposition the author is combating held
such exalted views of Moses and that the author is here countering these claims (cf. Meeks, *Prophet-King*, 297-301; Segal,
Two Powers, 213-214). If this is so then the reference to the
serpent may contribute to this polemic: Moses did not ascend
to heaven, he only lifted up the serpent, which was a figure of
Jesus (καθώς . . . οὕτως).

> This is not an example of "Moses-typology," for it is
> the serpent or, more precisely, the act of "lifting
> up" that is the *tertium comparationis*. . . . The main
> thrust of the passage is that what takes place through
> Jesus is parallel to, but far superior to that which
> was enacted by Moses. The bronze serpent was erected
> to save the Israelites who were dying from snake-bite
> (Numbers 21. 8-9), but "everyone who believes in him
> [*sc.* the Son of Man] will have *eternal* life" (Meeks,
> *Prophet-King*, 292).

Thus Moses here witnesses to Jesus not in the Scripture as such,
but by an action described in Scripture. Here also his own
personal role is played down.

Moses' witness is of the same sort in Jn. 6, and again there
is a possible polemic against exalted views of Moses. The context is the feeding of the multitude and a call by Jesus to

faith in himself (6.26-29). The crowd asks for a sign, drawing
upon the parallel with the giving of the manna in the wilderness
and quoting Scripture. That there is here polemic against Moses
is perhaps evident in Jesus' initial response to their request:
"Truly, truly, I say to you, it was not Moses who gave you the
bread from heaven" (6.32). This reference to Moses places
emphasis on him for he had not been mentioned previously in this
context, and the subject in the OT citation is YHWH. The source
of this citation is unclear, but in all the sources that have
been suggested, namely, Ex. 16.4,15; Neh. 9.15; Ps. 78.24; Wsd.
16.20, the subject is YHWH, not Moses. This substitution of
Moses for YHWH seems to tell us something not only about the use
of Moses in the Gospel's polemic but also something about the
nature of the author's argument itself. Indeed, it is only when
we have examined the structure of the argument that we will be
able to appreciate what is here said about Moses.

Looking first, then, at the structure of the argument, it
seems, as P. Borgen has argued, that the author is following the
Rabbinic exegetical pattern of changing the elements in a text:
"Do not read ___, but ___."[119] This shift from δέδωκεν to
δίδωσιν in 6.32 is similar to this Jewish pattern, though the
examples Borgen provides do not present a parallel to the introduction here in John of this reference to Moses. So, if the
author of the Gospel is following such a pattern his reference
to Moses is all the more emphatic since it is not a part of the
pattern. It seems, then, that Borgen has demonstrated "a recog-
nizable family likeness" (Lindars, *John*, 252) between Jn. 6 and
a Jewish homiletical pattern. So the whole of Jn. 6 is

> an exposition of a basic OT text, split up into parts
> and expounded in order, until a complete definition has
> been reached. It thus splendidly proves the point that
> was made in 5.30-47, that the Scriptures, when rightly
> understood, prepare for the revelation of God in Christ
> (ibid. 253).

The author, then, is not only using the Scriptures that he and
his opponents share in common in order to argue against them,
but he may also be using homiletical patterns familiar to them
to witness to Jesus. Or, as Meeks has said, "John uses Jewish
exegesis against the Jews."[120]

Some scholars, however, do not see this use of Jewish
exegesis as a part of the author's use of Scripture to witness
to Jesus. For example, Martyn has accepted Borgen's analysis,[121]
but considers, on the basis of the emphasis on the Father's
present activity,[122] that "John allows Jesus paradoxically to
employ a form of midrashic discussion in order to terminate all
midrashic discussion!" (*History*, 128). In other words,

> The issue is not to be defined as an argument about an
> ancient text. It is not a midrashic issue. By arguing
> about texts you seek to evade the present crisis. God
> is *even now* giving you the true bread from heaven, and
> you cannot hide from him in typological speculation or
> in any other kind of midrashic activity. You must decide
> now with regard to this present gift of God (ibid.).

Martyn further appeals to Jn. 7.15-17 where Jesus is described
by the opponents as having never studied (ibid. 122-123). As
Martyn notes, a Rabbi would agree with most of Jesus' defense of
himself:

> A Rabbi does not speak on his own authority. He could,
> therefore, utter both the first and the last parts of
> Jesus' saying: "My teaching is not mine . . . . I do
> not speak on my own authority." The Rabbi speaks, of
> course, on the authority of Moses. The force which his
> own words have, therefore, derives from his ability--
> gained from long study--correctly to interpret the writings
> of Moses.
>   It is clear that Jesus does not possess this kind
> of authority. Between the first and the last parts of
> Jesus' saying lie words which emphatically exclaim:
> *The criterion of midrashic accuracy is wholly inappli-*
> *cable to my teaching.* The issue is not midrashic, as
> both the Jamnia Loyalists and the secret believers sup-
> pose it to be. It is a decision of the will in the
> electing presence of God's emissary (ibid. 123).

Martyn here presents a very good statement of certain important
themes in the author's thought, but I do not see how his evidence
supports the contention that the author is denying the validity
of midrash. It seems, rather, that throughout the Gospel he is
using midrash to testify to Jesus.[123] In the author's context,
to show that Scripture witnesses to Jesus requires the use of
midrash, otherwise his case makes no impact. To use midrash to
deny midrash would be a possible line of argument, but I do not
see him taking it.[124] It is not the Scripture but the opponents'
interpretation of it that is denied.[125]

It seems evident that in Jn. 6 we find the author making
use of Jewish midrashic technique. What, then, is the function
of Moses in this context? Borgen suggests that the reason Moses
is here introduced is due to the association in Jewish thought
between bread from heaven and the Torah (*Bread*, 173). This suggestion is in keeping with the Johannine association between
Moses and the Torah, and lends support to Borgen's general point
that Jn. 6 follows a pattern of Jewish homiletical exegesis.
But this observation does not exhaust the significance of Moses
in this passage. Of even greater importance is the fact that
Moses is introduced in 6.32 in order to contrast him with the
Father, who gives the true bread of heaven that gives life to
the world. Thus, the contrast is not between Moses and Jesus,
but between Moses and God (see Martyn, *History*, 127). This
point clarifies the function of Moses in this passage. "*The*
point of the sign is not the Moses-Messiah typology but rather
God's gracious election" (ibid. 126). Once again, Moses' own
role is played down. He is an important witness to Jesus, but
not in his own person. Indeed, a great gulf is fixed between
Moses and Jesus, as is evident a few verses later. For in the
second assertion, that Jesus himself is the bread of life (6.35),
Jesus is placed in a completely different category from Moses.
Again, as in 3.14-15, the stress is on Jesus as the giver of
life to the world (6.33). When it is recalled that the question
of where life is to be found also enters into the witness of
Scripture (5.39), it will be seen that the principal effect of
the Moses testimony in John is to witness to the life present in
Jesus. Meeks has summarized very well the function of Moses in
John:[126]

> The Fourth Gospel is not so constructed that the reader,
> in order to understand it, would have to perceive that
> Jesus, the "Son of Man," is like Moses--that is the
> error of the numerous typological treatments of John that
> have proliferated in recent years. On the other hand,
> its form and content are such that, if the reader *were*
> acquainted with those Moses-traditions described above,
> he would recognize (1) that Jesus fulfills for the
> believer those functions elsewhere attributed to Moses
> and (2) that the Christian claims he does this in a
> superior and exclusive way, so that Moses is now stripped
> of those functions and made merely a "witness" to Jesus
> (like John the Baptist). Therefore one who had formerly

> accounted himself a "disciple of Moses" would now
> have to decide whether he would become instead a
> "disciple of Jesus." If he did not, then from the
> viewpoint of this gospel he had in fact deserted the
> real Moses, for Moses only wrote of Jesus and true
> belief in Moses led to belief in Jesus (*Prophet-King*,
> 319).

In the explicit references to Moses he is never used as a type
of Christ. He witnesses to Jesus in his role as writer of
Scripture and by his particular actions in the Exodus story.
Indeed, none of the OT characters are allegorized in John, unlike
their use in e.g. Philo (see Dahl, "Church," 107). Rather, they
all are used in their witness to Christ and/or as representatives
of God's gracious activity in the past. By his use of these OT
characters the author is both claiming the Torah as a Christian
revelation and showing the superiority of the revelation in Jesus
to that which has gone before.

β. *The Use of OT Symbols and Events to Witness to Jesus*

The use of the serpent and the manna as symbols of Jesus
as the giver of life raise the question whether the author makes
use of other events or images from the Exodus story to witness
to Jesus. Scholars have had no difficulty in finding such allusions. Indeed, it has even been suggested that the whole Gospel
is modeled on the book of Exodus.[127] In addition to the serpent
and the manna, the presumed references to the Tabernacle (1.14)[128]
and to the water from the rock (7.38),[129] as well as the image
of the vine (15.1-8)[130] and the shepherd (10.1-18),[131] the Lamb
of God (1.29)[132] and the image of light[133] have all been identified as Exodus motifs in that they have been taken to refer to
Moses or to some event during the Exodus. The vine is taken as
a less direct reference to the Exodus in that it is used in the
OT as an image of Israel coming out of Egypt (e.g. Ps. 80). Such
an indirect link with the Exodus has also been suggested for
various wisdom motifs in John, which are used elsewhere of the
Exodus.[134] That the Exodus should play such an important role
for the author is perhaps due to its role as the major example
in the OT of God's gracious love, since it is this that Jesus
also reveals of the Father (cf. Henderson, *Fulfilment*, 101).

To develop the author's use of various allusions to the
Exodus and the rest of the OT would require a careful study of
each alleged instance to determine its precise content and its
possible referents. Such a study, however, is not possible within
the scope of this dissertation, nor is it necessary. There is no
doubt that John's Gospel is thoroughly filled with biblical allusions and the general value of this feature of the Gospel for
the polemic with the Jewish opponents is clear. As has been
emphasized, the Scriptures are contested ground between the
author and his opponents. The fact that his presentation of the
story of Jesus echoes at almost every point the language and
stories of the OT could only serve to enhance his explicit claim
that the Scriptures bear witness to Jesus.

Another important aspect of the polemic which entails alluding to OT themes is the use of Jewish festivals. A number of
scholars would agree with R. Longenecker when he says, "John
appears to have thought of Jesus . . . as central in the life of
the nation and the fulfilment of its festal observances."[135]
G. E. Wright even goes so far as to say, "The controversies with
the Jews which John records are largely concerned with the question as to whether Jesus does not reveal the true significance
of the festivals which celebrate the Israelite deliverance and
wandering in the wilderness."[136] This use of the festivals is
what Brown has called "a theme of replacement" (*John*, 411), which
he summarizes as follows:

> On the Sabbath feast (ch. v) Jesus insisted that there
> could be no Sabbath rest for the Son since he must con-
> tinue to exercise even on the Sabbath the powers of life
> and judgment entrusted to him by the Father. At Passover
> (vi) Jesus replaced the manna of the Passover-Exodus
> story by multiplying bread as a sign that he was the
> bread of life come down from heaven. At Tabernacles
> (vii-ix) the water and light ceremonies were replaced
> by Jesus, the true source of living waters and the light
> of the world. Now at the feast of Dedication [10.22-39],
> recalling in particular the Maccabean dedication or
> consecration of the temple altar, but more generally
> reminiscent of the dedication or consecration of the
> whole series of temples that had stood in Jerusalem,
> . . . Jesus proclaims that he is the one who has truly
> been consecrated by God. This seems to be an instance of
> the Johannine theme that Jesus is the new Tabernacle
> (i 14) and the new Temple (ii 21) (ibid.).

The author, then, seems to imply that not only the Jewish
Scriptures but the Jewish cult in general witnesses to Jesus.[137]
The cult and the Scripture are closely related in that the feasts
celebrate the gracious activity of YHWH which is described in
the Scriptures. For the author the cult and the Scripture witness to Jesus because he is the ultimate revelation of this same
gracious God.

γ. *The Use of the OT in the Passion Account*

The final use of Scripture as a witness to Jesus to be
studied occurs in the Passion narrative. Here I will include
also 12.13,15,27 along with the four fulfillment texts in ch.
19. These verses in ch. 12 differ significantly from the other
texts, both in their position outside the Passion narrative and
in their lack of reference to fulfillment (apart from 12.14:
καθώς ἐστιν γεγραμμένον). But ch. 12 serves to introduce the
Passion, so this seems the best context in which to consider
these verses.[138]

The Triumphal Entry (12.12-19) is an important scene both
for the story and for the author's theology. Jesus has moved in
and out of Jerusalem earlier in the Gospel (cf. 2.13; 5.1).
Judea is the center of opposition so that it becomes dangerous
for Jesus to be seen there (cf. 11.7-8,16). In ch. 11 he returns
to Judea and raises Lazarus from the dead. This act results in
a further polarization of attitudes among the people about Jesus
(11.45-46), with the result that the authorities seek a way to
put him to death (11.47-53). Knowing this, Jesus withdraws to
the countryside (11.54). Thus, the tension between Jesus and
his opponents has reached its height. The people realize this
and are all wondering whether Jesus will attend the feast (11.55-
57). The author has masterfully described these tensions and
expectations with the result that Jesus' entrance is a climactic
event. By openly entering the city where he is a marked man,
Jesus has taken the first step toward the final confrontation.

It is through the citation of the OT at this point that the
author conveys the theological significance of this powerful
scene. The crowd comes to greet Jesus shouting two of the
phrases from Ps. 118.25-26: "Hosanna! Blessed is he who comes
in the name of the Lord." To this is added, "even, the King of

Israel!" (12.13), which most likely derives from Zeph. 3.15
or Zech. 9.9 (see Lindars, *John*, 424). In this way a song of
welcome to the pilgrim ascending to Jerusalem is applied to Jesus
as he enters the city. According to the author's thought this
line from the Psalms of Ascent applies to Jesus in a way it
never has to anyone else. Jesus, as the one who makes known the
Father, has come in the Father's name (5.43) and desires that it
be made known (17.6,26); of him it is uniquely true that he comes
in the name of the Lord.

This one who comes in the Lord's name is said to be the King
of Israel. Most commentators see here an indication of "the
complete misunderstanding of the crowds who believed on Jesus"
(Hoskyns, *Gospel*, 493). If this is the case then we probably
have here an instance of that same misunderstanding seen earlier
after the feeding of the multitude in the wilderness (6.14-15).
For the author, Jesus is indeed King, but not a political king.
The crowds come with palm fronds "as if they were welcoming
Jesus as a national liberator" (Brown, *John*, 461). But by referring to the young ass (12.14) *after* the ovation, "it may be
that he intended the selection of the ass as a correction of
the nationalistic enthusiasm of the crowd" (Barrett, *John*, 418).
Many commentators suggest that the author presents Jesus' kingship as one of peace (e.g. Lindars, *John*, 420-421), and this is
certainly a Johannine theme (cf. 14.27). But there is probably
more involved. In 18.36 Jesus explicitly refers to his kingship
and says that it is not of this world. Something of the significance of this assertion may be hinted at in the other citation from Scripture found in 12.15. Here Zech. 9.9 has been
modified by the reading "fear not" from Zeph. 3.16 (Lindars,
John, 424).

> The Greek words "Do not be afraid" occur frequently in
> LXX of Isaiah, e.g., xl 9; but the full expression that
> John uses resembles most closely MT (not LXX) of Zeph
> iii 16: "Do not be afraid, O Zion ['O daughter of Zion'
> occurs in iii 14]." The import of this passage in
> Zephaniah is to assure Jerusalem that "the King of Israel,
> the Lord" (iii 15) is in her midst. This may well be the
> source of "the King of Israel" which John xii 13 has
> added to the citation of the psalm (Brown, *John*, 458).

Such an interpretation would fit with Johannine theology for it
would mean that "They should not be acclaiming him as an

earthly king, but as the manifestation of the Lord their God
who has come into their midst (Zeph iii 17) to gather the out-
cast" (ibid. 462).[139]

Thus, by weaving together phrases from these various OT
passages the author has made a statement about the significance
of what is taking place--the Son of God is coming to his own.
A further consideration of the phrase "King of Israel" may help
substantiate this interpretation. Apart from 12.13, the terms
'Ισραήλ and 'Ισραηλίτης occur only in the first three chapters
(1.31,47,49; 3.10). The Baptist's witness to Israel (1.31) finds
an initial response in the confession of Nathanael, "an Israelite
indeed" (1.47), that Jesus is "the Son of God," "the King of
Israel" (1.49). This confession stands in marked contrast to
Nicodemus, "a teacher of Israel" (3.10) who is not able to understand "earthly things" (3.12), let alone "heavenly things"
(3.12). These first three chapters are thus characterized by a
concern with the initial witness to Israel and this motif comes
to a climax in the acclamation of Jesus as the King of Israel.
But 12.16 says the significance of this scene did not become
evident until after Jesus' glorification. This notion of later
insight will be discussed below with reference to 2.22 (pp. 101-
102). Suffice it to say, the author here presents characters
within the story using Scripture to speak of Jesus. In the
author's eyes these citations convey deep meaning, but only in
the light of Jesus' glorification.

Jn. 12.27 begins with the word νῦν, a reference back to
12.23: "And Jesus answered them, 'The hour has come for the Son
of man to be glorified." The perfect tense used here (ἐλήλυκεν)
contrasts with οὔπω ἐλήλυθεν ἡ ὥρα elsewhere in the Gospel (7.30;
8.20; cf. 2.4), thus denoting that a decisive turning point in
the action has been reached; "the crisis is already here" (Dodd,
Interpretation, 371). In presenting Jesus as faced with this
crisis, "the Psalms have been quarried to provide the words which
express Jesus' emotion" (Lindars, *John*, 431). The particular
Psalm drawn upon is uncertain. It could be 42.6, but is more
likely 6.3 since the words "save me" follow in 6.4.[140] Jn. 12.27
is a very important text in the Johannine theme of the obedience
of the Son. "Precisely in the overcoming of this trembling in

the presence of death is set the obedience of the Son to the
will of the Father. This obedience is the glorification of the
Father's name" (Hoskyns, *Gospel*, 497). Virtually every commentator considers the Johannine description of the Passion to differ
from those of the Synoptics in its lack of anguish.[141] It is
said that in John the emphasis is on triumphant victory, and the
total control of Christ over the situation. These are, indeed,
Johannine themes. However, while the anguish of Christ is not
presented as emphatically as it is in the Synoptics, it is not
correct to say it is lacking, for it is clearly stated in 12.27.
The author does not present Jesus' obedience as costing him
nothing, even if the emphasis is on the obedience as total and
the victory as assured.

But of what value is this incorporation of words from Scripture? Their value may be similar to that of Is. 6.10 in Jn.
12.40: "even for Jesus obedience unto death is costly; but the
cost, being expressed in the language of the Old Testament, does
not lie outside God's calculation" (Barrett, *John*, 425). Jesus'
agony is put in the context of the agony of the servant of God
in the Psalms (Hoskyns, *Gospel*, 497). Jesus' rejection is said
to be actually spoken of in Scripture and his agony is connected
with this rejection. If his agony is not actually spoken of in
Scripture,[142] at least it has antecedents.[143]

The first two uses of Scripture in ch. 19 are also from the
Psalms, again putting Jesus' Passion in the context of the experience of the Psalmist. First, in 19.24 it is said that the
soldiers' decision to cast lots for Jesus' χιτῶν is a fulfillment
(ἵνα ἡ γραφὴ πληρωθῇ) of Ps. 21.19 (LXX). This is a Psalm particularly well suited for this application, and was widely used
by Christians when speaking of the Passion.

> It is a poem of the righteous sufferer, and leads up to
> a promise of vindication. In this way it is suitable
> for the general apologetic position, that the sufferings
> of Jesus fit into a predetermined plan. . . . From this
> point of view it becomes a quarry for pictorial detail
> in writing the story of the Passion. Every detail of the
> tradition has its counterpart in prophecy, and so it
> cannot be objected that anything falls outside the
> divinely ordered scheme of redemption (Lindars, *Apolo-
> getic*, 90).

In particular, the author's use of Ps. 21.19 (LXX) shows this
same concern. Every detail of the verse is fulfilled, thus
suiting "John's purpose of suggesting that in the Passion all
that God has appointed is accomplished" (Lindars, *John*, 578).
Thus, both the choice of the Psalm and its use by the author
emphasize the notion that Jesus' death was God's will.[144] "Was
vielleicht als Hohn der Feinde verstanden werden konnte, zumindest
aber dem Glauben als anstössig galt, war *gottgewollt*. Schon
längst war dieser Zug der Passion Jesu durch das Alte Testament
vorausgesagt" (Dauer, *Die Passionsgeschichte*, 298).

In the second reference in ch. 19 that which is said to be
fulfilled (ἵνα τελειωθῇ ἡ γραφή) seems to be Jesus' statement
διψῶ (19.28).[145] In light of the mention of vinegar which follows (19.29) the text in mind is almost certainly Ps. 69.21.[146]
This was a favorite Psalm of the early Church in connection with
Jesus' Passion (see Lindars, *Apologetic*, 99-108). Once again
Jesus is seen in the person of the righteous sufferer of the
Psalms (see Reim, *Studien*, 50). The use of τελειωθῇ suggests
Jesus is completing all necessary aspects of his work which have
been revealed in Scripture. "The act that finishes (*telein*) his
work brings the Scripture to complete fulfillment (*teleioun*),
for both his work and the plan of Scripture come from his
Father" (Brown, *John*, 929). Τελειοῦν thus means "to bring to
completion what is appointed in Scripture for Jesus as the agent
of God's will" (Lindars, *John*, 580). The thirst he experienced
was not inconsequential, let alone scandalous. The Johannine
Christians need not be scandalized by Jesus' sufferings; they
are a sign of his fulfillment of God's will as revealed in
Scripture.

The final two citations occur in connection with the death
itself. The first reference (19.36) concerning Jesus' bones not
being broken is difficult, since the words used do not conform to
any one text in the OT. There is, however, agreement concerning
the two most likely sources, namely, Ex. 12.10,46 (LXX) (cf.
Num. 9.12), and/or Ps. 34 (33).21. A reference here to Ps. 34
(33).21 would continue the theme in the texts already examined
of Jesus prefigured in the righteous sufferer of the Psalms. If
the passage(s) from the Pentateuch is in mind then the reference

is to the Passover sacrifice. As many commentators note, there
are a number of allusions to the Passover in this context and
thus a reference to Ex. 12.10[147] would be in keeping with other
aspects of the author's presentation in the immediate context.[148]
It could well be that an allusion both to the righteous sufferer
of the Psalms and to the Passover is intended.[149]

The second citation in this passage (19.37) is certainly to
Zech. 12.10, but its significance is not entirely clear.[150]
There is much speculation concerning the subject(s) of the verbs
ὄψονται and ἐξεκέντησαν, but Barrett is probably to be followed
when he dismisses this speculation with the comment "John does
not indicate the subject of ὄψονται, or whether men look in
hatred, remorse, or faith (cf. 3.14f.; Num. 21.8f.). It is not
the look but the piercing that fulfils prophecy that interests
him" (*John*, 559).[151] As with the mention of the bones in the
preceding verse, this piercing also may allude to the Passover
(see Ford, "Mingled Blood," 337-338). Thus, the author's use
of the Scripture at this point serves to affirm that the details
of Jesus' death were foretold in Scripture. But the direct citations also emphasize these particular details, probably because
they are theologically significant for the author.

This emphasis is evident in all four of these texts in ch.
19. In each case the author has stressed elements in the story
which are more or less present in the Synoptics, though not
emphasized. In particular, he has added these texts from the OT
where they are lacking in the Synoptics (see Dodd, *Interpretation*,
427-428). Thus, the author seems to stress the Scripture in a
way his source(s) (whether the Synoptics themselves or common
traditions)[152] do not. Throughout the Gospel the OT is used to
substantiate the claims that Jesus does the will of the Father
and is *the* revelation of the Father. For the author, Jesus'
death is the center of this obedience and this revelation, and,
accordingly, citations from the OT play an important part in his
description of the Passion. The Scripture expresses God's will,
and Jesus is submissive to God's will, hence his activity fulfills
the Scripture (cf. Amsler, *L'ancien*, 39).

c. Conclusion

     In John's Gospel the OT is used as a witness to Jesus, both
by explicit citation and by the convergence of theological themes
with narrated events in Jesus' life.[153] Indeed, it has been
claimed that "in no other writer [in the NT] are the OT quotations
so carefully woven into the context and the whole plan of composition as in Jn." (Freed, *Quotations*, 129). His appeal to
Scripture as a witness to Jesus does not treat the OT as merely
a source of convenient striking phrases which can be claimed as
fulfilled prophecy. Rather, his use of the OT "shows an aware-
ness of the living tradition from which he derives his choice of
texts" (Lindars, *Apologetic*, 271). His polemical use of the OT
against his Jewish opponents shows "an intimate knowledge of
their arguments" (ibid.) and his own argument speaks to the issues directly.

     In this polemic there is no doubt that the author considers
that "the right interpretation of Scripture" exists "within the
community of believers" (de Jonge, "Expectations," 263). There
is a sense, then, in which, "as the fathers and the prophets
were witnesses to Christ before his coming, so the disciples have
to bear testimony to him after his departure, and thus to play
their role in the lawsuit of history" (Dahl, "Church," 116).
The Jewish opponents have indeed been judged and have been found
to be unfaithful in their possession of God's revelation to
Judaism. "Jesus reklamierte die Gottesoffenbarung der jüdischen
Schriften für sich. Und die Gemeinde des Johannes hat diese
Trennung mitvollzogen, hat sie noch radikalisiert: die Trennung
von Kirche und Synagogue ist endgültig. Die Polemik kennzeichnet
in zunehmendum Masse die Juden als falsche Sachwalter der Offen-
barung Gottes."[154]

     This description of the author's use of the OT assumes that
he has a very positive view of God's revelation within Judaism.
Not all scholars would agree with this interpretation, so before
leaving this first half of the polemic of the Gospel I will conclude with a consideration of the author's evaluation of the OT
and Judaism in general. His use of the OT is selective. For
example, he does not make use of the Law for commands (see
Smith, "Use," 53). But, as Smith notes, "paradoxically, John

evinces a more positive attitude to the Scriptures than to the
Law per se" (ibid.). The Scriptures witness to Jesus, but they
witness that he is greater than the characters in the OT and is
the fulfillment and focal point of all its imagery of God's revelation.[155] Thus, Jesus is superior to Torah, but he is also the
one of whom Moses wrote, so "the relationship is emphatically
ambivalent."[156] This ambivalence is expressed in the central
text in John concerning Jesus' relationship to the OT: ὅτι ὁ
νόμος διὰ Μωϋσέως ἐδόθη, ἡ χάρις καὶ ἡ ἀλήθεια διὰ Ἰησοῦ Χριστοῦ
ἐγένετο (1.17). Von Campenhausen is adamant that this is a case
of antithetical parallelism (*Formation*, 52-53). But others are
of the opinion that it is synthetic parallelism.[157] If there is
polemic in John against an exalted view of Moses, as already
noted, then the following verse (1.18) may well serve to deny
such views of Moses. But rejection of the exalted view of Moses
held by some within Judaism does not mean the author is rejecting
Moses entirely; obviously he does not. So Jn. 1.17 gives no
clear indication of the author's attitude toward Judaism and its
Scriptures. Does he think God was really known in Israel or
does the Torah only reveal God as it bears witness to Christ?
Many scholars would agree with Dodd when he says, "The evangelist
holds that the real revelation of God's grace and truth is not
in the Torah, but in Jesus Christ."[158] In fact, H. Seebass has
said that John "stands starkly opposed to Judaism,"[159] and von
Campenhausen is even more emphatic:[160]

> the Law, that is, the essence of the Jewish revelation
> and religion, does not lead to God: 'the Law was given
> through Moses; grace and truth came through Jesus Christ'--
> meaning, only through Christ, for the first time through
> Christ, who truly knew the Father, and absolutely never
> at any time through Moses and the Law. In thus setting
> the two side by side the author certainly does not
> imply a 'synthetic parallelism' with the old revelation;
> this is a clear antithesis, with the emphasis appropriate
> to a programmatic declaration (*Formation*, 52).

But apart from an appeal to the ambiguous Jn. 1.17, the other
explicit feature in the text most often appealed to as suggesting
such a negative evaluation of the Law is the reference to "your
law" (8.17; 10.34; cf. 15.25). But this reference to "your law"
should not be interpreted as disparaging the Law, but rather as

disparaging the Jewish opponents' use of it. Abraham is referred
to as "your father Abraham" (8.56), though obviously no dispar-
agement of Abraham is intended (cf. 8.39-40), but rather of their
appeal to him. Furthermore, the assertion by Jesus concerning
the passing of worship in Jerusalem and on Gerizim (4.21-24) is
an obvious claim that Christianity has superseded both Samaritanism and Judaism. But supersession is not necessarily a denial
of intrinsic value.[161] This same passage that speaks of Christianity's supersession also testifies to the value of Jewish
religion. This positive evaluation is found on Jesus' own lips:
"we worship what we know, for salvation is from the Jews" (4.22).
It is true, as virtually every commentator notes, that this salvation is the messianic salvation which has come in Jesus himself. But the second clause in this quote indicates the value
of the Jewish religion even if, as the following verse (4.23)
makes clear, the "role of Israel in the history of salvation is
. . . considered as a stage which has been left behind" (Schnackenburg, *John*, 1:436). But the significance of the assertion,
"we worship what we know" must not be overlooked. Here there is
a contrast with the Samaritans, of whom it is said, "you worship
what you do not know" (4.22). It would seem from this contrast
that it is possible to worship something without knowing it.[162]
But this is said not to be true of the Jews; they do have knowledge of that which they worship. So it would seem that the
Psalmist's boast is true, that God really is known in Judah (cf.
Ps. 76.1)--actual knowledge of God is available within Judaism.
So, while the author does not think that his Jewish opponents
have the knowledge of God which they claim, this lack of knowledge is not *because* they are Jews but *in spite of it*. The
Jewish opponents' ignorance is not the ἄγνοια of the pagans;
their ignorance of God is culpable precisely *because* God is
known in Israel (cf. Goppelt, *Christentum*, 256-258).

According to this Gospel, Jesus had no intention of breaking
with the Torah, but rather with its interpreters (cf. Baum,
Jews, 114). This difference over Scripture between Jesus and
his opponents, however, should probably not be interpreted in
Pauline terms.[163] Barrett, commenting on 5.39, says the problem
is that "the Jews regard their biblical studies as an end in

themselves" (*John*, 267, 270); they have made Moses "the author
of a final system of religion, and not, as he wished to be, a
witness to Christ" (ibid. 270). But the fact that they use
Scripture to evaluate messianic claims and seek eternal life
(5.39) would seem to call in question this assessment of the
problem; the Law, for them, does witness to the Messiah, it is
not an end in itself but a means to eternal life. The problem
is not so much a misuse of the Torah as it is a failure to recognize the Messiah to whom it testifies. As will become evident
below, according to the author, their problem is their view of
God himself. They have a false view of God and are thus led to
a false understanding of the Torah. So we see not misuse so
much as misunderstanding.

    While the author criticizes his opponents he would also
share with them a number of the attributes he gives them, in
particular their loyalty to Moses and the Torah (cf. Martyn,
History, 104). The reason for this is the essential continuity
between Jesus and the Torah which provides the ground for Jesus'
superiority over the Torah.[164] This essential continuity means
the Gospel and the Torah belong together. The following statement of G. Florovsky represents something of the author's
thought:[165]

> The Law and the Gospel belong together. And nobody
> can claim to be a true follower of Moses unless he
> believes that Jesus is the Lord. Any one who does not
> recognize in Jesus the Messiah, the Anointed of the Lord,
> does thereby betray the Old Dispensation itself. Only
> the Church of Christ keeps now the right key to the
> Scriptures, the true key to the prophecies of old.
> Because all these prophecies are fulfilled in Christ.

This view, in turn, means that the Torah has continuing, perma-
nent value for Christians (Enz, "Exodus," 212 n.19). In the
author's eyes it has this value for two basic reasons. First
and most obvious is his belief that the OT speaks directly of
Christ (1.45). But second, and perhaps less obvious but certainly of equal importance, is the author's use of the OT to
provide the context for appreciating Jesus and his revelation of
the Father. "The Jews worshipped what they knew (see 4.22); and
only as the outcome of this older knowledge, true but imperfect,
contained in the Old Testament, could the fuller knowledge of

God in Christ be manifested" (Tasker, *Old Testament*, 55). The
author's appreciation for the Torah is ultimately based on the
fact that the Father whom Jesus reveals is the God of Judaism
and its Scriptures. The OT *does* reveal God's graciousness,
truth and love.[166] It is because the Scripture reveals God that
Jesus, the revelation of God par excellence superseding all other
revelation, is said to fulfill Scripture. By showing Jesus to
be the fulfillment of Scripture, the author assures his readers
in their faith in Jesus; in following Jesus they are loyal to
the God revealed in Judaism.

Thus, the author has a very positive view of the OT. It
is his opponents' use of it in their rejection of Jesus that
he finds completely unacceptable. We have seen how he combats
their position, both directly by saying they themselves do not
keep the Law and indirectly by saying the Torah witnesses to
Jesus. Now we are ready to go further. Behind their claims of
loyalty to the Torah is a claim to know God. Correspondingly,
behind the author's rejection of this claim is the assertion
that they do not know God at all. This evaluation of the opponents is stated explicitly when Jesus says to them, "his [God's]
voice you have never heard, his form you have never seen"
(5.37b). The primary purpose of this verse is to separate the
opponents from Moses, for it was at Sinai that God was heard and
seen (Ex. 19.9,11) (cf. Pancaro, *Law*, 220-224).[167] The Father
had borne witness to Jesus (5.37a), not only through the Torah
(cf. Pancaro, *Law*, 217-227), but also internally (cf. Brown,
John, 227-228). But the opponents have not received this testimony.[168] The rejection of the opponents' claim to be loyal to
Moses and the Torah is essentially an assertion that they are
utterly alienated from God. This alienation is not left simply
implicit in this way. The explicit charge of alienation from
God is the substance of the second half of the polemic of the
Gospel, to which we now turn.

3. Polemic Against the Opponents' Claim to Be Children of God

a. Introduction

As we turn to a consideration of the author's attack on the
claim of the opponents to be children of God we come to the heart

of the polemic in John's Gospel. Our study of this part of the
polemic will begin with a consideration of the main text in
which the author explicitly rejects their claim, asserting that
the opponents are actually children of the devil rather than
children of God. From that which is explicit we will move to
the more implicit and see how this alienation from God is depicted
in the author's depiction of the opponents. The principal features of their alienation will then be clarified by seeing, in
contrast, the author's depiction of the docility before God of
those who receive Jesus. So we will see how the author uses
both explicit statement and narrative skill in driving home the
fundamental point in his polemic, namely, his opponents' utter
alienation from God.

b. *Principal Text: Jn. 8.31-59*[169]

In this passage the opponents' claim to be free children of
Abraham leads to their more basic claim to be children of God.
The passage begins with Jesus' introduction of the twin themes
of freedom and truth, claiming that they are available to those
who abide in his word (8.31-32).

1) They Are Not Children of Abraham

By saying they will have freedom and truth if they abide in
his word Jesus is obviously implying that apart from him they
do not have these blessings. The opponents are aware of this
claim by Jesus and counter it with the claim that they have never
been enslaved (8.33). It could be that their claim is political
as well as religious, perhaps somewhat like the thought expressed,
according to Josephus, by Eleazar at the siege of Masada: "Long
since, my brave men, we determined neither to serve the Romans
nor any other save God, for He alone is man's true and righteous
Lord" (*Jewish War* 7.323). But there is no indication in John
that the opponents are claiming anything like political freedom.
Rather, the reference to being the seed of Abraham (8.33) shows
their claim is to a religious freedom. They are claiming freedom
from idolatry and sin on the basis of the relation they have to
God through the covenant made with Abraham (Odeberg, *Gospel*,
296-297). "Abraham war für die Juden der Begründer der

Gottesverehrung, der den Schöpfer der Welt erkannte und ihm
treu diente" (Schnackenburg, *Johannes* 2:284). In response Jesus
says that anyone who sins shows thereby that he is a slave to
sin (8.34). This introduces the key distinction between external claims and internal reality. The truth about one's relation
to God is revealed by what one does. It is the interior reality
of the opponents' alienation from God underneath the exterior
appearances that the author is attempting to expose.

The formal claim to be Abraham's seed is at first accepted,
but their desire to kill Jesus is said to belie this claim (8.37).
In this way the reference in 8.34 to the test of deeds is repeated in v.39: "If you were Abraham's children, you would do
what Abraham did." They claim to be Abraham's seed, but in
seeking to kill the one telling them the truth of God they show
they are not like Abraham (8.40). The reference here is probably
to Abraham's reception of the divine messengers in Gen. 18,
though there may also be a more general reference to Abraham's
character (Brown, *John*, 357). If so, then Barrett's suggestion
that "Abraham's mind was not closed against the truth" (*John*,
347) has much to commend it in the light of 8.43. The characteristics of disciples of Abraham was a topic of interest within
Judaism. The comment in *Pirke Aboth* 5.22 is particularly noteworthy:[170]

> Every one who has three things is one of the disciples
> of Abraham our father. And *every one who has* three
> other things is one of the disciples of Balaam the wicked.
> *If he has* a good eye, and a lowly soul and a humble
> spirit, he is of the disciples of Abraham our father.
> *If he has* an evil eye, and a boastful soul and a haughty
> spirit, he is of the disciples of Balaam the wicked
> (*APOT* 2:709).

This description is of great interest since, as will be discussed
below (pp. 80-90) such humility is one of the hallmarks in
John of those who receive Jesus, and the opponents are depicted
as being full of pride. Of similar interest is the description
of Abraham in *Bezah* 32b: "whoever is merciful to his fellow-
men is certainly of the children of our father Abraham, and who-
soever is not merciful to his fellow-men is certainly not of
the children of our father Abraham." The author would agree
with this passage entirely. Indeed, the chief characteristic of

God for him is his compassionate mercy. Part of the author's
polemic against the opponents is that they do not share this
mercy, as is evident from their reactions to the healings which
immediately precede and follow ch. 8 (cf. 7.23 and ch. 9). This
lack of mercy demonstrates their alienation from God. Thus, the
author may agree with his opponents concerning the characteristics of Abraham and his disciples, but it is these very characteristics that he finds lacking in his opponents.

So this reference to doing the works of Abraham may already
contain implicitly the key elements in the indictment that later
become explicit. Be this as it may, the emphasis here is on
their rejection of Jesus, "a man who has told you the truth which
I heard from God" (8.40). The author here returns to the motif
of truth, which was the second theme introduced in the opening
section (8.31-36). Just as the opponents were said not to be
free, despite their own self-understanding, so now they are said
to be separated from the truth. Jesus has announced the truth
from God, but they have not received it because his word οὐ χωρεῖ
ἐν ὑμῖν (8.37). This statement could be a simple observation:
my word makes no headway among you (cf. BAGD 2, p. 889d). Alternatively it could be an indication of why they reject his
word: my word finds no place in you (cf. ibid.). The latter
interpretation is preferable since their internal disposition is
emphasized in the next section of ch. 8.

2) *They Are Not Children of God*

Jn. 8.41-47 is the very heart of the author's polemic. He
has denied that they are children of Abraham (8.39-40), but Jesus
now says that they are indeed doing the works of their father
(8.41). This assertion naturally raises the question of who
their father really is if it is not Abraham. So the opponents
counter that they have not been born ἐκ πορνείας, but rather ἕνα
πατέρα ἔχομεν τὸν θεόν (8.41). The nature of their self-understanding expressed here is well brought out by Brown:[171]

> when in 41 the Jews deny that they are children of
> fornication, they are denying that they have wandered
> from the true path of the worship of God. In stressing
> that God is their Father, they are reiterating the terms
> of the covenant with Moses whereby Israel became God's

child (Exod iv 22) and Yahweh became Israel's father
(Deut xxxii 6)--a theme reiterated constantly in the
prophetic preaching (Isa lxiv 8; Mal ii 10) (*John*, 364).

It is this claim to have God for a father which is attacked in
8.42-47.

The basic point in the rejection of this claim is quite
simple. Since Jesus has come from God and they have rejected
him, obviously they cannot know God: "If God were your Father,
you would love me" (8.42). Despite their claims, their rejection
of Jesus exposes who their real father is. Jesus' unity with
the Father, here expressed in terms of his origin and obedience
(8.42), makes it obvious in the author's eyes that anyone who
rejects him is rejecting God the Father.

The rest of the passage, 8.43-47, works out the implications
of this point just made. The lack of room for Jesus' word mentioned in 8.37 is now reiterated when Jesus says they are not
able to hear his word (8.43). This incapacity (οὐ δύνασθε) indicates that something is radically wrong with them. The next
verse, 8.44, is the central accusation: they have the wrong
father, they are of their father the devil.[172]

3) They Are Children of the Devil

De la Potterie has shown that v. 44 is the central element
in a chiastic pattern in vv. 42-47:

        A   The Jews and God (8.42a)
        B   The Jews and Jesus (8.42b-43)
        C   The Jews and the devil (8.44)
        B' The Jews and Jesus (8.45-46)
        A' The Jews and God (8.47)

"Au centre du développement . . . Jesus indique la raison profonde
de leur incrédulité: au lieu d'avoir Dieu pour père, ils ont pour
père le diable."[173] But unfortunately, v. 44 is perhaps as difficult to interpret as it is important for an understanding of
the author's polemic against the Jewish opponents. I will discuss first what he says about the devil and then look at how
this is applied to his opponents.

The key for understanding this description of the devil is
to see that it is describing one who is exactly the opposite of
Jesus. Both are described with respect to the beginning (1.1),

but Jesus is ἡ ζωή (14.6) and has life in himself and gives life
(1.4; 5.26), while the devil is ἀνθρωποκτόνος.[174] Furthermore,
Jesus speaks the truth (e.g. 8.40) and is the truth (14.6),
but the devil ἐν τῇ ἀληθείᾳ οὐκ ἔστηκεν, ὅτι οὐκ ἔστιν ἀλήθεια
ἐν αὐτῷ. This first clause in this negative description indicates "that in the whole course of human history the Devil remains outside the sphere of truth."[175] In the author's thought
ἀλήθεια refers both to the sphere of divine reality[176] and to
the divine revelation.[177] These two concepts of truth are united
in Jesus who both is the Truth (14.6) and speaks the truth (8.
40). Just as it is Jesus' very nature to be the truth, so it
is the devil's very nature that he lack the truth, as the second
clause says, οὐκ ἔστιν ἀλήθεια ἐν αὐτῷ. So for the author the
devil is the personification of what is exactly the opposite of
Jesus.

In these three clauses in v. 44 the description of the
devil moves from the exterior to the interior (de la Potterie,
La vérité, 921). The author begins with a reference to the
devil's external activity as a murderer, follows this with a
general reference to his alienation from the truth (ἐν τῇ ἀληθείᾳ
οὐκ ἔστηκεν) and concludes by asserting that this alienation
from the truth is thorough, to his very core οὐκ ἔστιν ἀλήθεια
ἐν αὐτῷ. The author then develops this theme of the devil's
alienation from the truth by use of the opposite term, ψεῦδος:
ὅταν λαλῇ τὸ ψεῦδος, ἐκ τῶν ἰδίων λαλεῖ, ὅτι ψεύστης ἐστὶν καὶ
ὁ πατὴρ αὐτοῦ. "Jean cherche donc à remonter jusqu'à la source
intérieure et secrète de l'action diabolique: c'est l'absence
totale, en lui, de la vérité" (ibid. 929).

It appears the author is concentrating on the interior disposition of the devil. The significance of his description in
the last sentence emerges when it is contrasted with his view of
Jesus. First, as already stressed, it is said the devil speaks
the lie and is a liar, while Jesus is the one who speaks the
truth and is the truth. But further it is said that the devil
speaks from himself (ἐκ τῶν ἰδίων), but this is exactly what
Jesus never does (cf. esp. 12.49).[178] Jesus always speaks from
the Father (e.g. 8.38) and all his activity and teaching is
dependent on the Father (e.g. 8.28,38,42,50). This contrast

between Jesus' dependence on the Father and the devil's independence from the Father is the crucial distinction between them,
that which characterizes each of them more than anything else.
In this context the conclusion that the devil ψεύστης ἐστίν is
a statement of his very being; he speaks lies (i.e. that which
is contrary to God and his revelation, especially his revelation
in Jesus the Truth) because (ὅτι) he *is* a liar (i.e. one who is
thoroughly separated from God).

The author concludes his description of the devil with the
statement, ψεύστης ἐστίν καὶ ὁ πατὴρ αὐτοῦ. This is a very difficult saying to interpret. It could refer to the devil and his
father, but this makes no sense in the context. Those who interpret ἐκ τοῦ πατρὸς τοῦ διαβόλου as referring to the devil's
father naturally find the same sense here. Most commentators,
however, accept an interpretation similar to that represented by
Barrett when he says, "The construction is very harsh but it
seems that there is no acceptable alternative to the rendering
'he is a liar and the father of it (that is, of the lie, or
falsehood)'" (*John*, 349). This interpretation fits the context
well. However, according to the grammar of the phrase, there
are three possible antecedents of αὐτοῦ. It could be neuter and
refer back to τὸ ψεῦδος, as Barrett and others suggest. It
could refer to the devil, though, as just noted, this makes little sense. The third possibility is that αὐτοῦ is masculine
and refers to ψεύστης, with the sense: he is a liar and the
father of the liar.[179] This interpretation would not materially
change the sense from the first option, but it could have the
advantage of fitting the context a little better since the main
point is that Jesus' opponents have the devil for a father, i.e.
the reference here is to persons rather than an abstraction.
In 8.55 Jesus actually calls them liars.[180] In any case, whether
αὐτοῦ is taken as masculine or neuter the general point is clear
enough: far from being related to God, the opponents are related
to him who is totally opposed to God.

Something of the author's understanding of the nature of
this relationship between the opponents and the devil is indicated in the first sentence of v. 44: ὑμεῖς ἐκ τοῦ πατρὸς τοῦ
διαβόλου ἐστὲ καὶ τὰς ἐπιθυμίας τοῦ πατρὸς ὑμῶν θέλετε ποιεῖν.

Many scholars think this is a reference to the 'origin' of the
Jewish opponents, in the sense that a father is one from whom
you "draw your being" (Westcott, *John* 2:21). According to this
interpretation the devil begets children in a way that is analogous to the begetting of Christians by God. While it is true
that there is a contrast here between the Fatherhood of God and
the fatherhood of the devil (cf. n.172 above), it is not at
all clear that the author attributes to the devil a spiritual
power working in the lives of individuals analogous to God's.
The strongest support for the view that such power is attributed
to the devil by the author(s) comes from 1 Jn. 3.8: εἰς τοῦτο
ἐφανερώθη ὁ υἱὸς τοῦ θεοῦ, ἵνα λύσῃ τὰ ἔργα τοῦ διαβόλου. If
the genitive, τοῦ διαβόλου, expresses possession then the devil
would seem to be responsible for all sin (cf. 1 Jn. 3.8a). But
even this text is ambiguous since the genitive could indicate a
more general description, i.e. it could refer to works like those
of the devil, who has been sinning from the beginning. So the
language allows the possibility that the author held the devil
directly responsible for sin, but this is not certain. Such an
interpretation, however, would run the danger of implying that
he held a view of cosmic dualism which included a strict determinism. Many scholars do indeed speak of Johannine determinism,
and such passages as 6.37,44 would seem to support them. But
the author's strong belief in God's sovereignty does not lead him
to deny that people must cooperate.[181] The opponents have not
been forced to reject God, it is something they themselves will
(θέλετε, Jn. 8.44). "Von einer 'Prädestination' zu Teufelskin-
dern ist nichts gesagt. Die Klassifizierung in Teufels--und
Gotteskinder ergibt sich aus dem Verhalten und Tun der Menschen
(vgl. 1 Joh 3,10)" (Schnackenburg, *Johannes* 2:288). The author's
thought is not really characterized by a determinist dualism but
rather is far closer to the Jewish notion of the two יצרים.
The belief that one must choose between the יצר הרע and the הטוב
יצר is already present in Sir. 15.11-17. In Rabbinic thought
the יצר הרע is identified with Satan (Odeberg, *Gospel*, 300), but
"the basis of sinfulness is not the yēṣaer hā-rā' in itself but
the domination of the yēṣaer over man, man's *slavery* under the
yēṣaer" (ibid. 299, cf. St-B 4:466-483). Such a conception, as

Odeberg notes (ibid. 301), corresponds exactly with the present
context in John which has spoken of freedom from sin and slavery
to sin (8.34).[182]

But if the author does not mean to imply that the devil is
the source of the opponents' sin, at least in any deterministic
sense, what then does he mean when he calls the devil their
father? As Schnackenburg has noted, in Johannine thinking εἶναι
ἐκ "affirms both origin and type of being" (*John* 1:371). The
devil as the origin, or source, of sin would seem to be a reference to his sin ἀπ᾽ ἀρχῆς. He is considered the first sinner,
and thus the source of sin in a general sense, rather than in
some deterministic sense in the life of any individual. But he
is also father in the sense of providing a "type of being," in
that he provides the pattern of sin. By referring to the devil
as the opponents' father the author implies a spiritual relationship. The devil would be their father in the sense that "the
child learns all that is decisive from his father," for the child
imitates the father.[183] This notion suggests a unity of mind.
So de la Potterie's suggestion that the καί in 8.44 is epexegetic
may be correct, with the result that when the author says the
Jewish opponents are ἐκ τοῦ πατρὸς τοῦ διαβόλου he *means* that
they wish to do τὰς ἐπιθυμίας τοῦ πατρὸς ὑμῶν (*La vérité*, 919
n.35). In seeking to kill Jesus they show that their wills are
in tune with the devil who is the murderer; in rejecting the one
who has told them the truth of God they show that their wills
are in tune with the devil who is the liar. The devil was a
murderer ἀπ᾽ ἀρχῆς and has no truth ἐν αὐτῷ, which is to say,
he is thoroughly alienated from God, evil to the very core. By
saying that such a one is the opponents' father the author implies that they are at heart alienated from God. At the center
of their own identity is their relation to God as Father. It
is loyalty to God as they know him that leads them to reject
Jesus. It is because their rejection is based on what is deepest
within them that the author asserts that at heart they are not
related to God at all but to the devil. They have nothing in
common with God. In essence the author *is* accusing them of
being ἐκ πορνείας in its religious sense of idolatry.[184]

4)   The Charge Reiterated and Confirmed

The final verses of this passage emphasize this indictment
by returning to themes already mentioned. It is the opponents'
lack of faith in the one who has spoken the truth to them that
condemns them (8.45). The freedom from sin and the knowledge of
the truth that they have claimed is now attributed to Jesus, and
is even admitted by the opponents to be true: "Which of you con-
victs me of sin?" (8.46). Finally, the indictment is reiterated
in utter simplicity: "He who is of God hears the words of God;
the reason why you do not hear them is that you are not of God"
(ἐκ τοῦ θεοῦ).

The truth of this charge is shown in their reaction (8.48).
By calling Jesus a Samaritan and demon-possessed they reveal,
for the author, the depth of their alienation from God (cf.
Blank, *Krisis*, 241-242). The context correlates having a demon
with glorifying oneself (8.49); in the opponents' eyes Jesus'
judgment upon them indicates that he thinks too highly of himself. They become convinced that this is the case when Jesus
goes on to say, "Truly, truly, I say to you, if any one keeps
my word, he will never see death" (8.51-52). His megalomania is
so great that he claims to be greater than Abraham (8.53-57).
But his self-glorification passes over into blasphemy when he
uses the divine ἐγώ εἰμι of himself (8.58-59). This reference
to δόξα and the matter of self-glorification introduces a key
motif in the author's polemic which must be examined further.
Jn. 8.31-59 has given clear expression to the main point in the
polemic, namely, the opponents' alienation from God. In turning
now to this theme of self-glorification I will begin to consider
how the author develops this point in narrative form.

c.   The Charge of Self-Glorification and Pride

Jesus denies the opponents' charge of self-glorification
expressed in Jn. 8.48-59. He claims, instead, to be glorified
by the one his opponents claim is their God (8.54). Thus the
author is developing the contrast he has made between Jesus and
the devil. Jesus' utter dependence on the Father has been contrasted with the devil's autonomy. The charge that it is this

devil who is the opponents' father is now worked out in terms
of their self-glorification. For not only is the opponents'
charge of self-glorification rejected, but also, in typical
Johannine irony, it is turned back upon the opponents themselves.
The central charge against them is that they glorify one another
and seek only human glory, thus lacking the humility necessary
to receive God's revelation in Jesus.

This charge is explicitly made in 5.41-44; 7.18 and 12.42-
43. In the first of these passages they are said to receive
those who come in their own name, but do not receive Jesus who
comes in the name of his Father. It would seem that, in the
author's eyes, there are only these two options. If one is not
commissioned by the Father then there is no other ground on which
to stand but one's own self. This same thought is presented in
the second passage, 7.18. Here seeking one's own glory is expressed in terms of speaking from oneself. Thus the seeking of
glory is a matter of one's interior disposition. They speak from
themselves while Jesus speaks from God. Jesus is one with God
while they are separated from him. They think they are in communion with God and speak for him, but they are really only in
communion with themselves and are speaking from themselves. This
same separation from God is emphasized in 5.41-44 when it is
said that they do not receive one who comes in the Father's
name. It is impossible for them to have faith in Jesus because
they only honor one another rather than seek the δόξα of the
only God (5.44). In this last accusation there is perhaps a
reference to the charges of blasphemy brought against Jesus.
They have accused him of making himself God and thus they seem
to be the champions of Jewish monotheism. But for the author it
is Jesus and the Christians who know the only God, not the Jewish
opponents. They are totally separated from him in that, as this
passage says, τὴν ἀγάπην τοῦ θεοῦ οὐκ ἔχετε (5.42). In the
ambiguity of this genitive are present the twin Johannine themes
of the opponents' lack of love for God and their lack of God's
own characteristic love. "Men seek the glory of personal distinction through the praise and esteem of their fellows: Jesus
reveals the glory of self-giving love which is the glory of the
Father and the Son" (Ramsey, *Glory*, 65).

Jn. 12.42-43 implies that this matter of seeking honor that
comes from men rather than that which comes from God was an important issue in the life of the Johannine community. This same
corruption in the heart of the opponents of Jesus was present
in the opponents of the Christians as well. But it was also
something that the Johannine Christians had to wrestle with in
their own hearts. Fear of the Pharisees who threatened to excommu-
nicate anyone confessing Jesus is described here as love of the
glory of men rather than of God. This is one of the passages
referring to ἀποσυνάγωγος; in deciding to confess Jesus and suffer excommunication they had chosen the glory of God rather than
men. It is implied that there were others who did not make this
choice. By describing their reticence with the same terms he
has used in describing Jesus' opponents the author is indicating
to these hidden disciples the implications of their position. For
the author it is impossible to refuse to confess Jesus and still
honor God. These hidden Christians, like the Jewish opponents,
are living only in communion with men, not God.

The author considers this self-glorification to be a form
of pride, as is evident from another passage, Jn. 9.39-41. Here
Jesus condemns the Pharisees for their claim that they see, when
in fact they are blind. Their inability to recognize their need
is emphasized. They are certain that they are children of God,
and their possession of the Law gives them the means of judging
religious matters, as has been noted. But the reception of
glory from one another has resulted in a closed-minded certainty.
It is this lack of openness and receptivity that indicates a
problem in their very hearts. They recognized Jesus as a Rabbi,
but they do not receive his teaching. Nicodemus confesses Jesus
to be a teacher come from God (3.2), but when Jesus then teaches
him, he cannot understand (3.9). But rather than accepting what
Jesus says, humbly acknowledging his own inability to understand,
instead he calls into question Jesus' teaching. This same confession of Jesus as teacher followed by rejection of his teaching
is seen on a wide scale in Jn. 6. Here the crowd calls Jesus
Rabbi (6.25) and asks for the Bread of Heaven (6.34) but when
Jesus' teaching goes beyond them they only question rather than
accept.[185] This lack of receptivity is evident among all those

who reject Jesus, both οἱ 'Ιουδαῖοι (6.41,52) and would-be
disciples (6.60). Indeed, to the opponents, receptivity towards
Jesus' teaching is tantamount to being led astray (7.45-49) (cf.
Pancaro, *Law*, 103). The problem is not intellectual but spiritual. As Jesus says, the Father must draw them (6.44,65), they
must be taught by God, hearing and learning from the Father (6.
45). Thus, once again the author's attack comes down to the
claim that those who reject Jesus are alienated from God. They
do not understand his teaching so they reject it, in contrast
to those, like Peter, who believe that Jesus has the words of
eternal life (6.68). But Peter's faith is not due to his having
understood Jesus' teaching. The author makes it very clear
throughout the Gospel that even Jesus' own true disciples did
not understand him until after the glorification and sending of
the Spirit (e.g. 2.22; 12.16; 14.26; 20.9). Rather, these disciples found something about Jesus' activity and teaching that
harmonized with what they knew of God and this led them to stay
with Jesus despite the incomprehensible, even outrageous things
he said and did. The contrast here between Peter and those who
are unresponsive to Jesus leads us to consider further the
author's description of those who are receptive of Jesus. His
depiction of the deep-seated pride of the opponents can be seen
more clearly when it is contrasted with the humble docility of
those who do receive Jesus.

d. The Contrast of the Disciples' Humility and Openness[186]

     Consider, as a first example of those who receive Jesus, the
figure of Nathanael. Nathanael's appearance on the Gospel's
stage is brief but highly significant since he is a major representative of those who come to the light. That the author intends Nathanael to have such a representative function is evident
from his position in ch. 1. In Jn. 1.35-51 there appears a
series of the first disciples coming to Jesus. Also in this section there are a number of titles applied to Jesus, Lamb of God
(1.36), Rabbi (1.38), and Messiah (1.41). Nathanael is the last
disciple in the series and his acclamation of Jesus as Son of
God and King of Israel (1.49) comes as a climax.[187]

He stands in striking contrast to the Jewish opponents. It
is most important to notice that he reacts to Jesus initially in
exactly the same way they do: "Can anything good come out of
Nazareth?" (1.46). That is, for Nathanael Jesus' origin disqualifies him from being "him of whom Moses wrote in the law and
also the prophets wrote" (1.45), just as it does for the opponents (7.41-42,52).[188] But unlike the Jews, he ends by confessing
Jesus to be the Son of God and King of Israel and is promised
even greater revelation (1.51). The reason for the difference
must lie in the fact that Nathanael is ἀληθῶς 'Ισραηλίτης ἐν ᾧ
δόλος οὐκ ἔστιν (1.47).[189]

The designation ἀληθῶς 'Ισραηλίτης marks him out in contrast
to the Jewish opponents. For the author "'Ισραήλ is the people of
God. To be related to it is to be related to God's people, and
consequently to God" (Gutbrod, "'Ισραήλ," 385). Thus, Nathanael
is a genuine[190] member of the people of God, while the opponents
consider themselves to be such but are not.

> A contrast is obviously being drawn between 'true
> Israelites', of whom Nathanael is the typical figure,
> and 'false Israelites'. The name 'Israelite' is
> reserved for those who are like Nathanael; those who
> are not may *call themselves* 'Israelite', but have
> no right to do so. Those who are unlike Nathanael are
> obviously the 'Jews'. It is they who refuse to
> acknowledge Jesus and maintain the skepticism
> Nathanael showed at the outset, hardening it into
> opposition and hatred (Pancaro, *Law*, 293).

Nathanael accepts Jesus despite his skepticism and thereby shows
that he is a member of the people of God. In contrast to the
opponents, whose rejection is traced to their relationship to
the devil in whom there is no truth (8.44), the author describes
Nathanael's internal disposition as one in which there is no
δόλος. It is difficult to know exactly what this term is meant
to signify. It may serve as an expression for all that which we
have seen attributed by the author to the opponents and which
keeps them from accepting Jesus. However, this interpretation
is only based on the more obvious general contrast between these
opponents and Nathanael.[191]

That which distinguishes Nathanael from the Jewish opponents
is a humble docility that is open to God (Walter, *L'incroyance*,
31; Brown, *John*, 86-87). Like the opponents, Nathanael

questions, but unlike them he comes to Jesus and "sees," a term
used in John for revelation.[192] This sight results in him confessing Jesus. The stimulus for this confession is Jesus' statement, "Before Philip called you, when you were under the fig
tree, I saw you" (1.48). It is not at all clear why this statement should elicit Nathanael's confession. But whatever the
specific reference may be, Nathanael accepts that Jesus has seen
into his heart (1.47-48a) and has seen him from afar (1.48b)
and this confirms the accuracy of Philip's claim to have found
"him of whom Moses wrote in the law, and also the prophets wrote"
(1.45).

In the light of 1.45 it is best to understand the titles
which Nathanael attributes to Jesus as messianic.[193] There is
some question, however, as to how much of the Johannine meaning
of ὁ υἱὸς τοῦ θεοῦ should be found in its use here. Perhaps
it is best to understand the addition of the term βασιλεὺς τοῦ
'Ισραήλ as indicating that ὁ υἱὸς τοῦ θεοῦ does not here have
the full significance it will have later in the Gospel. This
interpretation might be confirmed by the observation that
"Nathanael's faith is so far grounded only upon a miracle; such
faith, though it is real faith, is inferior to the faith that
needs no sign; cf. 4.48; 14.11" (Barrett, *John*, 186). And further confirmation would be Jesus' promise in 1.51, since, "as
it now stands 1.51 corrects Nathanael's confession which had affirmed that Jesus was the national-political liberator (cf. also
6,15; 18,36)" (Painter, "Christ," 361). Thus, Nathanael's confession is that of a true Israelite who recognizes his Messiah
but it is not yet the confession of a Christian who recognizes
"Jesus as the new 'locus' of divine revelation (cf. Gen. 28,16f)"
(Pancaro, *Law*, 304), which is the promise in 1.51. Nathanael has
a correct though limited understanding of who Jesus is, just as
the opponents also have a correct but limited view in their acknowledgment that Jesus is a teacher come from God (3.2). The
opponents continue to question (3.4,9) while Nathanael, instead,
whole-heartedly accepts and confesses. Nathanael is promised
further enlightenment, and it would appear that he is represented
as receiving it, since he is one of the group of disciples that
meet Jesus after the resurrection (21.2). The opponents, on the
other hand, go from questioning to antagonism to violent hostility.

Because of his function in John as a representative figure,
Nathanael is a particularly important illustration of the openness of those who accept Jesus. That Nathanael's openness is a
characteristic of those who receive will become more evident
through a consideration of other figures in the Gospel.

First, there is the description of the first followers of
Jesus. While the accounts in Mt. 4.18-20 and Mk. 1.16-20 depict
Jesus' first followers as answering a direct call from Jesus
himself, in John (cf. Lk. 5.1-11) there is no such initial call.
There is nothing but a declaration by John the Baptist, "Behold,
the Lamb of God!" (1.36). There is not even any indication that
the Baptist said this for the benefit of his two disciples who
were with him. The initiative is solely theirs, they heard and
followed (1.37). Indeed, far from calling them to follow him,
Jesus turns around and looks at them after they are already following him. He is going on ahead and they must catch up. His
question to them, "What do you seek?" (1.38), can reveal their
hearts by indicating their attitude toward Jesus and their reason
for following him. Their answer shows them to be very receptive
to Jesus: "Rabbi (which means Teacher), where are you staying?"
(1.38). They address him with a term of respect which indicates
that they regard him as a teacher, as the author points out. The
disciples' question, "where are you staying?" passes the initiative over to Jesus. His question to them, "What do you seek?",
would have allowed them to set the agenda. They could have
asked him, for instance, why the Baptist had called him the Lamb
of God. Instead, they accept the role of receivers and express
a desire to be with Jesus. Jesus' response, "Come and see"
(1.39), gives no information (such as the address where he is
staying) and again shifts the initiative back to the disciples.
It is an invitation, but it reveals nothing and promises nothing,
except that they will see where he is staying. This first part
of the story concludes simply: "They came and saw where he was
staying; and they stayed with him that day, for it was about the
tenth hour" (1.39).

When this opening scene is contrasted with the descriptions
in the Synoptics it will be evident how great an emphasis is
placed in John on Jesus' almost mysterious silence. Leading up

to the coming of the first disciples there is no heavenly Voice
identifying Jesus (Mt. 3.17; Lk. 3.22), no reference to the temptation of Jesus (Mt. 4.1-11; Mk. 1.12-13; Lk. 4.1-13), no
preaching of the Kingdom of God (Mt. 4.17; Mk. 1.14-15), nor
teaching in synagogues and healing (Lk. 4.14-41), and no call
for disciples (Mt. 4.18-22; Mk. 1.16-20; cf. Lk. 5.1-11). Instead, Jesus comes on the scene as one silently walking past
(Jn. 1.29,36). Instead of a Voice from heaven (which occurs
later, 12.28), there is only the human voice of John the Baptist,
applying to Jesus a term that will not be used again in the
Gospel (1.29,36). Far from teaching and preaching before calling
men to follow him, Jesus is presented as saying very little, being given only the lines, "What do you seek?" (1.38) and "Come
and see" (1.39). Thus, compared with the Synoptics' picture,
Jesus in John appears within the story as one hidden and aloof.
Instead of coming and preaching and calling men, he says nothing
and men must take the initiative to seek him out. These first
disciples are thus characterized by initiative and willingness
to examine claims they have heard concerning this silent one.
Most importantly, they are neither put off by his silence nor
do they seek to break it. Rather, they are receptive, seeking
only to be where Jesus is staying.

Something of the same characteristics can be discerned in
the author's depiction of the mother of Jesus at the wedding in
Cana (2.1-11). When the wine runs out Jesus' mother takes the
initiative and says "They have no wine" (2.3). There are significant similarities between this statement and the way the
first disciples relate to Jesus. The request that Jesus do
something about the wine shortage is entirely implicit. As the
first two disciples took the initiative in following Jesus, so
his mother now takes the initiative in speaking to him. But as
the response of the first two disciples (1.38) allowed Jesus to
set the agenda, so here his mother's statement does not dictate
what he is to do about the problem that has arisen. The implication is that she believes he is able to do something about it,
but whether he will do something and what it will be her statement leaves open for him to decide.

Jesus responds with a cryptic saying that tests his mother.
The phrase τί ἐμοί καί σοί (2.4) can express either a harsh

rejection or a milder form of disengagement, depending on the
context and/or the tone of voice (Schnackenburg, *John*, 1:328;
Brown, *John*, 99). Which is here implied seems impossible to determine. In either case Jesus is setting a distance between
himself and his mother, a distance also implied in the use of
γυνή (2.4). This is the same sort of coldness evident in his
question to the first disciples, "What do you seek?" (1.38).
This aloofness is followed by an enigmatic statement, "My hour
has not yet come" (2.4). This occurrence of the notion of Jesus'
hour is quite unintelligible to Jesus' mother, for it is a reference to his death and there is a thorough inability to understand
the necessity of Jesus' death throughout the Gospel. So it
seems best to take this as an entirely cryptic saying by Jesus.
As with the other cryptic sayings in John, it reveals everything
and nothing. It shows that even his signs in Galilee are to be
viewed in the context of his coming revelation in his death in
Jerusalem. But his mother does not grasp anything of this. Her
response is to tell the servants, "Do what ever he tells you"
(2.5). In the face of a thoroughly enigmatic statement by Jesus
she leaves the initiative entirely with him. His saying has
gone over her head. It sounds slightly or even completely negative, but since she does not know what this hour is she cannot
really be sure of what he means. She puts pressure on him to do
something about the problem but she does so in a way that leaves
him entirely free to respond as he will. Thus, a key element in
the character of Jesus' mother, as of the first disciples, is
this leaving of the initiative with Jesus. This is a form of
humility in that it is an openness to the will of another.

   One further example of the humble disposition of those who
receive, in contrast to the self-glorifying pride of those who
reject, is provided by the woman of Samaria. The conversation
between the woman and Jesus is instigated by Jesus. In contrast
to his encounter with his first disciples (1.37), he takes the
initiative and asks her for a drink of water (4.7). The woman
responds, "How is it that you, a Jew, ask a drink of me, a woman
of Samaria?" (4.9). The author adds the note, "For the Jews have
no dealings with Samaritans" (4.9). This ethnic barrier is the
first of a number of barriers between this woman and Jesus. As

the conversation progresses its chief interest is the description
of Jesus breaking down these barriers and revealing himself to
this woman. The story stresses that this ethnic barrier between
Jews and Samaritans is not one that God honors, since his Son
completely ignores it.

The woman has asked Jesus a question and he replies with a
characteristically cryptic saying: "If you knew the gift of
God, and who it is that is saying to you, 'Give me a drink,'
you would have asked him, and he would have given you living
water" (4.10). As with Jesus' other cryptic sayings, there is
no way the woman could understand this saying in the way a
Johannine Christian reading the Gospel could. But as with the
others, she could pick up something. The phrase ἡ δωρεὰ τοῦ θεοῦ
was used by the Rabbis of the Torah, by the Gnostics of life-
giving revelation and the power to see God and be like him, by
some early Christians of the Holy Spirit (Acts) and of righteousness, salvation and grace in general (Paul).[194] It seems that
"Δωρέα is a comprehensive term for anything that God bestows on
man for his salvation" (Schnackenburg, *John* 1:426). Thus, the
term ἡ δωρεὰ τοῦ θεοῦ should have at least indicated to the woman
that Jesus was talking about God's revelation. The term τὸ
ὕδωρ τὸ ζῶν also could have directed her thinking since it had
associations very similar to ἡ δρωεὰ τοῦ θεοῦ. As has been noted
(p. 45), the Rabbis and early Christians used it to refer to the
Holy Spirit. They also, along with the OT and the Gnostics, used
it to refer to God's revelation in general. On the basis of
such general associations of these two terms, within the story
Jesus could be understood to be saying, in effect, If you knew
the Scriptures and the salvation they reveal, and if you were
aware of my identity as Messiah, then you would ask me as the
bearer of revelation and salvation and I would give you revelation and salvation. From 4.25 it is evident that the woman does
have some knowledge of the gift of God in that she expects the
Messiah. The woman obviously would not understand the role of
the Holy Spirit and the death and resurrection, but she could
see that Jesus was speaking of the revelation of God and implying
that it was not just his request for water that was unusual but
that his own identity was unusual. The purpose of the conversion
is to reveal something of this identity.

The woman's reply (4.11) shows that she misunderstands Jesus entirely. She does not make any of these connections, but rather she thinks he is talking about physical water. This superficial level of reference is the second barrier to her belief. But one of the most interesting aspects of this conversation is how even this superficial reference is used to reveal to her Jesus' identity. She says, "Are you greater than our father Jacob, who gave us the well?" (4.12). That is, even on the level of physical water she recognizes that Jesus' cryptic statement implies he is greater than the patriarch Jacob. So the issue concerning water leads her to consider Jesus' identity. Jesus then continues to use the idea of water to lead her to an understanding of himself. He once again makes one of his testing statements, contrasting the water Jacob gives and the water he himself gives (4.13-14). What Jesus says about this water is very cryptic indeed: "Whoever drinks the water that I shall give him will never thirst; the water that I shall give him will become in him a spring of water welling up to eternal life" (4.14). The woman's response remains on the superficial level. All the cryptic elements in Jesus' statement concerning this water he offers go right over her head and she continues to think of physical water. But her response is also a profound movement forward toward faith, for even on the superficial level, by asking for this marvelous water that will mean that she need never again (a reference to εἰς ζωὴν αἰώνιον?) come to the well and draw water, she is actually putting faith in Jesus as one greater than Jacob. She believes in Jesus, albeit as yet on a superficial level.

Jesus then seems to change the subject entirely, though in fact he is responding to her request to give her this living water. That is, he begins to give her τὸ ὕδωρ τὸ ζῶν by revealing more of himself to her. She has shown an openness towards him to which he now responds. He indicates his special identity by revealing something of her own personal life, as he did with Nathanael (4.16-18, cf. 1.48). This preternatural knowledge indicates to the woman that Jesus is a prophet (4.19). With this realization she has come to the place Jesus' first statements about the gift of God and living water could have brought her right away. Her recognition of Jesus as a prophet

may imply much more than it would if she were a Jew, since the
Samaritans did not recognize a succession of prophets.[195] Rather,
their "Messiah" was the Prophet like Moses (cf. Kippenberg,
Garizim, 306-327). So her confession is highly significant, but
there are difficulties still to be overcome.

It is very significant that she does not react defensively
to Jesus' knowledge of her domestic relationships. Some interpreters see here an attempt to avoid the subject. Her interest
in pursuing religious questions, however, is in keeping with what
we have already learned of her, namely, her consciousness of differences between Samaritans and Jews and her pride in the patriarch Jacob. By implicitly affirming that Jesus is greater than
Jacob, her attention is being focused on his person, not her own.
So her attention remains on Jesus' person, even though her own
life is used to reveal something more of his identity. She now
returns to the original barrier between herself and Jesus, the
ethnic differences.

She does not ask about the relations between Jews and Samaritans, she simply states the differences in terms of places of
worship (4.20). Jesus' statement in return (4.21-24) contains
God's assessment of this division between Jews and Samaritans.
In essence he says that salvation is of the Jews but now with
the coming of the Messiah people will be able to worship in spirit
and truth, and this is the significant issue in worship rather
than its locale. This profound answer to the woman's question,
however, goes completely over her head. Jesus has spoken directly
to the issue she raised, but she could not hear it at all. "The
woman said to him, 'I know that Messiah is coming (he who is
called Christ), when he comes, he will show[196] us all things'"
(4.25). In effect, she says, I do not know what you are talking
about, but I believe Messiah will come and teach us about all
these things.[197] This reply is extraordinarily significant for
it reveals her basic openness and receptivity. Her response
epitomizes the appropriate response to Jesus and his cryptic
sayings. She is expecting one who will teach, which is to say
that she is open to revelation. Faced with such openness Jesus
reveals himself to her immediately, ἐγώ εἰμι, ὁ λαλῶν σοι (4.26).

The woman's response to this bald statement by Jesus is not
given. The disciples arrive on the scene and the woman heads to

town. In the background her response is hinted at: "Come see a
man who told me all that I ever did. Can this be the Christ?"
(4.29). So she is entertaining the possibility that Jesus is
Messiah but with some question still.[198] The woman's question
is the last we hear of her; we are not told whether it is a
question that results in faith like Nathanael's or rejection like
the opponents'. The impression left is favorable, both because
of what has been revealed of her heart at 4.25 and the the parallel between her and the first disciples. Like Andrew and Philip,
she is characterized by her testimony to others who come and see
and believe. Also, the Samaritans want Jesus to stay with them
(4.40) just as the first disciples want to stay with Jesus (1.38),
and the story concludes with a climactic confession reminiscent
of Nathanael's (4.42, cf. 1.49).

The woman's receptivity stands in obvious contrast to the
opponents' lack of such receptivity. As Nathanael began by
asking one of the very same questions later raised by the Jewish
opponents, so also the woman's question whether Jesus is greater
than "our father Jacob" (4.12) is identical with the opponents'
later question whether Jesus is greater than "our father Abraham"
(8.53). But the author makes it clear that

> the Samaritan woman, who is ready, seemingly, to
> desert her traditional religion (vs. 15b), is in
> reality faithful towards the element of truth re-
> ceived from the fathers, whereas the Jews, who, were
> apparently unswervingly loyal to the inheritance from
> their father Abraham and to the Tora of Moses, in op-
> position to the demands of J[esus], had already severed
> themselves spiritually and intrinsically from the way
> of Abraham and the Tora of Moses (Odeberg, *Gospel*,
> 178-179).

Thus the woman stands alongside the disciples as an example of
one who is receptive of Jesus. The docility before God and his
Law which figures so importantly in the opponents' self-understanding is actually present in the followers of Jesus. Through
his depiction of these various characters the author is assuring
his readers that they really do know God and are loyal to him.[199]
In contrast, his depiction of the opponents presents in narrative
form what is said explicitly in 8.31-59, namely, they are alienated from God.

e. Summary and Conclusion

The main issue at stake in the conflict between the author
and his opponents is the question of who is truly docile before
God, loyal to his revelation and, hence, who truly knows him.
We have now seen the main elements in the author's polemic. The
pattern of his polemic has been analyzed as an attack against
the two chief foci of the opponents' identity, their claims to
know God and to be loyal to his revelation. The author makes
use of the tradition he holds in common with his opponents to
reject their own claims for themselves and to undercut their
case against Jesus. Behind the issue of the acceptance or rejection of Jesus stands the basic theological point, their alienation from God.

While we have seen the main points of this polemic there
are certain elements that have not yet been discussed. In particular, appeal is made to a number of other witnesses besides
Scripture. Some of these other witnesses have been noted already,
though because of the opponents' claim to Scripture the use of
the witness of Scripture has been of primary interest. Now we
will turn to a consideration of these other witnesses. This
next section will not add any essentially new elements to the
general framework of the argument as it has already been described. Rather, it will fill out the picture, showing yet other
ways the author hammers home his point that the opponents are
not docile before God nor, indeed, do they even know him.

4. Further Witnesses in the Polemic

For the sake of analysis I will divide the witnesses into
two groups. I will first look at those witnesses, both human
and divine, who testify to Jesus, and then will turn to the
testimony of Jesus' own words and works.

a. The Witnesses to Jesus

1) The Voice from Heaven

The most overt instance of divine testimony to Jesus is the
Voice from heaven mentioned in 12.28. Jesus says this Voice is
for the benefit of the crowd (12.30), but the crowd is only

confused by it (12.29). Thus the direct experience of the Voice
of God is of no more help to them than is the word of God in the
Scriptures, concerning which they also have diverse opinions.
Perhaps the reference to this Voice should be seen in relation
to 5.37. The opponents have never heard God's Voice and now
even when God speaks it does the hearers no good. Furthermore,
their inability to receive the divine Voice is also to be seen
in relation to their inability to receive Jesus' teaching. As
with Jesus' cryptic sayings, the hearers of the Voice are divided. Some thought it was only thunder and some attributed it
to an angel. The latter, in relating the noise they heard to
the divine realm, were at least putting the event in the right
perspective, even if they still did not really understand it.
That which the Voice says, καὶ ἐδόξασα καὶ πάλιν δοξάσω, is a
very significant statement of the relation between the Son and
the Father. But as with the cryptic sayings, people do not understand. The people do not understand God's revelation in the
words of Scripture nor in the words of Jesus, and now they do
not even understand when he speaks directly.[200] Thus, this
story serves to illustrate the peoples' inability to hear, thereby implying that they are alienated from God.

2) The Baptist

     The testimony of the Baptist is first developed in 1.19-34.
This testimony is in two sections, first concerning himself
(1.19-28) and then concerning Jesus (1.29-34).

     His testimony is given "when the Jews sent priests and
Levites from Jerusalem to ask him, 'Who are you?'" (1.19). In
the other canonical Gospel most concerned with the Jewish opponents to Christianity, Matthew, the Pharisees themselves come to
the Baptist and they come in order to be baptized (Mt. 3.7). In
John, however, they only send their servants (1.19,24) and do
not seek baptism (cf. Lk. 7.30), which would imply acceptance of
the Baptist's authority. The leaders do not come and the servants only question. So this picture of the Jewish opponents
sending their servants to question the Baptist concerning his
identity at the outset of the Gospel's story hints at certain
characteristics of the opponents that have been noted, namely,

their self-satisfied superiority and belief that they are capable
of passing judgment concerning claims to speak for God.

The Baptist's testimony when he is interrogated by the religious Establishment is in two parts. The first (1.19-23) centers on the question "Who are you?" (1.19) and the second focuses
on his activity (1.24-28). The introduction of the Baptist's
answer to the question concerning his identity begins: "He
confessed, he did not deny, but confessed" (1.20). This observation puts great emphasis on his answer: "I am not the Christ"
(1.20). This stress in John on the fact that the Baptist is not
the Messiah is strong (cf. 1.8; 3.28) and it may be that the
author has in view contemporary claims made by disciples of the
Baptist on behalf of their martyred leader.[201]   In any event,
the primary effect of this denial in John is to strengthen the
emphasis on Jesus.

After the Baptist has denied that he is the Messiah, the
agents from Jerusalem try to connect him with other recognized
eschatological figures, Elijah and the Prophet (1.21). But the
Baptist does not fit into any of these categories any more than
Jesus fits the expectations of those who think they know how
God works. After exhausting their list the agents must repeat
the question, "Who are you?" (1.22). But, in contrast to
Matthew's picture just noted, they are not really interested
themselves, it is only that they might "have an answer for those
who sent" them (1.22). They demand, "What do you say about your-
self?" (1.22), thereby allowing the Baptist freedom to formulate
a description of his own identity. He does so by saying, "I am
the voice of one crying in the wilderness, 'Make straight the
way of the Lord,' as the prophet Isaiah said" (1.23). This reply
is a significant expression of the Baptist's humility, the central aspect of his character as it is drawn in John. He does
not answer in his own words but in the words of Scripture (Is.
40.3), and the figure he identifies himself with is no more than
a voice. His identity is his task and this is directed entirely
towards the Lord's coming and not his own.

This answer is also the first example of the author's de-
vice of the cryptic saying. The Baptist refers to the voice mentioned in Is. 40.3, a "figure" in the OT that had not been

incorporated into the common expectations. It is a highly significant expression of who he is, what he is doing, and why he
is doing it, but it goes right over their heads. His answer
does not register with them at all for they continue: "Then
why are you baptizing, if you are neither the Christ, nor Elijah,
nor the prophet?" (1.25). Evidently, in their expectations, to
be the voice mentioned in Is. 40.3 does not authorize one to
baptize. So the Baptist is now given a chance to say something
about his activity. Again he gives a cryptic answer that says
everything and nothing, and also expresses his humility. He
says nothing whatsoever as to why he is baptizing, he only
states as briefly as possible that he is doing so (1.26). He
then goes on to identify himself solely in terms of "he who comes
after me" (1.27). He begins by saying: "among you stands one
you do not know" (1.26). This sums up the picture of the opponents in the Gospel as a whole, as the reader already has been
prepared to expect from 1.10-11. This coming one who is among
them (already/not yet) is far greater than John the Baptist, as
he himself makes clear with the image of himself as unworthy
to untie the thong of his sandal. In this way the Baptist is
true to his task, for he is testifying to the light (1.7) even
when he is asked to testify concerning himself. Thus, this story
of the interrogation of the Baptist by the agents from Jerusalem
builds to a climax in 1.26-27 which has the effect of arousing
the expectations of the reader, for if the Baptist is doing
things which the Establishment in Jerusalem think important
enough to investigate, and if the Baptist says there is one coming
(although already among them) who is far greater than he, what
sort of person can this be and what will happen when he is revealed?

The reader does not have to wait long for the answer. In
the second section of the Baptist's witness (1.29-34) the focus
shifts from his own identity to that of Jesus. This testimony is
represented as taking place at a certain time (1.29), but no indication is given of who heard it. This section reads as a summary of the Baptist's testimony, consisting of two statements
(1.29-31; 1.32-34).

The first part of the testimony is in three sections. The
first consists in the statement "Behold the Lamb of God, who

takes away the sin of the world!" (1.29). The reference intended here is very difficult to determine for sure. Perhaps
the most satisfying interpretation is that which would find here
a variety of allusions, including echoes of the apocalyptic
figure of the conquering Lamb, as well as the Suffering Servant
and the pascal lamb (Brown, *John*, 63). The death of Jesus as a
sacrifice for sin is present in John (cf. 11.51), but it is not
emphasized.

The second section of the initial testimony comes in the
words, "This is he of whom I said, 'After me comes a man who
ranks before me, for he was before me'" (1.30). In contrast to
the reference to the Lamb, this saying has not only been prepared
for in John but actually given already at 1.15 (cf. 1.27). This
juxtaposition of the most familiar ("After me comes a man . . .")
with the least familiar (the Lamb of God) has the effect of
identifying the cryptic Lamb, even though it does not interpret
the Lamb's significance. The figure of the Lamb is not yet
understood, but we know who he is and therefore who to watch in
order to grasp the significance of the description.

Finally, the third section of the testimony: "I myself
did not know him; but for this I came baptizing with water, that
he might be revealed to Israel" (1.31). This element of the
Baptist's testimony begins with the very startling statement:
even I myself (κἀγώ) did not know him. What he asserted of the
opponents he now confesses of himself! Such ignorance is not
itself bad; everyone is initially ignorant of Jesus. Even the
fact that the cryptic saying of the Baptist went over the heads
of the opponents (1.23-25) is not necessarily an indictment of
them, since the same thing happens to the Samaritan woman (4.25).
But their ignorance and the Baptist's ignorance are two different
things; they thought they already knew all about the Messiah and
other eschatological figures, whereas the Baptist knows his ignorance and is looking for the one to be revealed. It is for
this very reason, according to the present text, that he came
baptizing, though exactly how this baptizing was to reveal the
coming one is not made clear.

We have already noted that these first three chapters can
be characterized as being concerned with the initial witness

to Israel (p. 60). Now we see that this announcement in 1.31
indicates the importance of the Baptist in this initial witness.
The Baptist dominates these first three chapters, being introduced in the Prologue and returning at the end of this section
(3.22-36). This repris has the effect of validating Jesus'
ministry and message, as will be noted below (p. 98).

In the second half of the Baptist's testimony to Jesus he
picks up the indication of his own ignorance of Jesus (1.31) and
describes his knowledge of Jesus. The section ends (1.34) as
it begins (1.29) with a pithy affirmation in the form of a title.

The admission in 1.31, "I myself did not know him," is repeated verbatum in 1.33. Now the Baptist says that God himself
indicated how he was to recognize Jesus: "he who sent me to
baptize with water said to me" (1.33). This way of putting it
stresses that his testimony to Jesus was the will of the same
one who commissioned him to baptize. So all those Jews who
thought that the Baptist was sent by God to baptize should also
see that he was sent to bear witness to Jesus, indeed this was
the purpose of his baptizing itself.

The way the Baptist is able to recognize Jesus as the Messiah is due to a revelation of God, though what exactly is meant
by, "I saw the Spirit descend as a dove from heaven, and it remained on him" (1.32) and "he . . . said to me" (1.33) is unknown.
Of more importance is the reference to the Spirit in connection
with the Baptist's witness because this reference joins the testimony of the Baptist with that of the Spirit. This connection,
along with the Baptist's testimony about Jesus as the one on
whom the Spirit remains and who dispenses the Spirit (1.33), is
part of the larger Johannine notion of the relation between Jesus
and the Spirit, and the function of the Spirit as witness, to
be mentioned again shortly (pp. 98-103).

This section of the witness of the Baptist concludes with
the essential element: "And I have seen and have borne witness"
(1.34). The use of the perfect tense here seems to impel this
affirmation into the present (cf. also the present μαρτυρεῖ in
1.15); the Baptist's witness stands for the Jews of the author's
own day as well as the Jews of the Baptist's day.

At the end of the third chapter (3.22-36) the Baptist returns and repeats what Jesus has just said to Nicodemus, thereby

effectively setting the Baptist's seal of approval on the ministry
of Jesus which has been launched from the context of the Baptist's
own ministry. This repris begins by noting that just as the
first disciples of Jesus came from the ranks of the Baptist's
disciples, so now the first real offense taken at Jesus in the
Gospel is on the part of the Baptist's disciples. It is said
that "a discussion arose between John's disciples and a Jew over
purifying. And they came to John and said to him, 'Rabbi, he
who was with you beyond the Jordan, to whom you bore witness,
here he is, baptizing, and all are going to him'" (3.25-26).
It is difficult to know how to interpret this reference to a
Jew in v.25. Because the discussion leads to their complaint
it seems most likely that this Jew is simply a figure representing those who came out to the wilderness seeking purification in
baptism. Because the Baptist's disciples saw a separation between themselves and Jesus, and considered Jesus to be more popular than the Baptist, it seems there were some differences between Jesus and the Baptist. If there were, then this Jew would
be one of those who was more attracted to Jesus, and in this case
the difference between the Baptist and Jesus was perceived as
having to do with purifying. This reconstruction fits neatly
with what is known of Jesus and the Baptist from the Synoptics.
One of the most obvious things about Jesus that a Jew would notice is his rejection of the various purificatory practices of
the Pharisees and his non-ascetical ways, compared with the
Baptist (cf. Mt. 11.18-19; Lk. 7.33-35). Thus, the Baptist's
disciples reject Jesus' teaching but they also reject their own
teacher's instruction. They admit that he has borne witness to
Jesus, but they do not accept this testimony. Like Nicodemus
(3.2), the Baptist's disciples use the term Rabbi without really
meaning it; they call him teacher but do not receive his
teaching.

So the Baptist repeats his testimony. Jesus' success is
confirmation of the Baptist's testimony (3.27-28) and it must
continue: "He must increase, but I must decrease" (3.30). Thus,
the Baptist is again seen as a model of humility. His statement
"no one can receive anything except what is given him from
heaven" (3.27) expresses exactly his attitude of open receptivity.

As in 1.19-34, he is completely self-emptied, being defined
solely in terms of Jesus. This humility stands in contrast to
his disciples' attitude (3.26). They are not open to their own
master's teaching, let alone to Jesus.

In 3.31-36 there is a shift from narrative to a general comment by the author on what has been described. In this more
general comment he begins by contrasting the one who "comes from
above" with the one who is "of the earth" (3.31). In the context
this reference is to Jesus and the Baptist. By putting it in
these terms we are back to the terms used in the Nicodemus story.
That is, this passage begins at the same point as 3.13, but now
Jesus' identity as the one from heaven is set in the context of
a contrast with the Baptist. The next statement, "He bears witness to what he has seen and heard, yet no one receives his testimony" (3.32), repeats what was said at 3.11. There then follows another of the author's explicit references to the alienation from God of those who do not receive (3.33). In the next
two verses (3.34-35) he ties together many of the major motifs
in ch. 3: "For he whom God has sent (cf. 3.2,16-17) utters the
words of God (cf. 3.11-12), for it is not by measure that he
gives the Spirit (cf. 3.5-8); the Father loves the Son, and has
given all things into his hand (cf. 3.27)." The final verse
summarizes the theme of judgment: "He who believes in the Son
has eternal life; he who does not obey the Son shall not see
life, but the wrath of God rests upon him" (3.36). This last
verse combines the central motifs of the two meditational passages in ch. 3. In 3.16-21 the issue is faith in Jesus himself
("believes in him" 3.16,18) and this is represented in the first
half of 3.36: "He who believes in the Son has eternal life."
In 3.31-35 the issue is receiving Jesus' testimony and this is
reflected in the notion of obedience in the second half of v. 36.
In this way the material in ch. 3 is rounded off and formed into
a distinct unit.

The final section of the initial witness to Israel, the re-
entrance of the Baptist, concludes the first major section of the
Gospel's story. The Baptist came that Jesus might be revealed
to Israel (1.31) and that is what the story of the first three
chapters describes. All of the major character types encountered

in the Gospel have been introduced in this first section.   Jesus
has begun the activity that will take him toward his hour and
he has given his first discourse to a representative of Israel.
By reintroducing the Baptist after this initial activity and
teaching of Jesus, and especially by including a meditation that
links Jesus and the Baptist and summarizes Jesus' teaching, the
impression is given that the Baptist is confirming that Jesus is
indeed the one who was to come.   By portraying Jesus' ministry
as emerging from the ministry of the Baptist the author is relating the ministry and message of Jesus, concerning whom the
Jews had a divided opinion, to that of one for whom most Jews
had a high regard.[202]   The Baptist's direct testimony to Jesus
is not, however, the extent of his function in the polemic.   He
also serves as an example of the humble disposition which is
receptive to God.   Thus, the author uses one who was highly regarded by the Jewish opponents not only to witness to Jesus but
also to condemn their own hardness of heart.

3)   *The Spirit*

One of the chief functions of the Spirit in John is as a
witness to Jesus.   It is the Spirit which testifies to Jesus
(15.26), leads into all truth (16.12-15, cf. 1 Jn. 2.27), and is
the means by which Christians can know that God remains in them
(cf. 1 Jn. 3.24).   Thus, as the Baptist was enabled to recognize
Jesus by the Spirit (1.33), so Christians can know the truth and
the presence of Christ with them by the Spirit.   The designation
of Jesus as "he who baptizes with the Holy Spirit" (1.33) is developed later in the Gospel when it is said that Jesus will send
the Spirit upon the disciples (14.16,26; 15.26; 16.7), a promise
fulfilled in 20.22.   This presence of the Spirit in the disciples
is yet another way the author makes his point concerning the internal difference between those who receive and those who oppose.
The utter separation from God in the hearts of the opponents
stands in contrast to the presence of the Spirit of God in the
hearts of believers.   But note that it is because of the presence
of the Spirit that believers are able to understand Jesus and
the testimony to him in the Scriptures.[203]   The Holy Spirit's
witness is thus used by the author in his attack on both foci of

the opponents' identity. The contrast just mentioned between
believers and opponents speaks clearly of the opponents' alienation from God. The function of the Spirit with regard to the
Scriptures is perhaps less clear. While this revelatory function
of the Spirit is explicitly stated in the passages just mentioned,
it will be of value to examine a story which seems to join the
Spirit's witness and that of the Scripture, and which also provides examples of other aspects of the polemic as well.

The author begins his version of the clearing of the Temple
by relating an account of the event itself (2.14-15), and then
gives a saying by Jesus which interprets his action: "Take these
things away; you shall not make my Father's house a house of
trade" (2.16). There are parallel accounts in all three of the
Synoptics, and each of them ends with a statement of Jesus consisting of a conflation of Is. 56.7 and Jer. 7.11: "It is written, 'My house shall be called a house of prayer'; but you have
made it a den of robbers" (Mt. 21.13; Mk. 11.17; Lk. 19.46).
Note, however, that neither this conflation nor either of its
members is found anywhere in John. Instead of Jesus using the
words of Scripture with the introductory γέγραπται, in John
Jesus himself authoritatively speaks. More significantly, instead
of contrasting God's house of prayer with a den of robbers, he
contrasts "my Father's house" with a house of trade. Here is
the first reference outside the Prologue (1.14,18) to the single
most important designation for God in the Johannine literature,
Father.[204] This reference to Jesus' Father is one of the most
significant aspects of the whole account for it implies Jesus'
identity as Son.

In each of the Synoptics the clearing of the Temple is one
event among others near the end of Jesus' ministry which results
in the heightened hostility of his opponents. In John also Jesus
is performing a very provocative act, but in John the act comes
at the beginning of his ministry and serves a very different
function. The emphasis in John is as much on the response to
this action as it is on Jesus' statement just mentioned. Significantly, the response is given not only of the Jewish opponents
but also of Jesus' own disciples. In contrast with the Synoptics'
accounts, in John Jesus speaks for himself and not in the words

of Scripture. But a text of Scripture does play the central
role in the disciples' response to Jesus' activity. As the author
tells the story, right in the midst of the event Jesus' disciples
"remembered (ἐμνήσθησαν) that it is written, 'Zeal for thy house
will consume me'" (2.17), that is, a verse of Scripture occurs
to the disciples which has the potential for putting this rather
enigmatic action of Jesus in its proper interpretive frame. Ps.
69.9 is spoken by the righteous one who is persecuted by those
who hate God, so this text relates Jesus' activity to a certain
strand of OT thought that we have already seen to be important
for the author (pp. 61-62). This particular text has the potential for revealing a great deal more about Jesus, but the disciples do not grasp this at the time.

Instead of an OT text that places Jesus in the light of
Scripture, however vaguely, in the case of the Jewish opponents
Jesus' action is met with a question: "What sign have you to
show us for doing this?" (2.18). This question is not hostile
and indeed they appear genuinely open to the possibility that
Jesus might be able to defend his audacious activity (cf. 3.2).
Presumably if a text of Scripture had occurred to them which
placed Jesus in relation to some feature of the Scriptural tradition then they would not have needed to ask such a question.
Furthermore, Jesus has already given them the answer to their
question, since it is his identity as Son that authorizes his
action. But as has already emerged, the opponents do not understand the Scripture because they cannot see Jesus' relation to
the Scripture (5.39) and they are also entirely unable to grasp
Jesus' identity as Son of the Father (8.19,27,42,55).

To their request for a sign Jesus responds with another of
his cryptic sayings that reveal everything and nothing: "Destroy
this temple, and in three days I will raise it up" (2.19). This
enigma tests their hearts. There is no way anyone could have
understood this saying at the outset of Jesus' ministry. By
responding with an incredulous question (2.20) they reveal their
response to Jesus. Nathanael also had heard something he considered unlikely, if not impossible, but he reserved final judgment, and came and saw, and ended by confessing Jesus. These
opponents on the other hand seem able only to question. They

cannot be silent and wait; they jump to conclusions, in contrast
with the disciples. So the opponents are left with questions
while the disciples have a vague but solid hint at the fact that
Jesus' action can be seen in the light of Scripture.

The author says no more in this story about the opponents;
they are left questioning Jesus' cryptic saying. He returns to
the disciples and something of the significance of their remembering the text of Scripture now becomes apparent. He first
interprets Jesus' cryptic saying about the Temple: "But he spoke
of the temple of his body" (2.21). In thus relating his own
body with the Temple, which is his Father's house, Jesus points
to his own special relationship with God and thus both in his
first statement (2.16) and in his cryptic reply (2.19) he does
give the opponents an answer to their question. But there is
really no way the opponents could have understood what he meant
by "Destroy this temple." Even the disciples did not understand
it until after the event: "When therefore he was raised from
the dead, his disciples remembered (ἐμνήσθησαν) that he had said
this; and they believed the scripture and the word which Jesus
had spoken" (2.22). This verse raises the question of the significance of the disciples' remembering and the relation between
this remembrance and the belief with which the story concludes.
That there is some connection between remembrance and belief
would seem evident from the fact that the object is the same for
each, that is, they believe the Scripture and the word of Jesus
after they have remembered a text of the OT and the saying of
Jesus concerning the destruction and raising again of the 'temple.' In John, to remember (μιμνήσκεσθαι, μνημονεύειν,
ὑπομιμνήσκειν) signifies not simply to recall but to recall and
understand.[205] After the climactic entrance into Jerusalem it
is said "His disciples did not understand this at first; but
when Jesus was glorified, then they remembered (ἐμνήσθησαν) that
this had been written of him and had been done to him" (12.16).
So in both of these instances the Scripture is related to an
event in Jesus' life, the Scripture interpreting the event.
Elsewhere it is added that the Spirit plays a part in such understanding, as we have seen. Thus, what emerges is that after
Jesus' death and resurrection the disciples are able, by the

presence of the Spirit, to recall Jesus' actions and words and
to interpret them in the light of Scripture. The insight arising
from this connection of Jesus' words and actions with Scripture
seems to be what is meant by believing the Scripture and the word
which Jesus had spoken (2.22), that is, faith in the old revelation and in the new.

This faith mentioned in 2.22 seems to be in the future. It
obviously is so with respect to Jesus' word about the Temple, but
is this belief in the Scripture in the future? What is the relation between their supposed recollection of a verse of the OT
in the midst of the event and this later belief in the Scripture,
after the resurrection? It seems that the disciples' recollection of this text from Ps. 69 indicates to them that Jesus' action
was in line with the previous revelation of God, even if they
could not understand what was happening and how it was in accord
with the OT. But if the recall at the time only indicates in some
vague way the significance of this activity, what would be the
later understanding of the Scripture after the resurrection?
The answer would seem to lie in the double meaning of "consume"
(καταφάγεται, 2.17). Presumably, in the midst of the action they
could understand it figuratively as referring to the extent of
his zeal, but after Jesus' death they could understand it as a
figurative reference to his death. If this interpretation is
accepted then the deeper meaning, both of the Scripture and the
word of Jesus which is believed after his resurrection, concerns
his death. So there are two notions communicated here through
the image of the Temple: the identity of the Temple as the house
of the Father of Jesus implies his identity as Son, and the identity of his body as temple points to his death. The significance
of this juxtaposition of Jesus' sonship and his death is perhaps
obvious. The death of the Son in Jerusalem at the instigation
of the opponents at a later Passover is already referred to in
this first provocation of the opponents at this earlier Passover.
Thus there are brought together here the witness of the Scripture
and of the Spirit to Jesus' death and resurrection. The inability
of the opponents to understand the Scripture is due to their lack
of this Spirit. This is yet another way of saying they are completely alienated from God.

The role of the Spirit is particularly important for the
author's polemic for the Spirit is the link between the story
of Jesus that he is telling and his readers' own experience.
During Jesus' own ministry, i.e. within the story, the Spirit
was not yet present (cf. 7.39), hence the emphasis on the disciples' lack of understanding. This lack of understanding continues throughout John, right up to the brink of the Passion
(cf. 16.29-33). It was impossible to fully understand Jesus'
revelation during his ministry because the supreme moment of
revelation, his death, had not yet occurred. Jesus' death was
the supreme manifestation of the Father's love and was followed
by the sending of the Spirit. The Spirit's presence with the
Johannine Christians accounts for their ability to appreciate
Jesus while the religious leaders of Israel reject him. Thus,
by referring to the Spirit the author helps his readers understand how it is possible that many within Judaism have failed to
recognize and accept the Messiah.

4) The Disciples

     The presence of the Spirit not only helps the Johannine
Christians understand the rejection they are experiencing, but
it is also explicitly related to their own witness to Jesus
amidst persecution. In Jn. 15.26, as we have noted, it is said
that the Spirit will testify to Jesus (p. 98). It is not spe-
cified who is given this testimony, but from the contrast we have
seen between disciples and unbelievers in terms of possession of
the Spirit, and from the other references to the work of the
Spirit (esp. 14.26; 16.7), it is most likely that it is the disciples who receive this testimony. Their reception of this testimony of the Spirit enables them also to testify to Jesus, as
the next verse makes clear (15.27). Thus the Spirit's witness
is given to the disciples and it is through them that it is
passed on to the world. If this is so then the difficult verses
which follow (16.8-11) perhaps also speak of this witness to the
world through the disciples. Jn. 16.9-11 focuses on faith in
Jesus, his going to the Father, and the judgment of the ruler
of this world. That is, the Spirit, by witnessing to Jesus,
shows that sin consists in the lack of faith in Jesus, that

righteousness is manifest in Jesus' relation to the Father (cf.
7.24 and p. 36 above), and that the judgment concerns the
ruler of this world. As we have seen, the devil is depicted as
one totally the opposite to Jesus, and to reject Jesus is to be
associated with the devil (pp. 72-74). Attention to the sub-
jects of the verbs in these verses also indicates the nature of
this witness of the Spirit. The sin is associated with "they"
who do not believe in Jesus, i.e. those outside the Christian
community (16.9). This assertion thus plays a part in the
author's attempt to help his readers understand that those who
reject Jesus are really alienated from God, no matter what they
claim to the contrary. The second assertion, that righteousness
is evident in Jesus' departure to the Father and consequently
"you" no longer seeing him (16.10), is part of the author's more
positive concern to assure his readers both of Jesus' relation
to the Father and of their relation to Jesus through the Spirit.
The third assertion is not about either of the parties in the
conflict. The author is describing the conflict in cosmic terms
and the reference to the ruler of this world speaks of the Spirit's witness to Jesus' victory as complete (cf. 12.31-32).
These verses, then, speak of the Spirit's witness to the community, enabling them to understand the truth about Jesus, the
devil, and their opponents. As they receive this testimony and
live in the light of it then they also witness to Jesus. In
John it is primarily the community's life together that witnesses
to Jesus, in particular their love (13.35) and unity (17.21).
In manifesting this love and unity they are manifesting the chief
characteristics of God himself, thus testifying that they are
indeed his children. In this way the Spirit testifies through
the community, exposing and thereby condemning (ἐλέγχειν, 16.8)
the alienation from God of those who claim to know him.

There is, however, a further factor associated with the disciples' witness. In addition to the role of the Spirit it is also
noted that their testimony is related to their presence with Jesus
ἀπ' ἀρχῆς (15.27). Above I noted the difference in the use of
ἀρχή when referring to the devil (p. 73 n. 174). Now there seems
yet another beginning in view, namely, the beginning of Jesus'
ministry (cf. 16.4). It is difficult to determine for sure the
significance of their presence with Jesus ἀπ' ἀρχῆς, but at least
two suggestions commend themselves. The reference could be

emphasizing their unity with Jesus (Barrett, *John*, 483); unlike
some (6.60), they have stayed with him despite their lack of understanding, thus revealing their faith in him despite difficulties. A second, not unrelated, emphasis could be on their own
witness of Jesus' words and works. The Spirit interprets Jesus'
life to those who have witnessed it, and through their interpretive account the Spirit bears witness to Jesus to others.

A relation to the witness of Jesus' words and works is
evident also in the case of the other two witnesses we have just
been examining. The phrase καὶ ἐδόξασα καὶ πάλιν δοξάσω used by
the Voice in 12.28-30 refers to Jesus' words and works, or at
least to his supreme revelation in his death (cf. Barrett, *John*,
426). The Baptist also points to Jesus' activity, his baptizing
in the Holy Spirit (1.33). What then is the witness of Jesus'
words and works, and how does their witness function in the
polemic?

b. The Witness of Jesus' Words and Works

1) The Witness to Jesus

The witness of Jesus' teaching is his revelation of the
Father and this is nowhere more evident than in the ἐγώ εἰμι
statements. In this phrase we have, if not a claim that Jesus
is to be identified with God, then at least the claim that "Jesus
ist Gottes eschatologischer Offenbarer, in welchem sich Gott
selbst zur Sprache bringt" (Schnackenburg, *Johannes* 2:69). The
ἐγώ εἰμι sayings use various images to proclaim the salvation
present in Jesus, as Schnackenburg has admirably summarized:

> Weil seine Offenbarung dem, der sie annimmt und sich ihm
> anschliesst, das Heil vermittelt, muss er darauf bestehen,
> das eine, wahre Brot aus dem Himmel zu sein, das der Welt
> das Leben schenkt (6,33.35), das Licht der Welt (8.12),
> die Tür, durch die man ins Leben eingeht (10,7.9), der
> gute Hirt, der für das Leben der Schafe sorgt (10,11.14.28),
> die Auferstehung, die gegenwärtig zum Ereignis wird (11,25)
> (ibid.).

This salvation is present in Jesus because of his relation to
the Father: "Er muss als der Sohn, der mit dem Vater in engster
Gemeinschaft steht und wirkt, den vollen und exklusiven Anspruch
erheben, der einzige Zugang zum Vater zu sein (14,6)" (ibid.).
This relation between Jesus and the Father is especially evident
in the absolute use of ἐγώ εἰμι. Whether this usage reflects

Ex. 3.14 or texts in Isaiah such as 51.12, the significance is
not radically altered.[206] The phrase "expresses the theme of ex-
clusive monotheism, in the sense that Yahweh alone is God. In a
similar way the absolute *ego eimi* expresses the same theme, in
the Johannine sense that the Son is one with the Father, yet God
remains one."[207] Thus these sayings are a focal point of Jesus'
claim to reveal God and the divine salvation. As such they are
central to the author's claims for Jesus in combating the opponents' rejection. One use of the ἐγώ εἰμι formula makes this
polemical aspect more explicit, Jn. 10.1-18.

Jesus as the Good Shepherd is contrasted to those who are
thieves, robbers and strangers. Barrett is probably correct when
he says we cannot "single out particular persons whom John may
have had in mind" in using the expression πάντες ὅσοι ἦλθον [πρὸ
ἐμοῦ] (10.18) (*John*, 371).[208] The most likely candidates, however, would seem to be the Jewish opponents.[209] They consider
themselves to be the leaders of Israel, but the author is here
claiming they are not good shepherds. Rather, they are the
wicked shepherds described in Ezk. 34 and there contrasted with
YHWH who will himself shepherd his people (see Brown, *John*
397-398). Also echoed here is a reference to "the watchmen of
God's people (cf. Jer. 6.17; Ezek. 3.17; 33.7; Isa. 56.10; 62.6)"
(Robinson, "Shepherd," 71). That which legitimates Jesus' claim
to be the Good Shepherd is his death.[210] Since Jesus' lifting
up, his death, is described as his glorification, perhaps the
reference to these others going up a different way (10.1) is a
part of the author's condemnation of their self-glorification and
pride. Be this as it may, we find in this passage a claim by
Jesus to perform a function attributed to YHWH in the OT which
directly challenges the opponents' view of themselves. They
consider themselves shepherds but Jesus denies that they are
even the Father's sheep (10.25-29) since they do not hear Jesus,
and he and the Father are one (10.30). So once again the emphasis is on Jesus' relationship with the Father. Indeed, the stress
on the relationship between Jesus and the Father points to the
primary characteristic of Jesus' words and works, their testimony to the Father.

2) Jesus' Witness to the Father

All of Jesus' words and works bear witness to the Father.
The works of Jesus testify that the Father has sent him (5.36,
cf. 10.25). Jesus' teaching is a declaration of what he has
heard from the Father (8.26), but people do not understand his
teaching concerning the Father (8.27). At the very end of his
teaching ministry Jesus admits that he has been speaking cryp-
tically (ἐν παροιμίαις) even to his disciples, but promises soon
to speak plainly of the Father (16.25). It seems this plain
speaking occurs immediately when he says, "the Father himself
loves you" (16.27). Apart from the references to the Father
sending the Son, present also in this context (16.27-28), this
is perhaps the clearest statement by Jesus concerning the Father
in the Gospel. The disciples even say as much: "Ah, now you
are speaking plainly, not in any figure (παροιμίαν)!" (16.29).
The central theme of John's Gospel is this revelation by the Son
of the Father's gracious love. The Father's love is his δόξα.
Jesus' works reveal this δόξα and his death is referred to as
δοξασθῆναι because in these works and in this death is revealed
the Father's gracious love.[211] In rejecting Jesus and his revelation of the Father the opponents show their alienation from
God. Since this charge against the opponents is the fundamental
point in the author's polemic I will conclude by examining more
closely Jesus' revelation of the Father, indicating how the
author's depiction of this revelation of the Father also reveals
the opponents' alienation from him.

5. The Revelation of the Father

Jesus' revelation of the Father's gracious love is explicitly stated in the Prologue and then depicted in the narrative of the story.

a. The δόξα and the χάρις (Jn. 1.14-18)

The δόξα that Jesus reveals is referred to at the outset
in 1.14. The δόξαν ὡς μονογενοῦς παρὰ πατρός speaks of the
unique expression of the Father's glory in Jesus. The next
clause, πλήρης χάριτος καὶ ἀληθείας, indicates the nature of

this δόξα. Jesus, the revelation of the Father, is characterized
by χάρις and ἀλήθεια. As I have already mentioned, in John
ἀλήθεια refers both to the divine reality and to its revelation,
both in Scripture and, especially, in Jesus the Truth (p. 73).
This word ἀλήθεια, which occurs twenty-five times in John, is
of obvious importance for the author, not least in his polemic
with his opponents since it is used to affirm that God really
is revealed in Jesus. In contrast, χάρις occurs only three
times, all in the Prologue. But while it is less frequent it
is no less significant for it defines this ἀλήθεια; the ἀλήθεια,
the divine reality that is revealed in Jesus, is the divine graciousness. "The glory of God is shown by his acting in faith-
fulness to his own character, and by his character's revealing
itself in mercy" (Barrett, *John*, 167, cf. Howard, *Christianity*,
100). The reference to πλήρης indicates the perfection of the
revelation of God in Jesus. The author goes on to say that from
this fullness (πλήρωμα) we have received χάρις (1.16), a notion
he clarifies (ὅτι) by a comparison with Moses and the Law (1.17).
As I have urged above (p. 65), 1.17 is not to be read as deni-
grating Moses and the Law. The relationship is one of fulfillment; the graciousness of God revealed in Scripture has now been
perfectly manifested in Jesus. The careful construction of 1.17
even allows us to say more precisely how this is the case. The
significant contrast in John is not between ὁ νόμος and ἡ χάρις
καὶ ἡ ἀλήθεια, since it is the same graciousness of the same
God that is revealed in both. Rather, it is the often noted
contrast between ἐδόθη and ἐγένετο. Ἐδόθη itself speaks of the
divine graciousness evident in God's gifts.[212] So these terms
do not contrast a negative and a positive. Rather the graciousness evident in the divine ἐδόθη is tremendously intensified in
the divine ἐγένετο. The same divine graciousness has now been
manifested in an entirely new mode: ὁ λόγος σάρξ ἐγένετο. So
there is a contrast with the older revelation, but it is one of
degree. As the author goes on to say, no one has ever seen God,
but in Jesus God himself is visibly manifested. He who is
uniquely related to God--μονογενὴς θεὸς ὁ ὢν εἰς τὸν κόλπον τοῦ
πατρός--it is this one who has made him known, ἐξηγήσατο. But
it is the same God and his same characteristic grace that is

revealed, or, as the author expresses it, ἐλάβομεν καὶ χάριν
ἀντὶ χάριτος (1.16) (cf. Hooker, "Prologue," 53).

As just noted, while the author uses ἀλήθεια throughout the
Gospel, χάρις is not referred to again, explicitly, outside the
Prologue. If, however, this χάρις is the δόξα that Jesus reveals
then we would expect to find the divine χάρις depicted in the
story. Taking the clue from 1.14 that it is precisely this divine graciousness which is the divine δόξα Jesus reveals, I will
look in some detail at Jn. 2.1-5.18, the section of the Gospel
which contains signs which are said to reveal Jesus' δόξα (2.11,
cf. 4.54) and which lead up to the beginning of hostility on the
part of the opponents.

b. *The Revelation of the Glory in Jn. 2.1-5.18*

I have already noted the humble openness evident in the request of the mother of Jesus at the wedding in Cana (p. 85).
In response to such a request Jesus provides wine in abundance
(2.6-8). Note also the stress placed on the fact that the servants know what has happened, in contrast to the steward and the
bridegroom who do not (2.9-10). The effect is to strengthen the
depiction of Jesus' unassuming place at the wedding. In this
story, then, a person close to Jesus, his mother, requests that
he help in an embarrassing predicament. He grants her request
abundantly, but those who reap the benefits do not realize what
has happened. What is striking in this story is the utterly
gratuitous nature of this deed. It may not be too fanciful to
infer from 2.1-2 that Jesus and his disciples were only at the
wedding because of his mother. In any case, he is not brought
into contact with the bridegroom or the steward and the miracle
takes place virtually in secret. Yet despite his humble place
at the festivity he provides an enormous amount of wine. It is
precisely this gratuitous generosity that is the glory revealed
in this sign (2.11).

I have already noted how the next story, the clearing of the
Temple, witnesses to the supreme manifestation of God's gracious
love in the death of Jesus (pp. 101-102). In this story we have
also seen contrasted the two responses to Jesus' teaching, the
Jewish opponents who question and the disciples who do not understand but who do recognize Jesus as somehow come from God (pp.
99-102). These two types of response are developed in the next
five sections of the Gospel.

The first two of these stories focus on those who do not
respond with a true faith, although they profess a faith. First,
the author mentions the enthusiastic response of the "many" to
various other signs Jesus did (2.23). Jesus does not entrust
himself to these people. He does so not because their faith is
based on signs,[213] but because there was something wrong with the
content of their faith. This becomes evident when we notice that
the description in 2.24-25 is the exact opposite of the description of Jesus in the rest of the Gospel. Jesus knows all men
and needs no one to bear witness of man (2.25), whereas no one
knows him and thus all need to have witness borne to him. Most
importantly in light of the interiority motif, he knows what is
in man, whereas men do not know him in that they do not recognize
him as Son of the Father. Thus, he knows a man's true identity
(cf. 1.47), but men do not know his. Since the notion of a political Messiah is in the background at various points throughout John, this is the best guess as to the specific misunderstanding that might be in view here. If so then this rejection
of the belief of the many in Jerusalem at this Passover would be
similar to his rejection of the attempt to make him king later
in Galilee (6.15), and both of these would be in contrast to his
final entry into Jerusalem at a later Passover when he is ac-
claimed King of Israel (12.12-13), and to his own claim at his
trial (18.33-37).

After this general statement that Jesus knew what was in
man the author next gives a closeup of one such man, a representative of the Jewish opponents: "Now there was a man of the
Pharisees, named Nicodemus, a ruler of the Jews" (3.1). I have
already noted that Nicodemus is an example of those who acclaim
Jesus as Rabbi (3.2) but who then respond to Jesus' teaching
with questions rather than acceptance (3.4,9) (p. 79). Nicodemus'
problem is precisely a lack of receptivity, as Jesus says (3.11).
If he really believed that Jesus was a Rabbi then he should have
received what he said. But he does not and he is thereby condemned. The signs had shown him that Jesus has come from God,
yet Jesus' teaching is not received as teaching come from God.

In these first stories the divine graciousness is evident
in the giving of signs and teaching to those who do not receive.

The people one would have expected to receive Jesus, at least
from a Jewish point of view, have not done so. Now in the next
two stories the divine gratuity is revealed in teaching and
healing given to those who, from a Jewish point of view, would
not have been considered worthy, let alone receptive.

The disciples' reaction when they find Jesus speaking to
the Samaritan woman is, according to Brown, "curious" since they
were more surprised by the fact that he was speaking to a woman
than that she was a Samaritan. He notes the reference in Sir.
9.1-9 about being careful not to be ensnared by a woman and
Pirke Aboth 1.5 and *Erubin* 53b that warn against speaking to a
woman in public (*John*, 173). To these could be added Prov. 5;
6.20-7.27 which warn about the adulteress. The reference that
it was noon (4.6) could simply be included to account for Jesus'
tiredness and thirst (Barrett, *John*, 231; Schnackenburg, *John*
1:424), but it is an unusual time for a woman to come to a well
(Brown, *John*, 169). It could be that she is there out of shame,
so as not to be met by her neighbors, since the other women would
presumably have little love for her. Her adultery seems well
known to the villagers (4.29), as one might expect. In any
event, her presence at the well at that hour is unusual and not
unnaturally would raise the disciples' suspicions. The function
of the disciples' unasked questions seems evident enough; they
point to the fact that Jesus has just revealed himself to a
Samaritan adulteress, which is to say, he has acted about as
scandalously as he possibly could. And this emphasis is therefore transferred to the underlying point, the scandalous grace
of God.

After providing a foil to highlight the scandal of what
Jesus has done the disciples next pose the question which leads
to Jesus' explanation of his action. They "besought him, saying
'Rabbi, eat'" (4.31). To this request Jesus responds with a
cryptic saying: "I have food to eat of which you do not know"
(4.32). The disciples do not get his point: "So the disciples
said to one another, 'Has any one brought him food?'" (4.33).
In this way the disciples repeat exactly the woman's incomprehen-
sion concerning living water. But whereas Jesus did not tell
the woman what he meant by living water, he does give an

explanation to the disciples: "My food is to do the will of him
who sent me, and to accomplish his work" (4.34). This saying
calls attention to what is significant about his encounter with
the Samaritan woman, and all of Jesus' activity: it accomplishes
God's work. And this work is his revelation of the Father. He
spoke to the woman of the worship which the Father desires and
in his relationship with her he demonstrated God's acceptance of
Samaritans. So in both his action and his teaching he revealed
God's love for the Samaritans and willingness to reveal himself
to them and receive their worship.

This same divine graciousness is evident in the story of
the second sign in Galilee. The chief character, along with
Jesus, is a βασιλικός whose son is ill. He is a servant at
Herod's court and as such could be either a Jew or a Gentile
(see Barrett, *John*, 247). If the latter then the graciousness
of God would be further heightened. What strikes one is the in-
appropriateness of Jesus' response to one who has asked for his
help (4.47-48). The request that Jesus heal his son implies the
official already believed, at least believed Jesus could heal,
and was willing to heal even his son, the son of a Herodian official. Ultimately, faith is belief that God is who and what
Jesus reveals him to be, i.e. the loving Father; this official
seems to have something of such a faith. This suggests an interpretation of Jesus' rather cryptic saying. In particular, it may
explain why a saying in the second person plural is said to be
addressed πρὸς αὐτόν (4.48). Perhaps this saying is directed
to the Jews of Galilee who would not think too highly of a servant of Herod. Jesus' statement may mean that they need to see
signs and wonders performed for such an undesirable before they
will understand that God loves him also and freely grants heal-
ing/salvation to him. In Galilee, with its "freedom-loving in-
habitants" (Schürer, *History* 2:341), the acceptance of a member
of Herod's court would perhaps be the best possible example of
God's gracious nature, especially if he were a Gentile.

This saying of Jesus seems particularly inappropriate if
addressed to this official. Not only does he seem to have some
faith even to come to Jesus for healing, but also his reactions
indicate the positive characteristics of Jesus' true disciples

which we have noted above. To Jesus' provocative statement the
official simply says, "Sir, come down before my child dies"
(4.49). Thus, he demonstrates perseverance, closely related to
the humble patience we have noted in Jesus' disciples. Jesus'
response is extremely ambiguous: πορεύου, ὁ υἱός σου ζῇ. The
official could have heard this as a simple command to go away,
especially since the word ζῇ need not necessarily imply healing.
Despite all of these possible barriers it says the man "believed
the word that Jesus spoke to him and went his way," thereby
showing again that Jesus' statement about needing to see signs
and wonders does not apply to this official; he believed Jesus'
word alone. Even though he had requested that Jesus come with
him to heal his son (4.47) he believes Jesus can do it without
coming with him. It is then told how he discovered his son's
recovery and it says, "he himself believed, and all his house-
hold" (4.53). What is the difference between this belief and
the belief in Jesus' word that he had at the first? There is a
great variety of types of faith in John and even for those who
have the truest sort of faith it seems to be something that must
be repeated rather than possessed once and for all. The best
example is the disciples. Already in the first chapter they are
confessing Jesus to be the Messiah and Son of God, among other
things, and this is called faith (1.50). But then it is said
of them at Cana that they believed in Jesus (2.11). Thus it
seems that faith is something that must be had over and over
again in the face of each new experience, revelation, event.
But there are varieties of faith, even as indicated by the Samaritans' contrast between believing because of the woman's testimony
and believing because of Jesus' own word (4.41-42). Ultimately
all pre-resurrection faith is immature. At the very end of Jesus'
time with his disciples, in the Upper Room just before his arrest, he indicates that even then they do not really believe
(16.31). For faith is not unrelated to its content and until
Jesus has died and risen again the core of the content is not
available in all its fullness.

    This story ends with the reference that "this was now the
second sign that Jesus did when he had come from Judea to Galilee"
(4.54). This saying lays as much stress on the geographical

motif as it does on the signs. Twice now Jesus has had to move
into Galilee, presumably due to pressure from the opponents.
Both times he has performed very significant signs. They both
have pointed to God's gracious generosity. The one was in a
presumably kosher Jewish setting and the other seems to have
involved a non-kosher healing. These two signs in Galilee contrast with the many signs he did in Jerusalem; each of these
signs was received in faith by someone, whereas the signs in
Jerusalem were not (cf. p. 110). These two signs that occur when
he has come from Judea to Galilee are not only a summary of what
has happened but an anticipation of what immediately follows.
Twice now Jesus has moved up to Galilee and twice he has revealed
God's glory and some have been able to receive it. Now he goes
down to Jerusalem once again and this time performs a revelatory
act that *is* grasped by the Jewish opponents. But as with all of
Jesus' actions and teachings, it is a provocative act. This
time, unlike his clearing of the Temple, they are aroused and
respond with hostility. Jesus' provocation has finally resulted
in confrontation. Up to this point in the Gospel there has been
no controversy as such, though we have been prepared for it by
the dualistic language (1.5,10-13; 3.18-20,32-36), the scandals
Jesus has caused (2.18-20; 3.4-10,36; 4.27), and the difficulties
that have had to be overcome even by those who do receive (1.46;
2.4; 2.17,22; 4.9-26,27,33,48).

There are certain similarities between the story of the
wedding in Cana and the story of the healing on the Sabbath of
the man who had been ill for thirty-eight years. As at the wedding in Cana, Jesus keeps a very low profile. "Now the man who
had been healed did not know who it was, for Jesus had withdrawn,
as there was a crowd in the place" (5.13). The mention of the
crowd seems to imply that Jesus does not want to reveal himself
openly yet, but it also means that the man does not know who he
is. Thus, the beneficiary does not know who helps him, as at
the wedding in Cana. In this case, however, Jesus later finds
him in the Temple and says, "See, you are well! Sin no more, that
nothing worse befall you" (5.14). This statement, in contrast
to Jesus' other statements up to this point in the Gospel, is
not at all cryptic. However, by the same token, it reveals

nothing about Jesus, merely telling the man the name of the one
who had healed him.

The man himself is not portrayed in a positive light. The
saying "sin no more that nothing worse befall you" (5.14) focuses on the man as a sinner, in contrast to the later healing
in which it is said there was no sin involved (9.3). This negative impression leads me to interpret what follows as more sinis-
ter than most scholars would allow. After the man learns Jesus'
name he "went away and told the Jews that it was Jesus who had
healed him" (5.15). Up to this point in the Gospel the opponents
have not persecuted Jesus so this man's informing could have been
in innocence. But 5.10 indicates that the man knew the leaders
were upset by Jesus and so in this man's informing on Jesus after
he had been healed by him we have prefigured the later informing
(11.45-46), and Judas' betrayal at a later feast (18.2-3). This
interpretation also is suggested by the contrast with the blind
man in ch. 9 who is a major representative of those who confess
Jesus (see Meeks, *Prophet-King*, 293). Thus, Jesus is healing one
who is totally unworthy; in doing so he reveals God's graciousness. In doing it on the Sabbath he provokes the Jewish opponents (5.16-18). Jesus' defense is that his Father is working
and he himself is working (5.17); another statement extraordinary
for its clarity, as opposed to being cryptic. And the opponents
are able to understand that he is claiming that God is his Father
and that he is uniquely related to God. From what has now been
seen of Jesus' activity leading up to this charge it is evident
that the work Jesus sees the Father doing and which he himself
does is characterized by gracious love. The opponents fail to
recognize this divine love at work in Jesus and thereby show the
depth of their alienation from God. Their rejection of Jesus
who reveals the Father shows that they have never heard nor seen
God (5.37) or else they would have recognized him in his Son.
They are utterly unlike this gracious God who is revealed in
Jesus; τὴν ἀγάπην τοῦ θεοῦ οὐκ ἔχετε ἐν ἑαυτοῖς (5.42).

In these stories in 1.19-5.18 we see revealed Jesus' manifestation of gracious love. In this way they provide the content
of Jesus' assertion that his Father is working and he is working
(5.17). Jesus gracious activity reveals the Father. The

gratuity of God's love becomes increasingly evident as his favor
is expressed to increasingly less worthy recipients until it comes
to a climax in one who has received Jesus' healing and yet be-
trays him. The rejection of Jesus by the man who has been healed
by him echoes the rejection by the opponents in that they themselves have been graciously offered divine revelation in Jesus.
Instead of accepting that which is graciously offered them by
Jesus the opponents seek to kill him (5.18). The story in 5.1-
18 is pivotal; it brings to a climax the revelation of grace in
these initial stories and it also triggers the opponents' hostility which leads to Jesus' death, the supreme revelation of
this gracious divine love. I will now turn to a brief consideration of this death, for in this death are found both the greatest
revelation of the divine love[214] and the clearest manifestation
of the opponents' alienation from God.

c. *Jesus' Death/Glorification*

The importance of Jesus' death for John is apparent from
the motifs of the hour, the lifting up, and the glorification
(see esp. Thüsing, *Die Erhöhung*). These occur throughout the
Gospel so that John can be described as one continuous Passion
Narrative.[215] Jesus' death is viewed as revealing God's love
and as making available eternal life, for to know God as he is
revealed in Jesus is eternal life (cf. 17.3). That Jesus' death
reveals the Father's love par excellence is most clearly expressed in Jn. 3.14-17.

I have already noted that Nicodemus calls Jesus Rabbi, but
is unreceptive to his teaching. Jesus emphasizes that Nicodemus
was right to call him Rabbi because he really does possess knowledge (3.11). He knows not only "earthly things" but also "heavenly things" (3.12) because he himself is from heaven: "No one
has ascended into heaven but he who descended from heaven, the
Son of man" (3.13). This is the first time since the Prologue
that Jesus' heavenly origin has been mentioned. This idea of
Jesus' heavenly origin plays an important role in the Gospel as
a key element in what it means for Jesus to be the Son.[216] It
is significant that this description of Jesus' identity is immediately followed by the mention of his coming redemptive death:

"And as Moses lifted up the serpent in the wilderness, so must
the Son of man be lifted up that whoever believes in him may have
eternal life" (3.14-15). Brown brings out the significance of
these verses in the context of ch. 3: "In vss. 14-15 Jesus pro-
ceeds to the actual answer to Nicodemus' question, 'How can things
like this happen?' Begetting through the Spirit can come about
only as a result of Jesus' crucifixion, resurrection, and ascension" (*John*, 145). So there is a shift from focus on Jesus'
testimony (3.11-12) to a focus on Jesus' identity (3.13). This
identity as the Son of man who descended from heaven is immediately juxtaposed with a reference to his coming death (3.14-
15) and in 3.16-17 the significance of this juxtaposition is
stated. In God's giving of the Son, both in the sense of Jesus'
advent and of his death, God's love is revealed (3.16). Thus, in
3.13-17 the author depicts the exalted identity of Jesus and this
puts in perspective Nicodemus' lack of faith (3.12). His unbelief is a rejection of the only Son of God, which is a rejection
of God himself, whose chief characteristic is gracious love.
This is the reason Jesus' words and works are witnesses, for they
reveal this love in action. Jesus is the visible expression of
God's characteristic gracious love in that his whole existence
is a humble self-denial. He humbles himself before the Father in
total obedience and he gives his body for the life of the world
(6.51). The idea that love *is* the laying down of one's life,
which is explicitly stated in 1 Jn. 3.16, is already evident in
the Gospel (cf. Jn. 15.13). This view of love explains why there
is such stress on the fact of Jesus' death (Jn. 19.34-35),[217]
for his death is the revelation par excellence of God's love,
which is to say, of God himself.

The opponents' rejection of Jesus becomes itself the occasion
of the greatest revelation of God by Jesus. This twist is perhaps the most powerful use of irony in the Gospel. We have seen
the irony of those who are so loyal to Moses and the Law actually rejecting the one witnessed to by Moses and the Law. Now
the irony that this very rejection itself is the occasion of the
climax of the revelation underlines the polemical point behind
all such irony in the Gospel, namely, that those who claim to be
so close to God are the farthest from him.

C. Conclusion

This gracious God is the God the opponents reject when they
reject Jesus. The Father revealed by Jesus is the same God who
revealed his grace and mercy to Moses (Ex. 33.19; 34.6-7). As
in Exodus so in John, God's glory (Ex. 33.18) is his goodness
(33.19).[218] By rejecting this gracious God the opponents show
themselves to be deluded. How can they be sons of God if they
reject the Son of God? Thus, behind the christological controversies in John there is the more basic theological argument.
The author's polemic against his opponents ultimately consists
of a charge of idolatry.

Faced with the Jewish attack on the Christians and the polarization between Christianity and Judaism, the author attempts
to strip away the appearances to show who is really a child of
God. The light comes and exposes the real state of affairs in
Israel (3.19-21). "Revelation brings to light what man really
is. This is the crisis."[219] Those who seem to be so virtuous
and who are so sure of their favor in the sight of God are found
to be farthest from him. Others who are considered to be distant
from God, such as the Samaritan woman and the Herodian official,
are found to be open to God, responsive to his revelation when
it comes. We have seen that what one loves and what one hates,
i.e. one's interior disposition, is the crucial factor,[220] so
that one's response to Jesus is ultimately a matter of the will
(7.16-18).[221] No matter how virtuous the leaders of God's people
may appear, nor what they themselves may claim, they are really
children of the devil. The κρίσις reveals the terrible possibility that even though one may be virtuous and have the very Scriptures of God, it is still possible to be alienated from God and
closed to him.[222] The Jewish opponents hate the light (3.20),
which is to say that they share the character of the devil. So
no matter how good their deeds may seem, these deeds separate
them from God and therefore the deeds are evil (3.19). This evil
which is the source of hatred of the light is the pride and self-
satisfaction of the religious people who think they know God and
yet are far from him. By unmasking the opponents' alienation
from God the author undermines their rejection of Jesus. He

assures his readers that they who believe in Jesus are the real
children of God.

The author considers the advent of Jesus to have caused the
κρίσις of the Jewish people.   In the next chapter I will discuss
1 John, where such a division takes place within the Johannine
community itself.   If the Johannine evaluation of those who reject Jesus is that they are not loyal to their own tradition
and are totally alienated from God, what is the Johannine evaluation of division within the Christian community itself?

3. JOHANNINE POLEMIC: THE LETTER

A. Introduction

There are a number of difficulties one encounters in studying this confusing document. To begin with, its style presents
a problem. It is a tightly written document in which everything
is interrelated. P. Minear is right in his assertion that the
author uses the various images, categories, motifs in parallel
with one another[223] in order to describe a central reality. This
reality is the referent of them all and thus they appear to be
parallel. But this does not necessarily, as Minear suggests, make
them interchangeable. Any one category is to be understood in
the context of the whole (which explains the style of writing
which so frustrates interpreters), but each must retain its distinctness as it harmonizes with the others. In such a document
in which no single element can be isolated from the rest the task
is to understand each part in the context of the whole. This
goal is appropriate for all documents but the closeness of the
weave in 1 John makes it particularly difficult.
    A further problem arises in determining the purpose of the
document. The major place given to combating the error of the
opponents has led some to see this as the sole aim of the document.[224] But others are surely correct in maintaining that the
author has his own positive message to present as well.[225] This
positive concern is expressed, for example, in the concluding
statement of purpose: "I write this to you who believe in the
name of the Son of God, that you may know that you have eternal
life" (5.13). Even in this text, however, the opponents are not
far from the author's thought; they are the ones causing the un-
ease among the community that necessitates his words of assurance
to his readers. Nevertheless, while the author is obviously very
concerned with what he sees as error threatening his readers, it
is important to understand that he is consciously presenting his
own positive message. He is presumably not simply taking his
cues from the opponents and reacting against them. Because of

121

this close connection the polemic in 1 John must be studied in
the context of the author's own positive thought.

Further problems arise from our lack of material written by
the opponents themselves.[226] The difficulties with trying to re-
construct the opposition's position from a controversy document
are notorious. In fact, to do so with certainty is simply impossible, for all we have is the author's own evaluation of the
situation and thus all we can really study with the slightest
objectivity is that evaluation. But even to understand his evaluation is exceedingly difficult because we know so very little
about the early Church and its setting. So caution is in order
and the tentative nature of the conclusions which may be reached
concerning both the author's own position and that of the opponents should be recognized from the outset. The reconstruction
of the opponents' position, however, raises the further problem
of recognizing an allusion to the false teaching when the allusion is not explicit. Fortunately, this problem is not too severe
in 1 John since it is evident that there is a false teaching being combated (e.g. 2.21-26; 3.7), and most of those passages
which are considered to be allusions to this teaching seem only
thinly veiled. So, while recognizing that there is always po-
tentially a problem with determining allusions to the false
teaching, the passages which are generally considered to be allusions seem a secure enough foundation upon which to build. There
are, then, three categories of material for reconstructing the
situation behind 1 John and the polemic involved:[227]

1. Specific statements of reasons for writing: 1.3-4; 2.1,12-
                                                 14,21,26; 5.13.

2. Direct references to the opponents and/or their teaching:
    A. Doctrinal: 2.22-23,26; 4.2-3,15; 5.6.
    B. Ethical: 1.6,8,10; 2.4,6,9; 4.20.

3. Allusions which fill out the picture:
    A. Tests of falsehood: 2.4,9,22; 3.6,10,14; 4.3.
    B. Tests of assurance: 2.3-6,10,24-25; 3.7-10,14,19-24; 4.2,
                           6,13-18; 5.2,12-13,18-20.

Note that the third section of this outline indicates again the
close relation between the author's own positive concerns and his
opposition to the false teachers in that tests of both falsehood

and assurance are given. Furthermore, the second section mentions references to both doctrinal and ethical errors. This is
significant for, as Häring has indicated in his influential outline of 1 John, the author's main concerns center in christology
and ethics.[228] I will begin this study with an examination of
these two topics, starting with christology. After examining
his criticism of his opponents' position I will then consider the
positive side of his polemic, his assurance of his readers.
This analysis of the negative and the positive sides of the polemic will then enable me to offer a suggestion concerning the underlying structure and ground of the polemic in 1 John.

B. The Polemic

1. *Negative Side: The Criticism of the Opponents' Position*

a. *Christology*

    The author's christological confession revolves around two
foci, Jesus as ὁ χριστός and Jesus as ὁ υἱός (τοῦ θεοῦ). The
primary christological passages are:
1. 2.22; 5.1 'Ιησοῦς ἐστιν ὁ χριστός.
2. 4.15; 5.5 'Ιησοῦς ἐστιν ὁ υἱός (τοῦ θεοῦ)
    (cf. 2.23; 3.23; 5.11-13,20).
3. 4.2 'Ιησοῦν Χριστὸν ἐν σαρκὶ ἐληλυθότα.
4. 5.6 οὗτός ἐστιν ὁ ἐλθὼν δι' ὕδατος καὶ αἵματος 'Ιησοῦς
    Χριστός κτλ.

1) χριστός *and* υἱός (τοῦ θεοῦ)

    The confession of Jesus as ὁ χριστός and as ὁ υἱός (τοῦ
θεοῦ) are closely interrelated, as is evident from 2.22-23. Although ὁ χριστός and ὁ υἱός (τοῦ θεοῦ) are virtually interchangeable,[229] de Jonge has probably gone too far when he describes
them as "synonymous" ("ΧΡΙΣΤΟΣ," 71). Nevertheless, to predicate
one of them of Jesus is to be conscious of the other also and to
deny one of Jesus is to deny the other as well.[230]
    What, then, is the significance for the author of confessing
Jesus as ὁ χριστός? This close relationship between ὁ χριστός
and ὁ υἱός (τοῦ θεοῦ) indicates, as de Jonge has pointed out,
that whatever the background of ὁ χριστός in Judaism, it is in

Johannine thought first of all a Christian term molded by Christian experience in the Christian communities.[231] Indeed, this
Christian use of ὁ χριστός is evident even in the Gospel, where
the main opposition comes from Judaism. In John ὁ χριστός is
used of the expected Jewish Messiah (de Jonge, "ΧΡΙΣΤΟΣ," 71-73),
but is also used in relation to ὁ υἱός (τοῦ θεοῦ). De Jonge concludes concerning the relation between these two terms in John:
"The terms ὁ υἱός τοῦ θεοῦ or ὁ υἱός, used in the typical Johannine way to express the unity of Jesus and God, qualify ὁ χριστός
and indicate how Christians should interpret the typical Jewish
term" (ibid. 74). Thus, in John, where ὁ χριστός is still used
with reference to Jewish expectations, it has already been interpreted in a distinctively Christian manner. In 1 John ὁ
χριστός has even less reference to Jewish expectations. Of the
nine instances of the term in 1 John, seven are in the phrase
Ἰησοῦς Χριστός. The other two instances (2.22; 5.1) are both
in contexts which bring out the almost interchangeable character
of ὁ χριστός and ὁ υἱός (τοῦ θεοῦ). So it is very difficult to
tell how much specifically Jewish content remained in the term
ὁ χριστός and how much it was modified by Christian thought. It
would seem unlikely that it would lose all contact with its
Jewish heritage, especially for an author (and, presumably, his
readers) who uses so many other "Jewish categories" (Robinson,
"Destination," 59-61). Be that as it may, the content of ὁ
χριστός is now influenced by that of ὁ υἱός (τοῦ θεοῦ).

        To confess that Jesus is ὁ υἱός (τοῦ θεοῦ) is primarily a
statement concerning his relation to God the Father. Here in
1 John, as we have seen also in John, Jesus as Son is primarily
the revealer of the Father. The Father and the Son are as inseparable in 1 John (e.g. 2.23) as they are in John (e.g. 10.30).
The revelation of the Father by the Son is focused in 1 John on
the crucifixion. The death of ὁ χριστός plays a central role in
the thought of the entire document and it is with the rejection
of this death by the opponents that the author is most concerned.
For it is through the death of Jesus, ὁ χριστός, ὁ υἱός (τοῦ
θεοῦ), that the Father's love and forgiveness are made known
(4.9-10). This crucial role played by Jesus' death in the theology of 1 John is the context in which the three most important
passages dealing with the christology of the opponents must be
studied.

2) 1 Jn. 2.22-23

The first of these passages refers to the confession of Jesus
as ὁ χριστός. The opponents are said to deny this. A good case
can be made that in doing so they are Jews who are following the
same line as the Jewish opponents in John, that is, that the
false teaching in view in 1 John is a simple denial that Jesus
is the expected Messiah.[232] There are no exegetical data that
conclusively rule out such an understanding of the false teaching.
However, it seems improbable given the subtlety of the author's
argument and the great danger of deception (2.26; 3.7). It is
difficult to imagine that Jewish denials of Jesus as Messiah,
which were present from the time the first claims for Jesus as
Messiah were expressed, should now pose some new threat which
causes the community to need instruction in order to discern its
error. But if it is not simply a Jewish denial of Jesus as Messiah, what is the threat?

In trying to determine what the opponents were actually affirming or denying concerning Jesus, all the problems of reconstruction mentioned above come to the fore. Are we to think that
the opponents said, in so many words, "Jesus is not the Christ?"
Or is this only the implication the author draws from their
teaching and/or their behavior, although they themselves would
not say such a thing? Again, it seems improbable that a group
of Christians would say "Jesus is not the Christ" (though perhaps this is not impossible),[233] and even less likely that the
rest of the community would have difficulty recognizing this as
an error. So it is most likely that the denial of Jesus as Christ
is an interpretation of the false teaching on the part of the
author. This view is further confirmed by the close relationship
between ὁ χριστός and ὁ υἱός (τοῦ θεοῦ) in 2.22-23. Given the
central role played by ὁ υἱός (τοῦ θεοῦ) in Johannine christology,
it is very unlikely that anyone saying explicitly "Jesus is not
the Christ" which would be the equivalent of "Jesus is not the
Son" would not be considered to be in error. So it seems the
opponents are teaching something which the author interprets as
a denial of Jesus as ὁ χριστός and ὁ υἱός (τοῦ θεοῦ), though
this is probably not how they would have expressed themselves.

3) 1 Jn. 4.2-3

The second major passage helps focus more sharply both the
author's own christology and that of the opponents. Here the
confession 'Ιησοῦν Χριστὸν ἐν σαρκὶ ἐληλυθότα is contrasted with
not confessing τὸν 'Ιησοῦν. The first thing to notice, which
was actually already present at 2.22 but now can be seen as crucial for understanding the issue at hand, is that the problem
concerns *Jesus* (cf. Wengst, *Spiegel*, 64). Presumably the opponents would deny, at least in the author's eyes, that which is
here confessed, namely, 'Ιησοῦν Χριστὸν ἐν σαρκὶ ἐληλυθότα.
As at 2.22-23, the threat may be simply Jewish. This clause
could refer to confessing that Jesus is the Christ come in the
flesh, that is, that the expected Messiah has arrived on the human scene and he is Jesus. Taken in this way, 4.2 would make
more specific the confession of Jesus as ὁ χριστός in 2.22.[234]

Given, however, the improbability of such an interpretation,
as mentioned above, many scholars take seriously the indication
that the issue concerns Jesus, but see here a reference to
Docetism. According to this interpretation, the author, on the
one hand, is affirming the true humanity of Jesus, the Christ,
the Son (of God), and the opponents, on the other, are denying
that Jesus was really fully a man--he only seemed to be one.
However, despite the attractiveness and widespread popularity of
this interpretation, there are difficulties with it. Part of
the problem is the vagueness of the term "Docetism." A. E.
Brooke, for example, distinguishes a wider from a narrower meaning of the term:[235]

> [Docetism] can be used in a more popular sense to
> characterize all teaching which denied the reality
> of the Incarnation, and therefore the reality and
> completeness of the Lord's humanity. It may also be
> used more precisely of teaching which assigned to the
> Lord a merely phantasmal body, maintaining that He had
> a human body, of flesh and blood, only in appearance.

He goes on to remark that "the language of the Johannine Epistles
does not necessarily presuppose the more precise Docetism"
(*Epistles*, xlv). A. Grillmeier is of the same opinion: "The
false teachers of the Johannines . . . are not docetists in the
strict sense. In other words, it cannot be demonstrated that

they already denied the reality of Christ's flesh."[236] Unfortunately, neither Brooke nor Grillmeier gives a very clear idea of what they mean by a wider sense of Docetism. It would seem that the wider sense refers to any denial of Jesus' humanity while the narrower sense refers to a specific theory involving his "appearance" in human form while in reality having only spiritual existence. Be this as it may, they are quite right that there is nothing in 1 John to demand such an interpretation. But if ἐν σαρκί does not indicate a Docetic denial of Jesus' humanity, what could it indicate? It is of value to look at the Gospel's use of σάρξ with reference to Jesus.[237]

The key passages are Jn. 1.14 and 6.51-58. In 1.14 the emphasis is on the contrast with Jn. 1.1. It is said that the λόγος which ἐν ἀρχῇ ἦν and ἦν πρὸς τὸν θεόν (1.1), σάρξ ἐγένετο and ἐσκήνωσεν ἐν ἡμῖν (1.14). The significance of 1.14 is brought out well by Barrett when he says, "Perhaps ἐγένετο is used in the same sense as in v. 6: the Word came on the (human) scene--as flesh, man" (*John*, 165). This interpretation catches the emphasis on movement in 1.14. The point emphasized is not in the first place the mode of the Word's coming but the fact of his coming.[238] The one who was with the Father in the beginning has now come among us.

While this interpretation proposes that the primary emphasis is on ἐγένετο, this does not mean that σάρξ is without significance. John quite clearly believes that Jesus was a man of flesh and blood, but he does not emphasize this in the way one would expect were Docetism in view. There are a number of references in John to Jesus eating, being tired, crying, and other flesh and blood activities, but these are not emphasized. Of particular interest in this regard is the post-resurrection account, in which some have found an emphasis on the reality of Jesus as σάρξ. Such an emphasis, however, is completely lacking, though the reality of Jesus as flesh and blood is evident through relatively incidental material. For example, in Jn. 20.11-18 Mary Magdalene mistakes Jesus for a gardener. The emphasis here, as throughout the post-resurrection narratives, is on the problem of recognizing Jesus' identity, not his σάρξ. That Jesus is flesh and blood is evident in this story from his command (or

request) μή μου ἅπτου (20.17), but this is incidental. In the
next section, 20.19-23, Jesus appears to his disciples. Jn.
20.20 might seem anti-Docetic, but again this is not the case
for the focus of attention is his hand and sides, i.e. not his
body as such but the distinguishing marks of the Crucified's
body. This emphasis in John stands in marked contrast to the
same story in Lk. 24.36-43. In Luke great emphasis *is* placed
on the reality of Jesus as flesh and blood, instead of he being
a ghost. Such an emphasis is missing in John not because the
Gospel is naively Docetic,[239] but because the reality of Jesus
as flesh and blood is not a problem for him. In this regard the
story of the walking on the water is also instructive. Luke
omits this story, while John has it but lacks the reason for the
disciples' fear as it is given in Mt. 14.26 and Mk. 6.49: ὅτι
φάντασμά ἐστιν. For the author of John there seems to be no
question but that Jesus is human. It is easy, however, to sym-
pathize with the disciples in Matthew and Mark, since anyone
walking on water seems somehow unhuman. Indeed, in John the
surreality of the scene is even heightened by the note: "Then
they were glad to take him into the boat, and immediately the
boat was at the land to which they were going" (6.21). While for
many people such an account calls into question Jesus' humanity,
it does not do so for the author of John--it does not question
his humanity but rather affirms his divinity.[240] That it is the
author's concern to affirm both humanity and divinity is evident
from the outset in the Prologue.[241] Thus, it is misleading to
call John naively Docetic. R. E. Brown is right when he says,
"If one must be anachronistic . . . I would see in John's description of Jesus more the danger of monophysitism than of
docetism."[242] Someone else might urge that John represents a
naive, unreflected form of Chalcedonian Christology, which is
to say that the emphasis in Brown's statement should be on the
word "anachronistic;" the Gospel lacks precision when compared
with later developments. It is precisely this lack of precision
that contributes to the problems faced in the Letter.

   The next part of the post-resurrection account in John, the
appearance of Jesus to Thomas (20.24-29), might seem most
strongly to suggest an anti-Docetic concern, but again this is

not the case--again the problem is identity and not corporeality
as such. The reference to Thomas feeling Jesus' hands and side
(20.27) makes no sense if Jesus is not flesh and blood. However,
the emphasis is not on his corporeality but on the reality of the
wounds. The point is not that Jesus has a body, but that the
obviously flesh and blood body standing there is the Jesus who
was crucified. The problem is the recognition of the Crucified
for who he is (20.28).

It is this same central concern with Jesus as the Crucified
that is behind the reference to Jesus' σάρξ in 6.51-58. In the
last chapter I noted the Johannine theme of the contrast between
the openness of those who receive with the closed questioning
of those who reject when confronted by a cryptic saying or action
of Jesus. This same theme can be traced in many passages in the
Gospel, including this one in ch. 6. During an introductory dialogue (6.26-34) the people show themselves to be open to Jesus
(6.28,30-31,34). As elsewhere in the Gospel, when Jesus finds
people who are open he reveals himself to them (6.35). But here
he also challenges them (6.36-40). The author next focuses on
the opponents' response to this challenge (note the shift from
ὁ ὄχλος, v.24 to οἱ ᾿Ιουδαῖοι, v. 41). They are closed; they
question and reject (6.41-42). Jesus' response to this rejection
is to repeat his emphasis on the divine initiative (6.43-46, cf.
6.37-40), thereby implying that his opponents are alienated from
God. He also repeats his claim to be the Bread of Life (6.47-51),
but adds a new element by referring to his σάρξ (6.51). This
additional revelation only deepens the opponents' rejection
(6.52). Faced with this rejection Jesus repeats his emphasis
on life-giving and the necessity of eating his σάρξ in order to
have life (6.53-58). The eating is related to abiding. This
life is from the Father and believers share it in Christ. Thus,
the reference to Jesus' σάρξ here forms part of a progressive
deepening of Jesus' self-revelation coupled with a corresponding
intensification of the rejection of him. It is this cryptic
saying referring to his death which tests peoples' hearts in the
same way such cryptic sayings function earlier in the Gospel. As
with the earlier cryptic sayings this reference to Jesus' σάρξ
cannot be understood until his death. But given the Johannine

motif that it is Jesus' death which gives life to the world it
seems the reference to σάρξ here is most likely an element in
this motif.[243] Thus, there is no clear indication that Docetism
is in view, since the reference to Jesus' σάρξ is explicable as
a cryptic reference to Jesus' coming death. As with the other
Gospel passages just examined, this reference certainly assumes
that Jesus is flesh and blood, but this aspect is incidental to
the main point that this flesh and blood Jesus has died.

If 4.2 is not confronting a Docetic denial of Jesus' σάρξ
then how is it to be interpreted? The interpretation here proposed would accept, in agreement with the interpretation that
envisages a confrontation in 1 John with Judaism, that 4.2 is
concerned with Jesus as ὁ χριστός. However, the opponents are
not to be understood as representing a simple denial of Jesus as
ὁ χριστός, as they would if they were Jews. Something more subtle
is involved. Furthermore, unlike the interpretation that envisages a confrontation with Docetism, the emphasis is not on
Jesus' σάρξ but on the σάρξ of ὁ χριστός. This important distinction is clarified by the last major christological passage,
5.6.

4)   1 Jn. 5.6

In this verse there is the most specific information concerning the nature of the false teaching, but also the most cryptic. There is a widespread opinion that 5.6 implies a position
similar to that held by Cerinthus, as represented in Irenaeus,
Against Heresies, 1.26.1. There are, however, many differences
between Cerinthus' thought as Irenaeus represents it and the
thought of the opponents in 1 John,[244] so it is very unlikely that
the author is combating either Cerinthus himself or disciples
who followed his teaching closely. Nevertheless, one of the most
recent major studies of the opponents in 1 John argues persua-
sively for interpreting 5.6 in the light of one aspect of Cerinthian thought.[245] The reference to both the water and the blood,
with the emphasis on the blood, makes one think of Cerinthus'
view that ὁ χριστός came upon Jesus at his baptism and left him
before his death. Such a view might claim to be loyal to the
Johannine tradition, perhaps as an interpretation of Jn. 1.32,34;

19.30. It goes contrary to the emphasis on the actual death of
Jesus in the Gospel, but the opponents, on this assessment of
their view, would not deny that Jesus died, but rather that ὁ
χριστός suffered death. The parallel with Cerinthus' thought is
the closest available to us at this time, but what relation the
Johannine opponents had with Cerinthian circles is altogether
unclear. 1 Jn. 5.6 implies some sort of denial of Jesus' death,
while accepting his baptism and thus appearing to have something
of a positive view of Jesus. Thus, the author would be arguing
against a teaching that he would interpret as a denial that Jesus
is the Christ, the Son (of God), but which would not be understood in this way by its proponents. In the author's eyes, to
deny that Jesus died as the Christ, the Son (of God) is to deny
the very center of Jesus' revelation of the Father and the
Father's love and forgiveness. Thus it is that 4.2 should be
interpreted as a denial not of Jesus' σάρξ but of the σάρξ of
ὁ χριστός, that is, here is a denial of the *essential* identity
of Jesus as the Christ, the Son (of God). This christological
confession of the essential identity of Jesus as the Christ, the
Son (of God), especially in his death, is fundamental for the
thought of 1 John, including, as we shall see, other aspects of
his criticism of the false teaching.

5) *Conclusion*

The christological problem is not a simple denial that Jesus
is the Christ, as 2.22-23 might imply. Nor is it a denial that
Jesus has come in the flesh, as 4.2 is often interpreted as implying. Rather, as 5.6 suggests, the issue concerns the death.
More specifically, the opponents are denying that Jesus died as
Messiah. They do not deny that Jesus is flesh but rather that
Jesus is the Christ come in the flesh (cf. 4.2), for they deny
his death (cf. 5.6). In the author's eyes such a view is the
denial of the very center of Christianity, for it is in the death
of God's Messiah Son that God the Father himself is revealed par
excellence.

b. *Ethics*

The differences in ethics between the author and his opponents can conveniently be discussed by examining the material in

1 John concerning sin and sinlessness. According to the author, the opponents claim to be sinless, and for this he condemns them. Yet he himself also speaks of believers as being sinless. Thus, as with the issue of christology, the ethical differences between the author and his opponents seem somewhat subtle. Before trying to distinguish the different views of sinlessness I will describe in more detail how very confusing the situation appears. If one group was antinomian and the other legalistic then the differences in sinlessness might not be so confusing. It appears, however, that both groups were concerned with the keeping of commandments.

1) Shared Ground: The Keeping of Commandments

Some scholars would disagree with this picture, considering the opponents to have been libertines instead of legalists (e.g. Robinson, *Redating*, 286). But there seems to be no evidence that clearly depicts them as libertines (cf. Brooke, *Epistles*, l-li). Brown does not call them libertines but he does think that they were indifferent to the commandments (*Community*, 128-130, 138). However, this view also seems inadequate in the light of 3.4: πᾶς ὁ ποιῶν τὴν ἁμαρτίαν καὶ τὴν ἀνομίαν ποιεῖ, καὶ ἡ ἁμαρτία ἐστὶν ἡ ἀνομία. Bultmann thinks that the claim to sinlessness (1.8,10) is precisely the reason they "make themselves guilty of 'lawlessness'."[246] The author and his opponents share "a common conception of 'lawlessness,' viz., that 'lawlessness' is a heinous sin" (Bultmann, *Epistles*, 50). Bultmann does not seem to think any specific indication of the nature of the opponents' attitudes with regard to the 'law' is indicated by ἀνομία since "in traditional parlance no difference existed between ἁμαρτία ('sin') and ἀνομία ('lawlessness')" (ibid. 50 n.26). W. Gutbrod agrees with Bultmann that ἀνομία is the more special and heinous term.[247] It would seem that ἁμαρτία has been weakened somehow and the author wants to make clear its evil character (Dodd, *Epistles*, 73). The key question is why ἀνομία has this force, and the fact that it here does have this force makes irrelevant Bultmann's comment that there is no difference between ἁμαρτία and ἀνομία in common parlance. Gutbrod's suggestion that ἀνομία means rebellion or revolt against God[248] is not specifically supported by 3.6b,9-10 since these say only that ἁμαρτία is

incompatible with the idea that one has seen God, known him, or
been born of him. In any event this comment is not very helpful
since it is ἁμαρτία that is so described in 1 John, and if we
are to take ἀνομία as an intensification of ἁμαρτία (i.e. that
it is what ἁμαρτία is only more so) this still does not explain
why ἀνομία has this significance in 1 John. The point Gutbrod
makes in n.3, however, is very helpful (see also Brooke, *Epistles*, 84-85). He mentions that for ἀνομία to be more heinous
than ἁμαρτία implies that those who hold such a view are not
antinomians or libertines, but the opposite. Thus it seems most
likely that the opponents, like the author, were concerned with
keeping the commandments. It must have been very difficult
indeed for the Johannine Christians to see any difference between the author's position and that of his opponents. Indeed,
the fact that 1 John was written at all indicates there was such
difficulty. The crucial question, therefore, is how the author
distinguishes between his own view of sinlessness and that of
the opponents.

2) The Opponents' View of Sinlessness

The sinlessness claimed by the opponents is generally considered to be in view in 1.8,10. In his recent study of perfectionism in 1 John J. Bogart has provided a useful insight for
understanding these two verses. He sets them in relation to the
other verses in the context which contain the phrase ἐὰν εἴπωμεν
ὅτι or ὁ λέγων (ὅτι) (1.6; 2.4,6,9). He notes four elements in
these passages which he describes as follows:

(a) The opening quotation formula.
(b) The apparent quotation of the opponents; (direct in
     the first four, indirect in the latter two). Also
     called assertions of the opponents.
(c) The statement of the actual behavior of the opponents.
(d) The statement of the consequences of that behavior,
     i.e., the present spiritual state of the opponents.

1:6, 2:4 and 2:9 have all four of these grammatical
elements. 1:8 and 1:10 both lack (c). 2:6 lacks (c) and
(d), but instead has a closing clause (e) which may be
designated as a simple statement of the moral obligation
of one who makes the quoted assertion (*Perfectionism*, 26).

For our purposes the most important aspect of Bogart's analysis

of these texts is the relation between parts (b) and (c) in 1.6;
2.4,9:

> The third element (c), the description of the opponents'
> actual behavior, when juxtaposed with the second element
> (b), the opponent's [sic.] assertions, effects a startling
> rhetorical contrast, which serves to highlight the oppo-
> nents' hypocrisy (ibid. 31).

So in these three verses there is nothing wrong with the claims
themselves (κοινωνίαν ἔχομεν μετ' αὐτοῦ, 1.6; ἔγνωκα αὐτόν, 2.4;
ἐν τῷ φωτί εἶναι, 2.9)--indeed, they are Johannine claims. The
author of 1 John criticizes not the claims but the hypocrisy
of those making the claims.

The text at 2.6 falls out of the pattern somewhat, as do
1.8,10. This change in 2.6 does not seem very significant for
the present study, but in the case of 1.8,10 the lack of (c) is
very significant, for it indicates that

> the assertions themselves are categorically denied as
> intrinsically wrong; unlike those in the other four
> sentences, these two have no qualifying explications
> surrounding them. This marks them off as not only
> different in form, but as dealing with a different
> problem: not the problem of hypocrisy, as in the other
> four, but here, the problem of heresy (Perfectionism, 33).

What, then, is this heresy? Bogart attempts to argue that it is
an understanding of sinlessness based on a Gnostic anthropology,
which he then contrasts with a Christian view:[249]

> Only a gnostic view of man, a view which saw man as
> intrinsically part of the Divine Essence, or a spark
> from the Divine Fire, a part of the Father who is above
> all, could claim that man had never sinned. It would be
> a claim of intrinsic human perfection, possessed by men
> as a right, not, as in the case of Christian perfectionism,
> given to repentant, sinful man as a gift from the forgiving
> Father.

Such a contrast between an "intrinsic human perfection" and the
perfection which is "a gift from the forgiving Father" may well
be in view in this passage since 1.7-10 indicate clearly that the
fundamental objection of the author is to the opponents' lack of
regard for the need of atonement and repentance. However, Bogart's assertion that the opponents' view of sinlessness is based
on a Gnostic anthropology is open to two objections. First, it
is disturbing that Bogart does not mention any positive exegetical

evidence in 1 John for such a view on the part of the opponents.
His only evidence for such a Gnostic anthropology is the tenses
in 1.8 (ἔχομεν) and 1.10 (ἡμαρτήκαμεν) (ibid. 33-34). He himself
chastises N. Turner for such "superficial exegesis,"[250] so Bogart
is aware of the weakness of such evidence. Presumably the reason
he would not see his interpretation as sharing in Turner's alleged superficiality is that he would consider himself to be
taking into account "the crucial historical and theological
questions" (ibid. 45). As this implies, the real evidence for
such a Gnostic anthropology is the satisfyingly coherent picture
it presents. It fits in well with the gnosticizing tendencies
evident in the opponents' christology and accounts for the seemingly irresolvable tension between 1.8,10 and the author's own
perfectionism.

The second objection is based on the lack of evidence for
such an anthropology at this period in the precise form Bogart
suggests. As Brown says, Bogart is "really introducing into the
period between the Gospel and the Epistles a development that we
can document only in the period *after* the Epistles" (*Community*,
127).

But the fact that Bogart's appeal to Gnosticism must be
questioned does not mean his analysis of the anthropology underlying the opponents' claim to sinlessness is necessarily wrong,
since this particular view of man as a divine spark is already
prefigured in Plato and the Orphics.[251] So some such notion of
man as intrinsically divine could well be behind their view of
sinlessness.

In any event, it is clear from the context of 1.8,10 that
the primary feature of their view is a claim to sinlessness apart
from God, Christ, and the atoning death. From their point of
view not only did the Messiah not die, there was no need for him
to do so.

One of the characteristics of such a view of sinlessness is
its extreme individualism. Individualism is prevalent in the
Gospel[252] and the opponents in 1 John seem to have developed it
into a form of elitism.[253] Brooke, for example, suggests on the
basis of 1 Jn. 2.4-6 that the opponents "must have claimed to
know God as ordinary Christians could not know Him, without

recognizing the obligation of complete obedience to the whole
of His commands, or of living a life in conscious imitation of
the life of the Master" (*Epistles*, li). He even goes so far as
to say: "They must have been unwilling to recognize that the
ordinary and less enlightened members of the community had any
real claims upon them. They may have preferred to stand well
with the more intelligent Jews and heathen in whose midst they
lived (μὴ ἀγαπᾶτε τὸν κόσμον), cf. ii.15,16" (Brooke, *Epistles*,
li). Elitism of some sort would appear to be implied by the un-
willingness to share ὁ βίος τοῦ κόσμου with members of the community who are in need (3.17-18). So the opponents would seem
to be somewhat separate from other believers, perhaps even in
their knowledge of God.[254]

In sum, the basic characteristic of the opponents' position,
as it is described by the author, is autonomy. They experience
both sinlessness and love quite apart from Christ's death and
the Christian community. In contrast, the author's own view of
sinlessness emphasizes both the death and the community.

3)   The Author's View of Sinlessness

The author's concept of sinlessness first emerges explicitly
in 2.1-6. Here he begins by saying "My little children, I am
writing this to you so that you may not sin" (2.1a), thus indicating that sinlessness *is* a goal to strive towards. But he
immediately adds, "but if any one does sin, we have an advocate
with the Father, Jesus Christ the Righteous" (2.1b). So he
recognizes a continuing need for the forgiveness (1.9) available
through Jesus' death (1.7; 2.2).[255] He then introduces the theme
of keeping Jesus' commandments (2.3-4, note the plural) and concludes by holding up Jesus as the example to imitate (2.6). It
is important to notice that there really is a moral perfection
encouraged here, for this fact is easy to lose sight of once the
more dominant motif in the Johannine understanding of perfection
is introduced. For the theme of sinlessness in 1 John cannot be
discussed for long without bringing in the motif of love, in
particular, love for the brothers.

While a moral perfection is taught in 2.1-6, it is immediately interpreted in 2.7-11 as love for the brother. This same

interpretation is clear in ch. 3 also. In 3.10 sin is explicitly
defined as μὴ ποιῶν δικαιοσύνην, which in turn is defined as
μὴ ἀγαπῶν τὸν ἀδελφόν. To love the brothers is to not sin.
These are the marks of those born of God.

The interpretation which understands sinlessness as love
must take into account another major passage in 1 John concerning sin:

> If any one sees his brother committing what is not a
> mortal sin, he will ask, and God will give him life for
> those whose sin is not mortal. There is sin which is
> mortal; I do not say that one is to pray for that. All
> wrongdoing is sin, but there is sin which is not mortal
> (5.16-17).

The clue to this puzzling text occurs in 3.14: "We know that we
have passed out of death into life, because we love the brethren.
He who does not love abides in death." This passage in ch. 3 suggests in the author's thought ἀμαρτία πρὸς θάνατον in 5.16 is the
breaking of fellowship. What one prays for is that the sinner
be given ζωή, but ζωή exists precisely within the community.
There is assurance only for those within the community, that is,
for those who are already within the realm of ζωή. According
to this interpretation the ἀμαρτία πρὸς θάνατον is the separation
of oneself from the community.[256]

Furthermore, since love is ποιεῖν τὴν δικαιοσύνην and μὴ
ἀμαρτάνειν, it is in 5.16-17 that the contrasting positions evident in 1.8,10 and 3.6,9 are resolved. Those in ch. 3 who are
said to be born of God and not sin are those who love the brother,
that is, who remain in the community which is the realm of light,
life, and love. Being a part of this community, however, does
not mean they have no moral failings (1.8,10) even though they
are to strive not to have (2.1). In 5.16-17 these moral failings
which do not separate one from the community are called ἀμαρτία
μὴ πρὸς θάνατον, while the breaking of fellowship, that is, the
putting of oneself outside the realm of light, life, and love,
is called ἀμαρτία πρὸς θάνατον. This is something ὁ γεγεννημένος
ἐκ τοῦ θεοῦ (3.9) and ὁ ἐν αὐτῷ μένων (3.6) would not do.

This in turn explains why the secession of some former members of the community has such an impact on the author in that
it indicates to him that ἐσχάτη ὥρα has arrived (2.18). He

interprets their withdrawal in line with the understanding here
proposed in that it is said that although they went out from the
midst of the community, they οὐκ ἦσαν ἐξ ἡμῶν, that is, they did
not share the abiding seed (3.9), almost by definition, since
μεμενήκεισαν ἂν μεθ᾽ ἡμῶν (2.19). Their going forth was that
their true character might be revealed (ἵνα φανερωθῶσιν, 2.19)
because οὐκ εἰσὶν πάντες ἐξ ἡμῶν. This last thought could be the
simple statement that none of those who went out were ἐξ ἡμῶν,
which would make it a rather obvious and therefore trivial observation, unless those who had withdrawn still claimed some sort
of tie with the community, which is possible. Alternatively, it
can mean that not all who are in our midst are really of us, that
is, more defections are possible and perhaps considered, unfortunately, probable. The latter interpretation is perhaps supported by 1.3, for here the author expresses his concern to
maintain fellowship with his readers: "so that you may have fellowship with us." He does so, as 5.13 indicates, by assuring
them of their current position, if only they will maintain it.
There are some who are in danger of losing such fellowship because they lack brotherly love. 1 Jn. 3.17 may not only refer
to the opponents but may also serve as a warning to some of the
readers, thus providing us with our only specific glimpse into
the community. There are those who are closing their hearts to
others in need (cf. 2.16). They claim to love God but their
hatred of the brothers belies this claim, since "every one who
loves the parent loves the child" (5.1).

This interpretation of sinlessness as meaning remaining
within the realm of life (the community) by loving is perhaps
further supported by 5.18. Here the perfectionism of 3.6,9 is
repeated (οἴδαμεν ὅτι πᾶς ὁ γεγεννημένος ἐκ τοῦ θεοῦ οὐχ
ἁμαρτάνει), but it is not contrasted with a clause such as ἀλλ᾽
ἔστιν τέλειος,[257] but rather: ἀλλ᾽ ὁ γεννηθεὶς ἐκ τοῦ θεοῦ
τηρεῖ αὐτόν, καὶ ὁ πονηρὸς οὐχ ἅπτεται αὐτοῦ. From what we have
seen of sinlessness in 1 John it is most natural to interpret
this text as referring to the believers being kept safe within
the community.[258]

The interpretation of sinlessness here proposed is corro-
borated by D. M. Scholer[259] though with one significant exception. As just suggested, he finds in 5.16-17 an indication of

how the seemingly incompatible texts (1.8,10; 3.6,9) are to be
understood. "For the author to say that believers do not sin
(5.18) immediately after a discussion of believers' sins (5:14-
17) can mean only that two different concepts are in view."[260]
These two concepts are identified in 1 Jn. 5.16-17 as ἁμαρτία
μὴ πρὸς θάνατον and ἁμαρτία πρὸς θάνατον, which Scholer interprets as being "the 'sins of the righteous,' i.e. those which do
not preclude membership in the believing community" and "sin
which *does* preclude membership in the believing community (i.e.
murder = hatred of believers and lying = denial of Jesus); it
is sin in the realm of death" ("Sins," 246). His interpretation
this far is along the lines of that here proposed. The point of
difference is that Scholer does not see ἁμαρτία πρὸς θάνατον
as referring to believers still in the community, but only concerning those who have already gone out and therefore are no
longer members. At the deepest level he is correct, that is,
by definition a believer is apart from the realm of death (3.14),
and thus is only susceptible to ἁμαρτία μὴ πρὸς θάνατον. But
the problem in the community is that some who appeared to be
members turned out not to be so after all (2.19), and the concern of the author is that those still in the community not depart also but rather have κοινωνία (1.3). The problem would
seem to be one of apostasy. Scholer, however, disagrees:

> In 1 John one is either a believer or an unbeliever;
> there is no reference to apostasy. This is made clear
> in 1 John 2:19, an important text for understanding the
> whole problem. After stating that many antichrists,
> already present and active (2:18; cf. 4:1-5), have come
> from the Christian community (2:19), the statement is
> modified in such a way as to negate it. In actuality the
> antichrists were not from the Christian community, for
> if they really had been, they would not have left it.
> The fact that the antichrists left the community was a
> good thing: it showed conclusively that they were never
> real members of it in the first place; they had been
> pretenders only. . . . Because the 'sin unto death' is for
> 1 John a sin of those who are actually disruptive,
> heretical outsiders, there is no concern at this point
> (in 5:14-17 where the concern is effective prayer for
> sin within the believing community) for prayer for the
> 'sin unto death.' The 'sin unto death' is mentioned as
> an aside in contrast to the 'sin not unto death,' which
> does in fact occur within the believing community
> (Scholer, "Sins," 242).

Scholer is right to stress that the concern in 5.14-17 is on
ἁμαρτία μὴ πρὸς θάνατον and this fact is thus another indication
that the author's primary concern is with edifying the community, although this must take place along with confrontation of
heresy. However, to demonstrate that the stress is on ἁμαρτία
μὴ πρὸς θάνατον is not to prove that the mention of ἁμαρτία πρὸς
θάνατον is simply an aside with no function of its own other
than as a contrast. Rather, it should be interpreted as an implied warning, which is made explicit a few verses later: "Little children, keep yourselves from idols" (5.21). The author
sees his readers as in danger of committing ἁμαρτία πρὸς θάνατον
in that they are in danger of being deceived by lying spirits
(4.1-6; 2.26), and there are some among them who do not love
the brothers (3.17-18). Thus, Scholer's interpretation of 2.19
does not take into account the two levels on which this verse
functions. On the deepest level of meaning the author can say
οὐκ ἦσαν ἐξ ἡμῶν, but that is precisely one of the points he
has to argue for his readers, since on the most obvious level
they certainly did ἐξ ἡμῶν ἐξῆλθαν and this, by definition, is
apostasy.

4) Conclusion

     The author's polemic concerning ethics is a charge that by
leaving the community the opponents have committed the sin unto
death in that they have turned away from the realm of life. The
ethical argument is basically an accusation of lack of love. The
opponents may have some form of obedience to commandments but
in their lack of love they show themselves to be strangers to
the very heart of the commandments. The commandments are characterized as an *imitatio Christi* (2.6), and the chief quality
of Christ's life was his revelation of God's love.

c. Summary

     Thus the opponents neither confess Jesus as Messiah nor
follow him in obedience. These features of their position are,
indeed, two sides of the same coin for they both are related to
their view of Jesus Christ's death. The death of Jesus the
Messiah both reveals God's love and atones for sin. The

opponents do not believe they are in need of this atonement and
they are also unwilling to follow Jesus' example by laying down
their lives for the brothers. Thus their belief and behavior
are inseparably intertwined. In the author's eyes it is obvious
that they have no right to consider themselves Christians.

I have now dealt with the key aspects of the christological
and ethical issues involved in the polemic in 1 John. In doing
so the passages listed in sections 2 A, 2 B, and 3 A of the outline of material in 1 John (see p. 122 above) have now been
covered, i.e. those passages directly referring to the opponents
and to the tests of falsehood. I now turn to what might be
called the positive side of his polemic. During the discussion
of the Johannine view of Christian sinlessness I noted the
author's belief that the community is the realm of life and light
and love. This view of the community is a part of his polemic
in that the opponents' secession from such a community in itself
says something about their identity. It is appropriate, therefore, to look more closely at what he says about the community.
In particular, the tests of assurance given in section 3 B of
the outline above can be seen to serve as a form of condemnation
of the opponents in that they provide criteria for the discernment of the opponents' error.

2. *Positive Side: The Assurance of the Johannine Christians*

How does the author view this community which is supposedly
the realm of light and life and love and yet has contained those
who οὐκ ἦσαν ἐξ ἡμῶν (2.19)? The secessionists have seemingly
split off completely from the community, but their influence is
still strong: "I write this to you about those who would de-
ceive you" (2.26, cf. 3.7). His readers stand in danger of being deceived, so the author writes to testify to "the eternal
life, which was with the Father and was made manifest to us"
(1.2), in order that they may (continue to) have fellowship with
him and with the Father and the Son (1.3). So there seem to be
at least some in the community dangerously susceptible to the
false teaching. But there is also much in the document that
suggests that the author considers the community to be composed
of strong, mature Christians.[261] For example, in 2.12-14 he

emphasizes their knowledge of God and their defeat of the evil
one. In 2.20 he says they have an anointing (χρῖσμα) from the
Holy One and they all know the truth (cf. 2.21; 5.20), and have
no need that anyone teach them (2.27). According to the author
they are the children of God (3.2; 5.19) and have eternal life
(5.13). Thus, it is evident that the author considers them to
be intimately related to God and in possession of all it takes
to keep from being deceived. These passages fill out the author's view that the community is itself the realm of light and
life and love. But how are they to keep themselves from being
deceived? This is where the assurance passages play their part
in his polemic.

a. Remaining in What They Have Been Taught

     Great stress is laid in 1 John on the readers remaining in
that which they have been taught. In 2.20-27 they are told that
they know the truth (2.20-21) and must remain in that which they
have heard from the beginning (2.24), i.e. from when they were
first Christians.[262] The author says they are able to do so
because of the χρῖσμα which they have received and which teaches
them about all things (2.20,27). Because what is said of this
χρῖσμα here is paralleled by statements in the Gospel concerning
the Spirit, most commentators see a reference here to the Spirit
(see Schnackenburg, *Briefe*, 151-154). These parallels are strong
enough to indicate that this identification must be correct.
Dodd, however, has suggested that the χρῖσμα is the word of
God, i.e. that which they have been taught (*Epistles*, 58-64).
This interpretation is supported in particular by the parallel
drawn between what is here said about the χρῖσμα and what is
said a few verses later about remaining (μένειν) in "what you
heard from the beginning" (2.24).[263] The arguments for both of
these interpretations are strong and prevent us from limiting
χρῖσμα to a single referent. In the light of what we have seen
of the Spirit's use of Scripture in John (above pp. 98-103) it
is perhaps best to see a similar notion in view here in 1 John.
De la Potterie in particular has developed an interpretation
which finds reference both to the teaching and to the Spirit:
"l'huile d'onction, c'est bien *la parole de Dieu*, non pas

toutefois en tant qu'elle est prêchée extérieurement dans la
communauté, mais en tant qu'elle est recue par la foi dans les
coeurs et y demeure active, *grâce à l'action de l'Esprit*."[264]

This teaching in which they are to remain is that communicated to them by the author. He lays great stress throughout
the document on the fact that he has testified to the truth (1.1-
3,5; 2.1; 3.11; 4.14). That he considers his teaching to be
absolutely authoritative is clear from 4.6: "We are of God.
Whoever knows God listens to us, and he who is not of God does
not listen to us. By this we know the spirit of truth and the
spirit of error." It might be argued that the reference here is
not to the author himself. However, "the change to the first
person ἡμεῖς strongly suggests that teachers are in the front
of John's mind, although the rest of the church is not excluded."[265] Thus, whatever the precise relationship between
the author and the earlier Johannine tradition, and whatever the
precise authority structure within the community(s), it is clear
that the community(s) has a teaching that should enable it to
discern error and avoid it, if only the readers will remain in
this teaching.

b. *Examination of Life-Style*

They can also discern truth and distinguish it from error
through examination of life-style. There are commandments to be
obeyed and these commandments can indicate both truth and error.
That is, if someone claims to know God but does not keep the
commands then he is thereby shown to be in error (2.4). On the
other hand, the keeping of God's commands indicates that this
obedient person does know God (2.5). These commands are summed
up as a life-style like that of Jesus--*imitatio Christi* (2.6).
Later it is said, "By this it may be seen who are the children
of God, and who are the children of the devil: whoever does not
do right is not of God, nor he who does not love his brother"
(3.10). As 3.10 illustrates, to speak of the commands is to
speak of love, for love is the supreme command (3.23; 4.20-21).
It is also a major criterion of discernment, for love indicates
that one has passed from death to life (3.14-15), and it indicates
that one is in the truth (3.18-19).

Thus, the tests of assurance provide two basic criteria for
discernment: (1) fidelity to the doctrine, especially, in the
present situation, the confession of Jesus as Christ and Son
(of God) (3.23; 4.2,15; 5.1-2,12-13), and (2) a life-style of
obedience to the commandments (2.3-6; 3.7-10,19-22; 5.18), which
means, in particular, love (2.10; 3.14,23; 4.16-18; 5.1-2).[266]

It will be noticed that the elements in these two basic
criteria for discernment are identical with the tests of falsehood already examined. As might be expected, the marks we have
examined, namely, right belief in Jesus the Son and sinlessness
(both as obedience to the commands and as love) serve both to
indicate the error of the opponents and to assure the Johannine
Christians. But, as we have seen, the author has had to instruct
his readers concerning the correct understanding of these marks
because the opponents assert very similar views. The danger of
confusion concerning these marks places all the more emphasis on
the other two sources of assurance/discernment that the author
mentions, namely, the Spirit and the author's own teaching.

c.   *Fundamental Sources of Assurance/Discernment*

In effect, the author is claiming to be a true representative of the Johannine tradition and his readers can be sure of
what is true by the Spirit within them. Such a claim is highly
significant if, as many scholars now believe, the author is fight-
ing opponents who claim to be loyal to the very same Johannine
tradition (see p. 4 above). According to this hypothesis the
Johannine tradition was ambiguous enough to give rise to a
gnosticizing interpretation of that tradition. Such ambiguity is
true to what we know of the tradition from the Gospel (see e.g.
Smalley, "Diversity"). Furthermore, this hypothesis finds confirmation in the very subtlety of the differences between the
author and his opponents that we have noted.

Indeed, the opponents not only claimed to be true representatives of the Johannine tradition, but also to be authorized
by the Spirit (4.1) (see Brown, *Community*, 138-141). So the only
unambiguous criterion the author uses in his argument is his
presentation of himself as the true representative of the tradition (4.6). The first person plural used in 4.6 would include,

as just noted, the community as a whole, but only as they remained in that which they were taught (2.24-27). The author, by
writing this document to interpret the tradition, shows himself
to be the true representative of the tradition (cf. Hoskyns,
Gospel, 98-104). The Prologue of 1 John makes this clear distinction between the author and his readers. The life was manifested to "us" and "we" in turn proclaim it to "you" (1.2). He
wants them to have fellowship with himself, and his fellowship
is with God (1.3).

The author claims a place at the very center of the community as the true bearer of its tradition. He does not, however,
simply make an authoritative statement and expect his readers
to accept it. Rather, he offers them a number of arguments, the
main details of which we have now examined. From 2.27 and 4.6
it seems he expects the Spirit to make clear to the readers that
his teaching is true. But this does not stop him from making
his own efforts to clarify the issues. So while he may say the
readers have no need that anyone teach them (2.27), his own efforts in this document indicate that this is not meant in any
absolute sense. Given his emphasis on his own authority and the
sufficiency of what they have already been taught (cf. 2.7,24),
when he says that they have no need of instruction he means
teaching from others besides himself and of matters other than
that which they have already been taught.

Thus the author puts himself forward as the authoritative
bearer of the tradition. He attempts to assure his readers by
affirming that it is they who agree with him who are really
remaining loyal to the tradition and thus are the legitimate
heirs of the community's claim to be children of God. We have
seen how the major elements in his argument concerning both belief and practice are interrelated. It now remains to consider
how they are all unified in the author's thought. I will begin
with the view of virtually all scholars that these elements are
brought together by the author in his view of Christ.

C. The Unity of the Argument

1. *The Place of Jesus, the Christ, the Son of God*

The confession that must not be denied is that Jesus, especially in his death, is the Messiah, for it is in his advent

and death that we know what love is (3.16-18) and see the very
love of God (4.9-10). The christological and ethical strands
are united in Christ in that Jesus functions for the author as
an example of the supreme command of love. Furthermore, he is
also the model for the other commands (2.3-6). Thus, Jesus is
the model of Christian sinlessness, both in its sense of obedience to the commands and in its sense of love for the brothers.
But he not only exemplifies such sinlessness; his death is also
said to be an atoning sacrifice for sin (2.2; 4.10). In this
way Jesus provides for the lingering sin in the community that
the community may be freed from sin. These various aspects of
the author's ethical case are all, therefore, directly related
to Jesus' death. It is Jesus' death that is at the center of
both the christological and the ethical arguments, and thus it
is Jesus' death that serves as the underlying point of union in
the author's argument. Even the more positive argument from the
nature of the Christian community is related to Jesus in that
the life of the Christian community is marked by sinlessness and
love, and Jesus is both the model and the source of these attributes. This deep relationship between the various aspects of
the author's argument should rule out the view that he had a cut-
and-dried confessional formula to which he appended some ethics.[267] Rather, 1 John must be seen as an extremely profound
response to a very difficult situation. The author has to argue
with his opponents on the basis of a common tradition to which
they both claim to be loyal. He has to draw attention to the
great gulf that separates his opponents from this tradition, as
it is correctly understood by himself, despite the opponents'
attractive appearance. The opponents claim to know God but by
their assessment of Jesus and their own relation towards the
community they belie this claim.

We have now seen the various parts of the author's polemic
and noted how they all form a christocentric whole. One last
aspect of the polemic in 1 John remains to be discussed. All of
the particular issues of christology and ethics are related to
the author's view of Jesus, but behind Jesus there is the Father.
As in the Gospel so in 1 John, Jesus is viewed above all as the
revelation of the Father. In a final section of this chapter,

therefore, I turn to a consideration of this underlying theological argument. Behind the particular issues of christology and
ethics the basic element in the author's polemic concerns theology proper, i.e. the understanding of God.

2. *Theology: The Opponents' Alienation from God*

While the author's use of theology is of very great importance for an understanding of his polemic it is not a difficult
motif to discuss briefly. All the issues we have considered,
both christological and ethical, are gathered up in the two great
theological affirmations of the document: God is light (1.5) and
God is love (4.16).

a. *God Is Light*

As with their christology so with their theology, the opponents seem to have held a view sufficiently similar to that of
the author to make it difficult for some in the community to
see any difference. Most scholars assume that "God is light" is
a catch phrase of the opponents and perhaps is even taken over
by the author from them. It is impossible to determine whether
this is the case, but in any event it seems they both used the
phrase. In fact, 2.22-23 may well indicate that the opponents
thought they were united with the author in their theology,
sharing the same view of God. In 2.22b the opponents are said
to deny both the Father and the Son, but it is clear from 2.23
that this was not the intention of the opponents but rather the
implication drawn by the author. The opponents did not deny the
Father, but this is what the author claims on the basis of their
denial of the Son.[268]

The statement that God is light comes just after the introduction: "This is the message we have heard from him and proclaim to you, that God is light and in him is no darkness at
all" (1.5). It is not at all clear what exactly is meant by
saying that "God is light and in him there is no darkness at all"
is the "message" proclaimed by the Son.[269] The symbolism of
light pervades the Gospel (Dodd, *Epistles*, 19), but neither there
nor in the Synoptics is such a message given in so many words.
However, it is clear from 1.5b, and the entire context which

follows, that the phrase "God is light" is primarily ethical
(cf. Mussner, ΖΩΗ, 169-170), conveying the idea that God is
pure and holy, that is, sinless. Perhaps this is the Son's message in the sense that he "appeared to take away sins, and in
him there is no sin" (3.5). One of the major motifs throughout
1 John is that Christians are to be sinless like the Father and
the Son, and this sinlessness is possible precisely because of
the death of Jesus (2.1-2; 3.5-8; 4.9-10,14; cf. 5.18). Thus
Jesus' death is closely related to the notion that God is light.
Jesus both reveals God's holiness and provides the means by which
believers are able to share in that holiness. But over against
the author's own positive concept of Christian sinlessness there
appears also a mistaken concept of sinlessness held by the opponents (1.8,10). In addition to what we have already seen of the
author's response to this claim it is important to note that his
criticism is ultimately based on his theology. This is behind
his assertion that the opponents, in their claim to sinlessness,
ψεύστην ποιοῦμεν αὐτόν (1.10). "We make God a liar (i.e., we
declare him to be such), because the assertion of sinlessness
does not recognize him as the one who, as πιστὸς καὶ δίκαιος
('faithful and just') in v 9, is the forgiving God" (Bultmann,
Epistles, 22). In their claim to sinlessness, the opponents deny God not only by not sharing in his sinlessness but also by
rejecting his forgiveness. But as we have seen, sinlessness for
the author means, above all, love. Thus we are led to the second
great theological affirmation in 1 John, God is love.

b. God Is Love

    I have already noted the Johannine view that love is the
laying down of one's life and this love is seen par excellence
in the death of God's Son (3.16-18; 4.9-10). It only remains
now to point out that the author says this love is a characteristic of God's very nature (4.7-10). The opponents lack this
love, but then even the Johannine Christians themselves must be
exhorted to love (4.11-12). So there is a certain lack of love
among the Johannine Christians just as there is a certain sinfulness. But they, unlike the opponents, have remained within
the community. Their imperfect love thus differs from the hatred
evident in the secessionists.

The polemic in 1 John, then, is ultimately based on the author's understanding of God. God's light and love are lacking in the opponents and this shows that they are alienated from God. In this way God's character can be seen to be the ultimate criterion in the author's argument against the opponents. They do not reflect his character, which is to say that they do not share his life. This motif of the divine ζωή brings us to the central referent for the thought expressed in 1 John. A consideration of this motif will provide a summary of this chapter on 1 John.

3. ζωή (αἰώνιος)

The issue at stake in 1 John is the question who truly shares in the divine ζωή. Ultimately the truth that the author is contending for in the face of error is the right understanding of the very life of God in which the believers share. All the major aspects of the author's thought revolve around this motif of ζωή (αἰώνιος). The promise to believers is life (2.25) and this life is in the Son (5.11-13), for Jesus is this life (1.1,2; 5.20). The ethical marks we have examined are characteristic of this life in that life is love of the brothers (3.14-15) and forgiveness (5.16). Indeed, the author can say that to obey the commands is to live in God (3.24), and to confess that Jesus is the Son of God is to live in God (4.15), and to love is to live in God (4.12,16). Ultimately, to remain in the truth by remaining in the doctrine and in love, *is* to remain in the Father and the Son (cf. 1.3).

The motif of ζωή (αἰώνιος) is introduced at the outset of the document: "That which was from the beginning, which we have heard, which we have seen with our eyes, which we have looked upon and touched with our hands, concerning the word of life" (1.1). The series of relative clauses circle around their subject until finally it is clearly stated: περὶ τοῦ λόγου τῆς ζωῆς. The use of λόγος probably has typically Johannine double meaning (cf. Marshall, *Epistles*, 101-103, esp. 102 n.10). It refers not just to a message, as ὃ ἀκηκόαμεν would lead us to expect, but to a person, Jesus,[270] as the other relative clauses intimate and 1.2 expresses more clearly: "the life was made

manifest, and we saw it, and testify to it, and proclaim to you
the eternal life which was with the Father and was made manifest
to us" (1.2). Jesus, the Christ, the Son (of God) as eternal
life which has now come among men and made eternal life available
to them is the fundamental framework behind 1 John. The purpose
in writing is "that you may know that you have eternal life"
(5.13). The author says this life is available in the Son:
"God gave us eternal life, and this life is in his Son. He who
has the Son has life; he who has not the Son of God has not life"
(5.11-12, cf. 2.25). Since this life is in the Son one must be
truly related to the Son. It is in the Son that God is truly
present and the divine life truly available, as is emphasized in
the conclusion: "And we know that the Son of God has come and
has given us understanding, to know him who is true; and we are
in him who is true, in his Son Jesus Christ. He is the true
God and eternal life. Little children, keep yourselves from
idols" (5.20-21). Here are evident both the author's assurance
to his readers and his warning against the danger. The center
of his thought is "his Son Jesus Christ." He is described again
(as in 1.2) as "eternal life," but now also as "the true God."[271]
Thus, the motif of eternal life is used to assert that those who
do not have a right understanding of Jesus, i.e. the opponents,
worship idols. As J. Miranda has well said:

> John is not talking about erroneous or defective
> doctrinal conceptions of God that permit people to
> worship the true God albeit with an imperfect conceptual
> instrument. John says, 'Be careful of idols,' and,
> 'He does not have God either.' He is not talking
> about imperfect awareness of God, but about the
> *denial* of God, even by persons who sincerely believe
> that they are worshipping the true God. The dilemma
> is this: God or idolatry (*Being*, 194-195).

In contrast, however, those who remain faithful to the teaching
(2.24,27) and who lay down their lives for the brothers (3.16-
17) remain in the community and thus remain in the realm of life,
and indeed they remain in God. For God, as revealed in Jesus
and especially in his death, is light and love, and to know him
is eternal life.

D. Conclusion

Behind the author's polemic is his understanding of God's
character, and his belief that the very life of God is revealed
in Jesus and is present in the Christian community. The opponents claim to know God, but the author makes use of the community's tradition to show that, far from knowing the Father, they
are in reality idolators. These same two basic characteristics
were also found in the polemic in the Gospel. There also the
author had to demonstrate how a common tradition actually supports his position rather than that of his opponents. There also
the argument went behind all of the points of difference to claim
a fundamental difference of theology. In the next chapter I
will look in some detail at the similarities and differences
between John and 1 John with regard to their polemic.

4. JOHN AND 1 JOHN COMPARED

A. Introduction

In this final chapter we come to an analysis of the material
presented in the first three chapters. The relation between John
and 1 John is one of those problems of NT criticism that seems
impossible to solve to the satisfaction of a majority of scholars.
Even the nature of the problem has changed greatly since the
beginning of this century. The older form of the question was
whether the same person wrote both documents. Now the issue is
tremendously complicated by the various source theories which
have been developed for both the Gospel and the Letter. It is
not my present purpose to review all of the details of this discussion, but rather to determine what contribution this study of
the polemic makes to the larger question of the relation between
John and 1 John.

I will begin the present comparison of John and 1 John by
noting the various differences in thought that scholars have
found and evaluating these differences in the light of the working hypotheses I have proposed for the two documents. This evaluation will serve as a test of these working hypotheses since it
is these very differences between the documents which form the
basis for the hypotheses. I will next mention further similarities and differences which the present study highlights. This
analysis in turn will serve to introduce a comparison of the
central elements of the polemic in John and 1 John.

The two documents have been compared and contrasted by
scholars both with regard to the linguistic features and with
regard to the ideas expressed in each. Study of the linguistic
features of grammar and vocabulary has demonstrated the great
similarity between the documents, but has also brought to light
certain differences. By highlighting these differences the linguistic data pose the problem of the relation between the documents, but they are of little value in solving it since so many
different interpretations of the data are possible.[272] Even

those who stress the differences admit that linguistic uniformity
is not to be expected if a number of years have elapsed between
the two documents and/or there has been a change in circumstances
(e.g. Dodd, *Epistles*, liv-lv). What is needed is to form a
plausible hypothesis that can account for these differences
(ibid. lv). Such a hypothesis must be developed from the more
substantive differences between the documents. Accordingly,
the differences in thought between the two documents are far more
significant than the strictly linguistic features (cf. Marshall,
Epistles, 33-34). Therefore I will limit the present discussion
to alleged differences in thought between John and 1 John.

B. Evaluation of Differences Between John and 1 John

In the previous two chapters it has been proposed that
John and 1 John are addressing two very different problems. The
Gospel is telling the story of Jesus for the benefit of Christians whose faith is severely challenged by Jewish opponents,
while the Letter is restating certain basic themes of Johannine
thought for the benefit of Johannine disciples in order to assure
them and warn them of a subtle erroneous teaching that has arisen
in their midst. In the Gospel the threat comes from outside
the Christian community while in the Letter the threat comes from
those formerly within the community. In the Gospel the opponents
do not accept that Jesus has come from God in any sense, while
the opponents in the Letter do accept Jesus as the Messiah,
though the author of 1 John finds their understanding of Jesus
entirely unsatisfactory. These general remarks present the fundamental differences in the circumstances behind John and 1
John. How, then, are these differences in circumstance reflected
in the differences in thought which scholars have found between
the two documents?[273]

1. The OT

One of the most frequently noted differences is the lack of
reference to the OT in 1 John.[274] The sole explicit reference
in 1 Jn. 3.12 stands in sharp contrast to the all-pervasive
presence of the OT in the Gospel. In the Gospel the author must
use the OT to assure his readers and combat the Jewish opponents

because it is to the OT that the opponents appeal in their attack against Jesus and his followers. The author decides to
make use of the religious tradition he holds in common with his
opponents in order to counter their attack. In 1 John, however,
there is no indication that the opponents are appealing to the
OT. Rather, they seem to appeal to the Johannine community's
own traditions. The author also appeals to these same traditions,
claiming to give the true interpretation of them. This lack of
reference to the OT in the Letter highlights a fundamental similarity in the form of argument in the two documents. In both
cases the author(s) confines himself almost exclusively to arguing on the basis of the particular traditions that are in dispute. It seems that he is concerned not simply to make his
points on the issues in dispute, but also to claim these traditions for his side. He could have argued against the Jewish opponents in the Gospel by denying the validity of the OT entirely.
That he did not do so underlines his well known belief that the
OT witnesses to the true God and to his Messiah Son. The question arises, however, if the OT was so important for this au-
thor(s) why did it not play any significant role in 1 John? The
answer may be that the author of the Letter is not concerned
simply to counter the opponents' views but also to reclaim the
Johannine tradition from them. The issue in the Letter is not
a difference in the interpretation of the OT, as it is in the
Gospel, but a difference in the interpretation of the community's
tradition. In such a controversy the author could perhaps have
bolstered his argument by appealing to the OT. Whether he chose
not to do so because it would have distracted from his argument,
or because it was unnecessary, or for some other reason, we cannot say. But this absence of the OT in 1 John need not indicate
a very different view towards the OT from that in John; it might
be due to the conciseness of the argument in 1 John. In any
event, by not appealing to the OT but solely to the community's
traditions the author's concern to claim the Johannine tradition
for himself is emphasized.

2. *Signs of Jesus' Messiahship*

     There is a second difference which also concerns the cri-
teria appealed to in the arguments. Given such different

circumstances it is not so surprising as Moffatt thinks that the
signs of Jesus' Messiahship are not repeated in 1 John (*Intro-*
duction, 592). Moffatt believes the author(s) is arguing in
both documents that the historical Jesus is the Christ. We have
seen reason to believe, however, that the position of the opponents in 1 John is far more subtle. They do not deny that Jesus
is the Christ, but rather that Jesus died as the Christ. They
would be in complete agreement with the author(s) that the signs
show Jesus to be the Messiah, and thus an appeal to these signs
in 1 John would serve no purpose.

3. Atonement

Another of the more obvious differences between the documents is their depiction of the significance of Jesus' death.
The reference to ἱλασμός in 1 Jn. 2.2; 4.10 is not paralleled
in the Gospel. Some scholars, however, have overemphasized this
difference. For example, Forestell offers a very helpful study
of the exemplarist view of Jesus' death in the Gospel, but he
ignores the references to the atoning significance of Jesus'
death (1.29,36; 10.11,15,17-18; 11.50-52). He says,[275]

> If these notions do appear in some texts of the Gospel
> we would insist that they are entirely secondary and
> peripheral and should not be allowed to deform the
> properly Johannine theology of salvation by assuming
> a position which they do not have in the distinctive
> thought of the evangelist.

Forestell here admits that he is not studying the author's
thought but only that which is distinctive, thereby following
a procedure reminiscent of the criterion of dissimilarity. In
doing so he does not allow the references to the atoning significance of Jesus' death to deform that which is distinctive,
but his own study obviously only offers a "deformed" version of
the thought expressed in the Gospel. Dodd also suggests too
wide a gulf between the documents on this issue ("First Epistle,"
145-146). He deals only with the reference to the Lamb of God
in Jn. 1.29, trying to deny there is reference here to the pas-
chal lamb. All of his argument from the background is completely
beside the point, however, since, as Howard points out ("Authorship," 295), Jn. 1.29 explicitly states that this Lamb is to

take away the sins of the world. So there is not a complete
contrast between the documents on this point; it is rather a
difference of emphasis (cf. Brooke, *Epistles*, xviii). Indeed,
the οἴδατε in 1 Jn. 3.5 seems to indicate that the atoning significance of Jesus' death was an element in the Johannine tradition. But how, then, is this difference of emphasis accounted
for on the basis of the hypotheses of the present study? In
the Gospel the atoning significance of Jesus' death is a very
minor theme. Far more stress is placed on the complete separation of believers from the world (e.g. 15.19; 17.16), their experience of salvation now (e.g. 11.25-26; 17.3), and Jesus' com-
mandment of love (13.34-35; 14.15,21; 15.10,12,17). As we have
seen, the opponents in 1 John claim to be without sin. Such a
view might draw upon these aspects of Johannine thought in the
Gospel which stress the difference between believers and unbelievers, and the love command, which could imply that anyone who
loves is sinless and therefore not in need of atonement. The
opponents do seem to believe they have love (cf. 1 Jn. 3.14-18)
and they also believe they keep the commands, as we have seen.
On this assessment, the opponents are stressing certain elements
in the Johannine tradition. He counters their position by
stressing the atoning significance of Jesus' death. In his eyes
they are deluded if they think they have no need of Jesus' death
for atonement. Furthermore, they are deluded in their claim to
have love, since love is the laying down of one's life, and this
is something they are not willing to do (1 Jn. 3.14-18). Thus,
the opponents' error is all related to Jesus' death. They do
not believe the Messiah has died and therefore they have understood neither the atonement accomplished nor the revelation of
God's love manifested. The interpretation of Jesus' death as
atonement and as example are evident in both the Gospel and the
Letter. The emphasis on the atoning value has been strengthened
in the Letter because this aspect has been denied by the opponents.

4. *Faith*

     Another difference noted concerns the notion of faith.
"While in the gospel faith is equivalent to the coming of man to

the truth and light of God in Christ, or to a reception of the
words of Jesus in the heart, the writer of the epistle . . .
tends to resolve faith into a confession of Jesus as the Son of
God" (Moffatt, *Introduction*, 591-592). Actually, the Gospel also
mentions confessing Jesus (9.22; 12.42), but Moffatt is right
that in the Letter the issue is very much more narrow. The issue now revolves around confessing something very specific about
Jesus. In the Gospel, to have faith is basically to recognize
the Father in the Son. Even in the Gospel the content of the
faith is not insignificant, as though faith were mere trust without reference to its object. In the Letter, however, the content is much more precise, for a distinction is being drawn between different beliefs about Jesus (cf. Conzelmann, "Anfang,"
195). In the Gospel the issue is belief that Jesus reveals the
Father; in the Letter there is more stress on how Jesus reveals
the Father. As we have seen, the death of Jesus is central in
both documents, but its significance and correct interpretation
is more explicitly emphasized in the Letter. Thus, this nar-
rowing of the notion of faith reflects the different polemical
setting in 1 John. Because the Letter addresses a controversy
among Christians, the issue is not simply acceptance of Jesus
but a correct acceptance of Jesus.

5. *Christ as* λόγος *and* ζωή

The difference in the nature of faith in Christ leads next
to a consideration of alleged differences in the conception of
Christ's person. Moffatt believes the description of Jesus as
λόγος in the Gospel is replaced by ζωή in the Letter (*Introduction*, 591). The difference is not nearly as sharp as Moffatt
suggests since, as we have seen (p. 149), the reference to λόγος
in 1 Jn. 1.1-2 seems to refer to Jesus as well as to the message
about him. Furthermore, Jesus is referred to as ζωή in the
Gospel itself (1.4) (cf. Marshall, *Epistles*, 35). Moffatt also
asserts that the notion of λόγος is less personal in 1 John.
Brooke notes that, while this may be so with regard to this
particular term, "the personal distinction of υἱός and πατήρ
is as clearly marked in the Epistle as in the Gospel" (*Epistles*,
xvi). R. Law, however, strongly rejects the view that λόγος

is less personal in 1 John (*Tests*, 354-355). But he actually
confirms what he denies by noting that the emphasis in the
phrase ὁ λόγος τῆς ζωῆς is on τῆς ζωῆς, "because the theme of
the Epistle is to be the Life, not as to its historical manifestation in the Incarnate Logos, but as to its essential qualities,
in whomsoever it exists" (ibid. 355). So the use of λόγος is
less personal in 1 John. It is not, however, entirely impersonal since it does refer to Jesus. Furthermore, while the motif
of ζωή is central in both documents, it is more prevalent in the
Letter. We have seen how the author of 1 John seems to consciously link all of his major themes to this central referent
(above pp. 149-150). He does so explicitly in the Letter, while
in the Gospel the central role of ζωή is present, but not so
explicit. The purpose of both documents is expressed in terms
of this ζωή (Jn. 20.31; 1 Jn. 5.13). So there is a difference,
but it is one of emphasis.

6. *Believers' Relation to God and Christ*

There is also an alleged difference between the documents
in their conception of the role of Christ. Moffatt says that
in the Gospel people are related to God through Christ (cf.
10.7,9; 14.6; 15.5), while in the Letter the relationship between believers and God is more direct (2.5; 3.21; 4.4; 5.14)
(*Introduction*, 590). Once again Moffatt overstates his case,
since "the Epistle makes it quite clear that nobody can have a
relationship with the Father unless he believes in the Son"
(Marshall, *Epistles*, 35, cf. Brooke, *Epistles*, xvii). Furthermore, near the end of Jesus' teaching in the Gospel he stresses
the direct relationship between his followers and the Father
(16.27).[276] Even if there is not a major difference between the
documents on this point there does seem to be a shift of emphasis; "the Gospel being a narrative of the redemptive ministry of
Christ, and the Epistle an analytical study of the Divine Life
as it exists in God and in the children of God" (Law, *Tests*,
356). But why, then, is not more made in 1 John of the role of
Christ in the believers' relationship to God? Probably because
this point is not disputed. There is no evidence that the opponents denied any and every role in salvation to Jesus. Rather,

in the eyes of the author their view of Jesus' role in enabling
God to be known is completely inadequate, based on an erroneous
view of Christ. So once again we have a shift in emphasis due
to the different situations in view. In both documents Jesus'
role in revealing the Father is stressed and in both documents
the author'(s) fundamental polemical point against the different
opponents is their alienation from God because they have not
understood Jesus aright. In the Gospel the issue is acceptance
or rejection of Jesus, while in the Letter it is acceptance of
a particular view of Jesus and his role, and the rejection of
another view which claims loyalty to Jesus.

7. φῶς

Another difference to account for occurs with respect to
the use of the word φῶς. In the Gospel it always is used with
reference to Jesus, but in the Letter there seems to be a variety of uses. The use of φῶς in 1 Jn. 2.8-11 is very closely related to its use of Jesus in the Gospel's Prologue, especially
in the contrast with σκοτία, and in the use of τὸ φῶς τὸ
ἀληθινόν in v. 8 (cf. Jn. 1.9). In contrast with the Gospel,
however, the Letter uses φῶς of God as well as of Jesus. This
usage is somewhat confusing in that it is first said that God
is φῶς (1.5), but then that he is *in* the φῶς (1.7). Actually,
both of these forms of expression are making the same point,[277]
so the principle difference is that φῶς is here used of God rather
than of Jesus. What is the significance of this difference?
Again, the difference in situation and purpose between the two
documents could account for this difference (cf. Marshall, *Epistles*, 38). In the Gospel the reference to Jesus as φῶς refers
to his role as the revelation of the Father. There is no indication in the Letter that the opponents would deny that Jesus
reveals the Father. It is possible that they would even be
willing to refer to him as the φῶς. So perhaps the author of
1 John does not stress the view that Jesus is the φῶς because
it is not contested in 1 John, in contrast to John. As for the
shift of reference of φῶς in the Letter from Jesus to the Father,
this seems to be a response to the use of φῶς by the opponents
(see Wengst, *Spiegel*, 76 n.184). They claim to be walking in

the light, by which they mean that they know God. The author
attacks this claim by playing on the associations which the term
φῶς has in the OT and throughout the culture in general. The
opponents use the term, as does the Gospel, to refer to revelation and salvation (cf. Marshall, *Epistles*, 109). The author
of 1 John, however, draws upon the ethical associations of the
term which convey the notion of holiness. In particular, as we
have seen, he says the opponents' claim is repudiated by their
lack of fellowship, or as he says later, their lack of brotherly
love. So the author uses the motif of φῶς to make the same point
he makes in a number of other ways in the Letter, namely, if they
knew God they would live the life of God. There is, then, a
shift in the use of φῶς in 1 Jn. 1.5,7 from its use elsewhere
in John and 1 John. The point it is used to make, however, is
common to Johannine thought. This shift is accounted for by the
claims being made by the opponents.

8. Spirit

       From the differences that have to do with the Father and
the Son we turn to differences that concern the Son and the
Spirit. There are two main differences noted: the shift in the
use of the term παράκλητος from referring in the Gospel to the
Spirit to referring in 1 John to Jesus, and the seemingly impersonal use of πνεῦμα in 1 Jn. 4.1-6. Dodd says the use of the
phrase "spirit of truth" is impersonal inspiration in 1 Jn. 4.1-
6, but is personal in Jn. 14.17; 15.26; 16.13 ("First Epistle,"
147).[278] These two basic differences introduce shifts of emphasis rather than entirely new concepts. The mention of ἄλλος
παράκλητος in Jn. 14.16 indicates that the Johannine tradition
did not use the term παράκλητος solely of the Spirit, even if
this is how it is used in the Gospel as we have it. This use of
ἄλλος has the "obvious implication that Jesus has been a Paraclete, since the other Paraclete is coming when Jesus departs"
(Brown, *John*, 644). Indeed, even in the Gospel the reference
to Jesus as παράκλητος is primary, since "the Spirit of Truth
is a Paraclete precisely because he carries on the earthly work
of Jesus" (ibid. 1140-1141). So again we see the author of 1
John emphasizing an element already present in the tradition.

What purpose, then, would this shift serve in 1 John? The emphasis on Jesus as παράκλητος might be a part of the rebuttal of
the opponents' claim to be inspired by the Spirit. As the
author of 1 John stresses, not every πνεῦμα is from God; the
πνεῦμα that comes from God is the one confessing Jesus (1 Jn.
4.1-6). The opponents are claiming the Spirit, but they are
denying Jesus. Since the Spirit, according to the Johannine
tradition, is the *alter ego* of Jesus (Dodd, "First Epistle,"
146), the opponents' claim must be wrong; their inspiration is
counterfeit. This same claim by the opponents is perhaps also
the reason for the less personal use of πνεῦμα in John, though
it should be noted that not all references to πνεῦμα in the
Letter are entirely impersonal (e.g. 3.24; 4.13), nor are all
references in the Gospel necessarily personal, as Dodd admits
(ibid.). The effect of these changes, then, is to emphasize the
Spirit's close association with Jesus.[279] This motif is strong
in the Gospel but has been heightened in the Letter in response
to appeals to the Spirit's inspiration which had the effect, in
the author's eyes, of denying Jesus and his revelation of God.

In addition to these shifts of emphasis in the depiction of
the Spirit there is another alleged difference concerning the
Spirit that should be mentioned, only to be completely rejected.
Moffatt believes that the Spirit in the Letter is merely a witness to correct belief rather than an indwelling presence
(*Introduction*, 592). It is probably true that the Spirit's
witness to correct belief is focused more specifically in the
Letter than in the Gospel, as we have seen, but it is not true to
say that the Spirit is not conceived of in the Letter as an indwelling presence (cf. e.g. 2.20,27; 3.9,24; 4.13) (cf. Marshall,
Epistles, 35). All major features of the picture of the Spirit
in the Gospel are present in the Letter, though with differences
of emphasis (cf. Scott, *Spirit*, 211).

9. Eschatology

Recently, alleged differences in eschatology have come to
the fore in scholarly discussions. Interestingly, these differences emphasized by recent scholarship were considered by Moffatt
to be rather unimportant since they do not, in his opinion,
"constitute any radical difference" (*Introduction*, 592). These
differences in eschatology have been developed in particular by

Dodd, Conzelmann, and G. Klein.[280] These scholars tend to over-
emphasize the gap between the documents, but they have highlighted certain shifts of emphasis that are significant. Dodd's
contribution is the general contrast he has noted between the
'realized eschatology' of the Gospel and the future eschatology
of the Letter. The future orientation, however, is not entirely
lacking in the Gospel (5.21-29; 12.47-48),[281] nor does the Letter
neglect the belief that believers even now share in the life of
God (e.g. 1.3; 3.2; 5.13). Dodd has shown a difference between
the documents, but he has not advanced very far the analysis of
this shift of emphasis. Conzelmann has noted the change in the
use of ἀρχή from the Gospel where it is used to refer to the
beginning of the world, to the Letter where it is used to refer
to the beginning of the community. Once again this is not an
absolute difference of usage since the Letter's usage is similar
to that in Jn. 6.64; 15.27 and 16.4 where it refers to the beginning of discipleship (Marshall, *Epistles*, 35). Nevertheless,
Conzelmann's observation does point to the fact that there is
more concern in the Letter than in the Gospel with the history
of discipleship. Klein has provided further evidence for this
shift, though he also has overstated the difference. He contrasts the concern with history in the Letter with the Gospel's
concern for that which is atemporal and existential. For example, he contrasts the atemporal φῶς of Jn. 1.4 with the use in
1 Jn. 2.8, which anchors the φῶς in history ("Licht," 269-291);
he contrasts the atemporal or transtemporal ὥρα of the Gospel
with the reference to the ἐσχατή ὥρα in the Letter (2.18), which
seems to refer to a temporal series (ibid. 291-304); and he
contrasts the καινή of Jn. 13.34 with the καινή of 1 Jn. 2.7-8,
where the καινή of the Gospel is now also παλαιά (ibid. 304-307).
The last of these three main points is not objectionable, but
the first two should be questioned. Klein focuses on the use of
φῶς in Jn. 1.4 and denies that the Prologue and Gospel as a
whole is concerned precisely with the coming into history of this
φῶς. But concern with history is evident already in the use of
φῶς in Jn. 1.9. What was said earlier about Bultmann (p. 14) applies also to Klein, namely, he does not see that the author is
using cosmic language to make a comment about history. The

emphasis in the Prologue is on motion (cf. 1.9 ἐρχόμενον and
1.11 ἦλθεν, cf. 3.19; 12.46). Even the more atemporal references
in 1.4-5 view the φῶς not as an abstract entity, but in its relation to mankind (cf. Mussner, ΖΩΗ, 164-171). Indeed, even the
references to the Baptist in the Prologue, which seem to many
scholars to be clumsy insertions, actually "serve to link the
subsequent historical statements with the metaphysical truths
there outlined."[282] The Gospel, then, is an interpretation of
human history using cosmic symbols. There is in the Gospel a
distinction between the time before the coming of the φῶς and
after it has come. So when Klein interprets 1 Jn. 2.8 as implying
that "bis Christus waltete ausschliesslich Finsternis, und zwar
nicht nur aufgrund faktischer Entscheidung des Menschen für sie,
sondern prinzipiell" ("Licht," 282), it must be noted that such
a view is not absent from the Gospel as well, even if it is more
starkly stated in the Letter. Thus, the two documents are not
nearly so far apart with regard to their notions of time as Klein
suggests.[283]

   Nevertheless, there are differences. These can be discussed
by turning to another of Klein's main points, the use of ὥρα.
The differences Klein finds with regard to ὥρα are misleading.
The use of ὥρα is not as atemporal as Klein seems to suggest
since it is used to refer to a specific event (cf. Jn. 12.27).
The more significant comparison is not between ὥρα and ἐσχάτη ὥρα
but between ἐσχάτη ἡμέρα and ἐσχάτη ὥρα. The difference in
eschatology between John and 1 John is not, as Dodd and Klein
would suggest, a difference of kind, but rather a difference of
degree. That is, in both the Gospel and the Letter there is a
present eschatology and a future eschatology. But to the ἐσχάτη
ἡμέρα of the Gospel is now added the ἐσχάτη ὥρα of the Letter.
The difference is a shift from a general eschatological hope to
a more complicated view of the details of the end. Thus, while
I disagree with much of Klein's interpretation of the Gospel I
agree with his basic point concerning the Letter, namely, that
here there is more concern with the details of a chronology of
the end. Such a concern is evident in the Gospel at 21.20-23
so it is not possible to say it was not present in the community
even before the Gospel was finalized in the form we have it.

Indeed, that the belief concerning the antichrist(s) did not
arise at the defection of the opponents is evident from 1 Jn.
2.18 itself. This verse says that this defection has happened
καθὼς ἠκούσατε. The defection is not a surprise; it even has a
very specific meaning. So the detailed vision of the end is an
element in the community's tradition to which the author now refers since he believes it is coming to fulfillment.

Dodd, Conzelmann, and Klein are right to say that the Letter
is far closer than the Gospel to the eschatology we find in Paul,
the Synoptics, and elsewhere in the NT. But while the Letter is
closer to other writings of the NT in its concern with chrono-
logical details of the end, there is also another way in which
it is closer to John. Brooke has suggested that both the Gospel
and the Letter are characterized by what he refers to as a spir-
itualizing of eschatology (*Epistles*, 37). In the Gospel the
future coming of the Lord is already experienced spiritually,
while in the Letter the expected antichrist is already present
in the opponents' teaching (ibid. xviii). Brooke's comparison,
however, is not entirely satisfactory, for, as we have noted, the
realized eschatology of the Gospel is not lacking in the Letter.
Even more to the point, the author of 1 John does not just spir-
itualize by referring to anti-Christian *teaching*. Rather, he
also "historicizes the mythical figure" (Bultmann, *Epistles*, 36)
by applying the term antichrist to former friends of those in the
community. This same historicizing is also evident in the depiction of Judas in the Gospel. In particular, there is the
reference to him as ὁ υἱὸς τῆς ἀπωλείας (Jn. 17.12), which echoes
Paul's reference in 2 Thes. 2.3.[284] So in both documents eschatological material is used to interpret present experience. In
both cases the eschatology is both spiritualized and histori-
cized; the community is now, within history, experiencing both
eschatological blessing and danger.

There is, then, great similarity between the documents concerning eschatology, but also something of a difference. This
difference seems to be due to the different sort of crisis faced
in the Letter from that in the Gospel, for "the difference between the Gospel and the Epistles is the change from a vague
prophecy to a clear recognition of its fulfilment in the supreme

danger to which the Church is now exposed" (Howard, *Christianity*,
127). To meet this crisis the author of 1 John focuses more
sharply the meaning which ἀρχή and ἐσχατή have in the Gospel.
He interprets what his community is experiencing by referring to
details in the community's belief concerning the ἐσχατὴ ὥρα. He
tries to meet the challenge by referring to the community's traditions, that which they have heard ἀπ' ἀρχῆς.

10. *Individualism*

C. F. D. Moule believes the emphasis on realized eschatology
in the Gospel is in part due to the Gospel's focus on individuals, whereas "as soon as we turn to I John, which is addressed
to a community, the future type of eschatology comes back into
prominence."[285] He sees this difference as a shift of emphasis
and finds "no difficulty in believing the Epistle to be by the
same author as the Gospel":

> In the Gospel he is concentrating mainly on the individual's
> relation to Christ and shows, in generalized terms, that
> this is, in its essence, a matter of life and death.
> Consequently, the future tense recedes. In the Epistle
> he is addressing a specific--and collective--situation,
> and immediately the future tense comes back into greater
> prominence ("Factor," 159).

Such a view is in keeping with the other shifts of emphasis between the Gospel and the Letter noted above. However, according
to the present hypotheses, even this careful distinction is over-
drawn. The Gospel is not simply concerned with individuals but
with two communities in conflict. Even the individuals of the
Gospel may be representative figures (cf. e.g. Leroy, *Rätsel*,
171-172), though, as we have seen (above pp. 16-17), some scholars
overdo this interpretation. On the other hand, the Letter is
obviously addressed to a community, but often it addresses the
individuals within that community. For example, such passages
as 2.20,27 and 3.2 may betoken an individualism. Even the exhortation to love, which could be an exhortation to the community
in general, is often addressed to the individual (e.g. 2.10).
In particular, the very frequent use of an articular masculine
nominative singular participle serves to stress the individual.
So the Letter is addressed to individuals to a greater extent

than Moule seems to allow. This, however, is not to deny his
main point that in the Letter there is a heightened emphasis on
the community. The threat to the community's existence from
within could account for this shift of emphasis, but a certain
aspect of the opponents' position may also have been a contrib-
uting factor. As we have seen, the opponents have stressed their
autonomy as individuals to the neglect of their identity as members of the community (above pp. 135-136). So once again we see
an aspect of Johannine thought developed in what the author of
1 John considers an unacceptable way. His stress on communal
love and adherence to the traditions (as he interprets them) may
be, in part, an attempt to respond to the unbalanced individualism of the opponents.

11. Conclusion

   Such, then, are the major differences scholars have found
between John and 1 John. In each instance we have seen that the
difference noted is not the introduction of something totally
new but rather a shift of emphasis, a development in the Letter
of some aspect of the community's tradition as it is represented
in the Gospel. Because these shifts of emphasis match up with
various features of the opponents' position as we have it reflected in the Letter it seems likely these shifts were made in
response to the threat posed by the opponents. These opponents
claim to be loyal to the Johannine community's tradition. As
such they claim to know God, to be loyal to Jesus, to be inspired
by the Spirit, and to be without sin. Since they claim to be
loyal to Jesus there is a shift from the simple belief in Jesus
in the Gospel to a correct confession of him. Both the atoning
significance of Jesus' death and its exemplary value as revealing
God's love are more explicitly stated in the Letter by way of
combatting the opponents' claim to sinlessness. Their appeal to
the Spirit is attacked by stressing the close relation between
the Spirit and the Jesus they are denying. In addition to these
refutations, all basically christological, the crisis caused by
the opponents' secession has also led to more explicit concern
with the nature of the community. There is a heightened stress
on its authoritative tradition and now its history must be

interpreted in eschatological categories in a way it is not in
the Gospel (cf. Jn. 15.18-16.4). But most of all there is re-
newed emphasis on the divine nature of the community. The believers' relationship with God the Father and the experience
within the community of the divine ζωή are major motifs in both
documents, but are more sharply stated in the Letter. This divine character of the community is severely challenged by both
the Jewish opponents and the former members of the community and
so this motif is of great importance in both documents. In the
Gospel the stress is on the revelation in Jesus of this divine
ζωή, while in the Letter the stress is on the presence of this
ζωή in the community that confesses Jesus truly.

Thus, these various shifts can be explained by reference to
the different settings of the two documents. The present study
of the polemic in the Gospel and Letter provides a working hypothesis which accounts for these differences. It also highlights further similarities and differences, to which I now turn.

C. Further Differences Related to the Polemic

We have now seen in this study of the polemic in John and
1 John the very sharp contrasts the author(s) draws between
those who are children of God and those who are utterly alienated
from God. Because this polarization is an essential feature of
the polemic in these two documents it is of particular interest
for the present study to consider whether or not there are any
differences in the dualism found in John and 1 John.

1. *Dualism*

Johannine dualism has received much attention from scholars
and there have emerged three main evaluations of this aspect of
Johannine thought. First, there are those who believe the dualism
to be essentially Gnostic; it is a mythological polarity in the
cosmic realm with little reference to the contingency of history.
We have already noted that such a view is held by Bultmann (above
p. 14). One of the most significant presentations of such a view
is that offered by L. Schottroff.[286] She believes the author
worked with a Signs Source, modifying it to conform to his own

Gnostic outlook. According to Schottroff, the author saw two opposing camps, with people called to make an existential decision
for one or the other. People are either in one camp or the
other. What is of importance is faith. The particular content
of the various terms used to describe the two camps is not significant since these terms are interchangeable. What is of importance is the polarity and the call to decision.

The same year that Schottroff published her study, another
work appeared which offered a very different interpretation from
that of Schottroff. Instead of a cosmological Gnostic dualism,
G. Stemberger finds what he calls an ethical dualism.[287] The
distinction presented in the Gospel is that between good and
evil. These are not, however, two opposing camps in the same
sense Schottroff suggests. Rather,

> Les termes que Jean oppose deux à deux ne doivent pas
> être considérés comme des possibilités équivalentes
> entre elles. Jean ne connaît en fin de compte qu'une
> seule réalité: le bien, le salut, ce qui est de Dieu. . . .
> Par rapport au bien, le mal n'est pas seulement *une*
> *autre façon d'être*, il est purement et simplement
> *non-être* (Stemberger, *La symbolique*, 239).

While there are two camps and people must choose between them,
there is no cosmological dualism since only one of these camps
has existence; "Jean montre le chemin qui va du dualisme au
monisme" (ibid. 240). Thus, Stemberger considers the realm of
evil to be less substantial for the author of John than does
Schottroff. The divine reality is also conceived of differently.
For Stemberger it is anchored in history. He finds in the Gospel
an emphasis on movement. The light comes and there is a battle
between the forces of good and evil, with evil being vanquished.
Thus, Stemberger sees the author of John working with a concept
of salvation history, where Schottroff sees atemporal cosmological
mythology.

A third view of Johannine dualism would combine certain aspects of these two extreme positions. Schottroff's emphasis on
the starkness of the categories used and their reference to basic
types of existence is more representative of the author's

thought than Stemberger's emphasis on morality, which runs the
risk of reducing the sharpness of the tension in the dualism.
This is evident, in particular, in Stemberger's assertion: "Avec
la venue du Christ, la séparation ciel/terre, haut/bas s'est
estompée" (La symbolique, 98). This statement can be very misleading. The fact that the light has come and people can come
to the light from the darkness does not mean that the difference
between light and darkness has been blurred. On the other hand,
Stemberger's stress on the concern with history and movement is
true to the thought of the author of the Gospel in contrast to
Schottroff's atemporal cosmological dualism. Indeed, the fact
that Schottroff believes she is able to separate out a Signs
Source which has been modified by a Gnostic redactor indicates
that the Gospel as we have it does not conform to her view of
dualism. This same indirect evidence is found in another recent
study of Johannine dualism which takes somewhat the same line as
Schottroff. W. Langbrandtner distinguishes between a Grundschrift which represents a radical cosmological dualism and
stresses the need for faith, and a later Redaktion which relaxes
this tension and introduces this-worldly concerns such as ethics,
sacraments, and bodily resurrection.[288] By attempting to distinguish a Grundschrift from its Redaktion Langbrandtner testifies to the presence in John of both strong mythical categories
and concern for the contingencies of history.[289] In keeping with
the concerns of the present study, rather than comparing the
dualism of the Gospel with that of its hypothetical sources, I
will compare this complex dualism of the Gospel as we have it
with the dualism in 1 John. I will begin with the macrocosmic
and then discuss the microcosmic,[290] i.e. from the division among
people to a certain division within persons.

a. Macrocosmic Dualism: The Polarization of Mankind

     In the Gospel macrocosmic dualism, the polarization of man-
kind, is both static and dynamic. It is static in the sense that
very stark categories are used: life and death, light and darkness, above and below, truth and error/lie, good and evil, love
and hate, children of God and children of the devil. Such
language implies that everything is black or white; there seems

to be no room for an ambiguous grey. The mythic quality of some
of these terms gives the impression that all of mankind is in
one camp or the other. One's decision about Jesus is decisive
and there appears to be no possibility of sitting on the fence.
This Johannine view is epitomized in the depiction of Pilate.
"Pilate, the would-be neutral man, is frustrated by the intensity
of the participants. Having failed to listen to the truth and
decide in its favor, he and all who would imitate him inevitably
finish in the service of the world" (Brown, *John*, 864). So mankind is divided between believers and ὁ κόσμος. Ὁ κόσμος appears to be simple, undifferentiated, totally negative. God
loves the world (Jn. 3.16) and the Christian community is to
bear witness to the world (17.23), but salvation consists in
being called out from the world (15.18-19; 17.6,9) (cf. Böcher,
Dualismus, 146). But the fact that people can be called out of
the world indicates that while the categories used may be stark
and thus appear to be static, nevertheless, the Johannine dualism
is also dynamic. Mankind *is* divided into two camps, but there
is movement between these two camps. Furthermore, while the
categories seem to paint everything in black and white, the actual descriptions of various individuals and groups in the Gospel
show that the author has a great appreciation of the greyness
of the human situation. For example, no group within the Gospel
is described as totally good or totally evil. It is not surprising that the crowd is said to be divided on account of Jesus
(7.43), for this is to be expected. What is more surprising is
that the Pharisees are also said to be divided over Jesus (9.16).
Most striking of all is the description of οἱ Ἰουδαῖοι as
divided over Jesus (10.19). Οἱ Ἰουδαῖοι is such a negative
term in the Gospel and yet even this group is not totally bad.
The same complexity characterizes the groups on the positive
side. Many of Jesus' disciples leave him (6.66), and he is betrayed by one of his inner circle of disciples, whom he has chosen (6.70-71). Jesus must urge his disciples μένειν ἐν ἐμοί,
that they not be cast out, lifeless (15.6). Thus, while the
Jewish opponents and the disciples are contrasted with one another as being evil and good respectively, neither group is
simply and totally good or evil.

This same complexity, even ambiguity, characterizes various
individuals. As we have noted, it is never said explicitly that
the Samaritan woman is a believer; we even leave her still questioning whether Jesus could be the Messiah (4.29). Likewise,
Nicodemus is an ambiguous character. We are not given his response to Jesus during their first interview (Jn. 3). We leave
him questioning, but we do not know whether it is questioning
that ends in faith like Nathanael or questioning that ends in
rejection like the opponents. Nicodemus later defends Jesus
against his fellow Pharisees (7.50) and thus he seems to appear
in a positive light (cf. esp. 9.22; 12.42-43). His desire to
anoint Jesus' body seems also to be creditable (19.39). M. de
Jonge, however, presents a very different interpretation.[291]
He notes the link in 3.1 between Nicodemus and the unfaithful
believers of 2.23-25 ("Nicodemus," 339-340). Further, he believes the reference in 7.52 is negative; Nicodemus here "takes
part in an inner-Jewish discussion and does not take up one of
the themes which were [sic.] developed by Jesus in his own way
in the course of this chapter" (ibid. 344). The desire to anoint
Jesus is negative; it depicts Joseph and Nicodemus "as having
come to a dead end; they regard the burial as definitive" (ibid.
343). Thus, according to de Jonge, Nicodemus is not portrayed
positively. It is said that none of the Pharisees believed in
Jesus (7.48), yet later this is modified; some did believe but
loved the glory of men rather than that of God (12.42-43).
Nicodemus seems to be an exception, but for de Jonge he is not.
Rather, Nicodemus is one of these secret believers who represent
secret believers within the Synagogue of the author's own day.
"The sympathetic, even believing Jews like Nicodemus are on their
way to Jesus. But they should know, and Christians who speak
with them should know, that a far more incisive decision will
have to be made before they really understand who Jesus is and
what salvation he brings" (ibid. 357). Even if one thinks the
portrait of Nicodemus is more positive than de Jonge allows,
nevertheless, de Jonge has shown that Nicodemus is portrayed
more ambiguously than appears at first sight.

The Gospel, then, presents us with stark, simple, clear-cut
categories combined with ambiguous descriptions of individuals

and acknowledgement of the complexity of groups of both believers
and unbelievers. Such a combination is not carried over into
1 John. Here we do find the same stark, simple, clear-cut categories, but the other aspect of the picture in the Gospel is
missing. In 1 John there is movement, but it is only the movement from the community to the world (2.18-19; 4.5). Indeed, as
we have seen, one of the author's purposes is to prevent others
in the community from moving in this same direction. There is
nothing comparable to the complexity of the opponents in the
Gospel. In the Letter the opponents are thoroughly bad, there
is no ambiguity about them, there is no hint of secret believers
among them. Indeed, the author goes so far as to deny that there
ever was anything good about the opponents (2.19), even though
they were at one time within the community. The description of
the community itself retains something of the dynamic element
found in the Gospel. As we have seen, the community is characterized as the realm of sinlessness and love and yet the members
must be exhorted to confess their sins and to show love toward
one another. So there is in both documents a combination of
indicative and imperative that makes the seemingly static description more dynamic.

The main difference, then, between the documents with regard to macrocosmic dualism is the depiction of the group of
opponents in 1 John as totally bad. As with the other differences we have noted this difference may be due to the different
polemical settings. The opposition in the Gospel comes from
outside the community. There is always hope that some of these
outsiders may come into the community. Not all of those outside
the community are necessarily against Jesus; they may be uninformed or undecided. In the Letter, however, the opposition
comes from former members of the community. There is no possibility that they are uninformed or undecided. The very fact that
they have gone out indicates that they recognize the differences
separating them from the community and have chosen to go their
own way. The author of 1 John recognizes that the issues which
separate him and the opponents are subtle, but he believes they
are fundamental; there is no place for honest differences of
opinion on the issues in view. Those who have gone out cannot be
of the truth. They must be deluded for they have gone out.

b. Microcosmic Dualism: Divine Will and Human Will

When Böcher (*Dualismus*, 72-75) and Otzen ("Sektenschriften,"
135-142) discuss microcosmic dualism they are interested primarily in the notion of the two spirits within man struggling for
mastery, the יצר הרע and the יצר יטוב. We have noted that this notion of the two יצרים seems to lie behind at least certain por-
tions of the Gospel (p. 75). Yet this struggle of the two יצרים
is never explicitly developed in either John or 1 John; it plays
no part in the author'(s) own thought.[292] However, while the
notion of the two יצרים within man is not developed by the
author(s) there is much said, as we have seen, about the interi-
or disposition of individuals. In this section I will discuss
the relation between what is said about peoples' disposition and
what is said about the sovereign will of God. This section is
about microcosmic dualism in the sense that it is concerned with
the struggle within individuals, even though one of the two participants is not merely internal in the way the יצרים are in the
Jewish notion. What, then, is said in the Gospel of the relation
between God's sovereign will and the will of man? On the one
hand there are strong explicit statements mentioning sovereignty,
such as Jn. 6.37, "All that the Father gives to me will come to
me" and 6.44, "No one can come to me unless the Father who sent
me draws him." On the other hand there are texts which emphasize
the role of the human will, such as Jn. 5.40, "yet you refuse to
come to me that you may have life," and 7.17, "if any man's will
is to do his will, he shall know whether the teaching is from
God or whether I am speaking on my own authority." Indeed, some
of the strongest texts are set right next to each other (cf. 9.39
with 9.41 and 12.39 with 12.42-43). Thus, in the Gospel peoples'
response to Jesus is spoken of both in terms of a divine call
(6.70; 13.18; 15.16,19) and in terms of the human will, what one
loves and what one hates (e.g. 3.19-21).[293]

A shift takes place in 1 John. There is still much concern
with peoples' interior disposition (cf. Malatesta, *Interiority*)
and the Letter contains imperatives that speak to the human will.
But the strong explicit references to the divine will found in
the Gospel are entirely lacking in the Letter. This is not to
say that there is no reference to divine initiative. The divine

will is evident above all in the sending of the Son (4.9-10,14).
It is also evident in the divine gifts: the Spirit (3.24; 4.13;
cf. 2.14,20), love (3.1), eternal life (5.11); and the Son's
gift of διάνοια which enables the readers to know him who is
true (5.20). God's activity is also evident in the references
to being born of God (1.29; 3.9; 4.7; 5.1,4,18).[294] So we do not
find a radically different view of God in the two documents.
What we do find lacking in 1 John is the use of one of the more
important arguments used in the Gospel. This lack of reference
to the divine will to account for the opponents is somewhat surprising since, as we have seen, the ultimate polemical point of
both documents is the utter alienation from God of the opponents.
This being the case, why then do we not find in 1 John a statement similar to that in the Gospel that God has blinded the eyes
of the opponents (Jn. 12.40)? Indeed, in a very similar passage
in 1 John it is said that it is the darkness which blinds (1 Jn.
2.11). This reticence to speak of the divine will might reflect
a failure of nerve on the part of the author of 1 John, caused
by the shock of the departure of some who supposedly were elect.
Such an explanation of this difference, however, is unlikely
since, as we have seen, the tradition as we have it in the Gospel
was fully aware of the weakness of the first disciples (6.66,
70-71) and the possibility of defection from the community (Jn.
15.6, cf. 1 Jn. 2.18). Another explanation for this lack might
be that the opponents themselves were referring to God's sovereign will. We have seen that their appeal to the Spirit has
caused the author of 1 John to modify his own appeal to the
Spirit; the same might be true of this reference to the direct
activity of God. We have seen that the opponents were claiming
to know God and have fellowship with him and yet were standing
off from other believers (pp. 135-136 above). Whether they not
only considered themselves to be elite but also appealed to divine election must remain uncertain. If they did so then this
might account for the lack of appeal by the author to divine
election.

Such are the main differences in the dualism of the two
documents. As with the other differences we have examined, these
are shifts of emphasis rather than radical breaks. The

discussion of the relation between the divine will and the human
will leads to a consideration of yet another difference between
the documents which is closely related to dualism. I turn now
to look more closely at certain aspects of the depiction of the
human will in John and 1 John. In particular, for the topic of
Johannine polemic it is worthwhile comparing the characteristics
of those in the Gospel who receive and reject with the characteristics of those in the Letter who remain and depart.

2. *Characteristics of the Christians and Their Opponents*

As we saw in ch. 1, the chief characteristic of those who
receive Jesus in the Gospel is an openness to that which is
new. The Jewish opponents, on the other hand, are characterized
as being closed to the new out of loyalty to that which they have
already received, i.e. the Torah. So, in the Gospel, being open
to the new is a virtue and being closed out of loyalty to tradition is a vice. When we come to the Letter, however, the evaluation is reversed. Now it is the opponents who are open to that
which is new, as least in the author's eyes, and the community
members who are encouraged to be loyal to that which they have
received. Such a complete shift raises the question of whether
the author of 1 John has a totally different view from that in
the Gospel. Does the author of 1 John come under the same condemnation as the Jewish opponents in John? The opponents as they
are depicted in the Gospel think they know God and his ways and
have in their tradition all that is necessary for evaluating
Messianic claims. They are depicted, as we have seen, as being
self-assured and self-deceived. They believe they know God and
care for his glory but they do not know him and actually care
only for the glory they give one another. Might not some or all
of these same charges be leveled against the author of 1 John?
His claim to know God is as strong as that of the opponents in
John. More significantly, his claim to be the authentic bearer
of the community's tradition (e.g. 1 Jn. 4.6) seems as comprehensive and heavy-handed as the similar claim of the Jewish opponents in the Gospel (e.g. Jn. 7.47-52). What, then, is the
significance of such a complete reversal? Why is that which is
a virtue in one document a vice in the other? The answer would

seem to be that openness to that which is new has no intrinsic
value for the author(s). Being open to the new or closed due
to loyalty to that which has been received are either positive
or negative characteristics depending on *what* one is open to and
what one is loyal to. In both John and 1 John it is the ultimate
revelation of God in Jesus that determines whether openness and
closedness are a virtue or a vice. Openness to Jesus and loyalty
to him are virtues, closedness and disloyalty to him are vices.
It is the belief that God is revealed in Jesus that determines
the view of the opponents in both documents. In both John and
1 John the central issue is a correct evaluation of Jesus on the
basis of the received traditions. We are led, therefore, to a
comparison of that which is central in the polemic of both documents, namely, the appeal to religious tradition and the understanding of God. Up to this point in this chapter we have been
assessing various differences between the documents. I will now
draw upon the results of the previous chapters to describe the
fundamental unity between the documents in their polemic.

D. Fundamental Similarities in the Polemic of John and 1 John

1. *Tradition*

     We have seen that in both documents the author(s) is con-
cerned to claim for his own side the tradition that he holds in
common with his opponents. He is presented as the authoritative
interpreter of tradition. Both in John and 1 John, then, the
key principle evident in the polemic is continuity of tradition.
In the Gospel the Jewish opponents believe Jesus is condemned by
the Torah. John argues that Jesus is not condemned by Torah but
rather is vindicated by it. The OT witnesses to Jesus so he
does not destroy Torah but fulfills it. What Jesus does destroy
is the Jewish opponents' interpretation of the Torah. It is
these opponents who are disloyal to the tradition; Jesus is fully
in harmony with it. When we turn to 1 John we find this same
basic principle of continuity with tradition. But whereas in
the Gospel the concern is to show that Jesus does not contradict
the Torah, in the Letter the concern is to show that the opponents' position does contradict, even destroy, the community's
tradition about Jesus. The opponents appear to believe they are

loyal to the tradition, but the author shows that what seem only
subtle differences between himself and them actually destroy the
very center of the Johannine community's belief about Jesus.
Thus the underlying principle of the polemic we have studied in
detail above is loyalty to the received tradition; the Torah witnesses to Jesus rather than supporting the Jewish opponents in
John, and the community's traditions support the understanding
of Jesus held by the author of 1 John rather than that of the
opponents. So the key principle is loyalty to the tradition, the
central subject of which is Jesus.

2. *Theology*

The similarity of the polemic of the two documents goes even
deeper. The study in the previous chapters has shown that not
only the principle and the subject are the same but there is also
reference in both documents to the same ultimate criterion,
namely, theology proper, the understanding of God. We have seen
that in both documents the ultimate issue at stake is the gracious love of God revealed in Jesus. It is this love that is the
ultimate continuity between the Father, as he is revealed in
Scripture, and the Son, Jesus. This gracious God has been revealed in Jesus' words and actions, above all in his death. This
theme in the Gospel is also central to the Letter. God's love
is revealed in the death of his Messiah Son, for love is the
laying down of one's life. To follow the opponents and deny that
the Messiah Son died when Jesus died is to destroy the very center of Johannine theology, the revelation of God's love in the
death of the Son. Thus, although John and 1 John are addressing
very different situations, and there are many shifts of emphasis,
nevertheless the central criterion in the polemic of them both
is identical. Both groups of opponents are attacked for their
destruction of that which is central to the Johannine vision of
God. Such is the underlying similarity of the polemic in John
and 1 John. In both documents the argument is taken down to
bedrock, the understanding of God himself.

The fact that the conflicts involve very different views of
God accounts for the intensity of the polemic. The polemic in
both John and 1 John is presented as a life and death struggle

in which no compromise is possible. In both cases what is at
stake is not a mere cut-and-dried doctrinal position but the
presence of the very life of God. Even the doctrinal confession
presented in 1 John is only an aid for guidance and protection
from error. The dogma does not itself constitute the truth, for
in both John and 1 John the truth is personal, it is God and his
Son.[295] Knowledge of truth refers in Johannine thought to experience of the living reality of God. Notice, for example, the
coordination of knowledge and life in Jn. 17.3 and 1 Jn. 5.20.
Hence the emphasis on the internal work of the Spirit in both
documents; certainty comes not just from intellectual harmony
but also from the assurance of the heart and the inner vision of
God. As we have seen, in Johannine thought Christians are in the
realm of light and life and love, they indwell the Father, the
Son and the Spirit. It is because the author(s) sees the opponents as denying God himself and as working against the very life
of God revealed in Jesus and experienced by his followers that
these opponents are said to be completely alienated from God.
We have seen that this charge is made explicitly in both documents. This evaluation of the opponents reflects the stark polarity of the dualistic categories used in *both* documents. Does
such an evaluation of the opponents indicate the author(s) could
only think in terms of an absolute dichotomy? Would he ever be
willing to try to reason with his opponents and come to a common
understanding of the Faith? According to the hypotheses of the
present study the controversies reflected in John and 1 John had
both reached crisis proportions at the time these documents were
written. In both cases there had already occurred a division
between the groups involved, the Christians had withdrawn from
the Synagogue and the opponents had withdrawn from the Johannine
community. Did such division on the social level influence the
dualism of the author'(s) conceptual framework? Possibly so,
though it seems impossible to conclusively substantiate such a
view.[296] The author(s) of John and 1 John may well have had
such a dualistic framework prior to the division that occurred,
but even if he did there are hints that his attitude was not
always as separationist as it now appears. In particular, recall the point made above in ch. 2 that as the story is told in

the Gospel it appears that the separation from the Synagogue was
not desired by the Christians (see pp. 7,10). This does not
necessarily mean that they were not uncompromising in their witness to Jesus; their expulsion suggests they were. But it does
indicate a willingness to live together with those with whom they
disagreed. Indeed, complete withdrawal from the world is not
advocated in John (cf. 17.15). Similarly, the author of 1 John
says that it was the opponents who left the community (1 Jn. 2.18-
19), thus placing the blame on them. As in the Gospel, this
statement might imply a willingness to coexist with those who
disagree. But it seems that neither separation would have occurred if the Johannine Christians were not uncompromising. Thus,
it is unlikely that their sectarianism is a matter of principle,
but they are uncompromising on at least some issues. There seems
to be no reason to think they would have been willing to negoti-
ate concerning these. In the conflicts reflected in these documents there is no place for debate, only confession. How the
author(s) would have responded to other opinions or other conflicts is impossible to say. Perhaps the author(s), like Paul,
would distinguish between non-negotiable matters and other matters on which opinions could differ.[297] It is possible that the
virtue of being open to that which is new, which is presented in
the Gospel and is there said to characterize the community in
the future (e.g. Jn. 14.12; 16.13), is not necessarily negated
in the Letter. The polemical stance we have seen in the Letter
comes across as a simple conservative traditionalism. This concern with tradition, however, need not mean being closed to all
that is new. What we do see is a decided rejection of the particular developments proposed by these opponents. There is no
reason to think that because the polemic in both of these documents is basically a charge of alienation from God, therefore the
author(s) would view everyone who disagreed with him as being
alienated from God. His judgment on these particular opponents
is based on the particular positions he believes they held. These
opponents strike at the very heart of Christianity and therefore
have called forth the strong, profound responses examined in this
dissertation. The issue concerns one's knowledge of God and experience of his life. There can be no compromise.

E. Summary

In summary I will recapitulate the main points that have
been stressed in this study. The author(s) of John and 1 John
finds himself faced with a situation in which people are claiming
to speak for God in such a way as to cut at the heart of Christianity as he understands it. Both groups of opponents are
making strong and convincing appeals to the same traditions that
the author(s) himself considers to be authoritative. Both groups
of opponents also have an appearance of holiness; they keep commandments and are fervent in their loyalty to God as they know
him. The author(s), however, considers them to be self-deceived
and to be deceiving others. He attempts to uncover their error
by appealing to the traditions he holds in common with them. In
his loyalty to these traditions he seeks to demonstrate how he
is in continuity with the traditions and how they are not. This
continuity of tradition is the key working principle of his polemic in both documents. In both John and 1 John the differences
between the author(s) and his opponents concern the interpretation of the significance of Jesus. In the Gospel his main point
is that Jesus as Messiah Son is the revelation of God par excellence and in particular his characteristic gracious love. In
the Letter the issue is focused more sharply; it is Jesus' death
as Messiah Son that is the revelation of God par excellence. In
both documents the argument about Jesus is related to the underlying differences the author(s) sees between himself and his
opponents concerning God himself. His key criterion for assessing his opponents' positions is his central theological vision
of the gracious love of God. He interprets the gulf between
himself and his opponents in cosmic and spiritual terms. One is
ultimately either of God or of the devil, and he says as clearly
as possible that he considers his opponents to be utterly alienated from God. One's response to the truth of God is related to
one's interior disposition. The opponents cannot receive the
truth because their wills are not in tune with God's will. Even
though the former members of the community at one time appeared
to have receptive hearts, their defection revealed what was
really within them. In both John and 1 John there is a theme of
the exposure of one's heart which is effected by one's response
to Jesus (e.g. Jn. 3.19-21; 1 Jn. 2.19).

In the eyes of the author(s), then, the danger is extreme.
He is facing opponents who have many of the beliefs and practices
which are in common with the truth. But they are deceived and
are deceiving others for under the surface they do not share the
life of God; they only have certain trappings of this life. For
the author(s) this life of God is present in Jesus in the Church.
This life is evident in the experience of the Spirit within the
community, but it is also testified to by the traditions. The
internal witness of the Spirit is necessary, but this does not
preclude appeal to more objective criteria. In this dissertation
we have seen something of the nature of this appeal as it is
presented in John and 1 John.

F. Conclusion

1. *The Present Study and Johannine Studies*

The present study is an attempt to contribute to our understanding of early Christian apologetic and Johannine Christianity. I have attempted not so much to break new ground as to
build upon ground that seems secure, at least as secure as any
ground can be in biblical studies. Since I have tried to build
on the work of various scholars, to the best of my knowledge only
a few of the particular exegetical points made in the first three
chapters are not duplicated elsewhere. I have gathered together
commonly recognized aspects of Johannine thought and, working
with commonly accepted hypotheses concerning the setting and
purpose of the documents, I have attempted to discover how these
aspects of thought would have been of use in the polemic reflected in the different documents. The present study seeks to
provide an understanding of the overall structure and rationale
of the polemic in each document. In doing so it has also provided confirmation of these commonly accepted hypotheses.

The present chapter has moved on from an attempt to contribute to an understanding of the individual documents to an assessment of important features in the relationship between them. I
have attempted to show that behind various shifts of emphasis
the two documents actually share the same basic principle of
argument, namely, loyalty to the tradition held in common with
the opponents. Their common appeal to the same basic criterion,

theology proper, is particularly noteworthy. In both documents
the opponents' positions are evaluated in the light of the implications of their position for the understanding of God, and
that vision of God is identical in both documents. The Johannine
polemic is based on God's love revealed in the Son's death and
God's life present in the Christian community. This fundamental
agreement in the form and content of the polemic of the two documents suggests that they are more closely related to one another
than has sometimes been allowed. I do not think that the close
similarities I have discussed necessarily indicate common authorship. However, if they were not both written by the same person,
then the similarities in the polemic that I have noted at least
indicate that 1 John is very close indeed to the mind and spirit
of the Gospel.

2. *The Present Study and NT Studies*

     The present study touches on a number of larger issues of
interest in NT studies generally. To conclude I will note three
such areas, briefly suggesting in general terms something of the
possible significance of this study for our understanding of
these topics. It will be evident that each of these topics has
wider implications for the Church today, though these are not
here explored.

     One of the most obvious topics touched on by the present
study is the question of unity and diversity within the NT and
within Christianity generally. The diversity within the NT has
long been recognized and recently it has become increasingly
popular to conclude from this phenomenon that the canon canonizes
diversity.[298] It is said that the NT, far from witnessing to a
monolithic view of Christianity, actually supports a variegated,
pluriform view. I believe there is a great deal of validity to
this line of thought. The present study offers the reminder,
however, that the canon canonizes not only diversity but also
boundaries.[299] This study has examined how two of the writings
of the NT mark out these boundaries. Where and how they are to
be drawn today is a difficult question, but that they are to be
drawn is the implication of both the canon and many of its
various writings, not least John and 1 John.

There is a certain modern resistance to this drawing of
boundaries for to do so seems to some people to reflect a lack
of love. So a second general topic touched on by this study is
the notion of love, especially its character within a polemical
setting. In this connection Brown has referred to "the great
anomaly of the First Epistle":[300]

> No more eloquent voice is raised in the NT for love
> within the Christian brotherhood and sisterhood. . . .
> Yet that same voice is extremely bitter in condemning
> opponents who had been members of his community and
> were so no longer (*Community*, 132).

Brown considers this attitude something of a disaster:

> Those who believe that God has given His people the
> biblical books as a guide should recognize that part
> of the guidance is to learn from the dangers attested
> in them as well as from their great insights. . . .
> In his [John's] attitude toward the secessionists in a
> passage like II John 10-11 he supplied fuel for those
> Christians of all times who feel justified in hating
> other Christians for the love of God (ibid. 135).

What Brown describes in 1 John is also present in the Gospel.[301]
Brown's assessment would probably be shared by many people; few
today would argue that those with whom they disagree are utterly
alienated from God and, indeed, are worshipping idols. But is
this Johannine attitude of uncompromising exclusivity an unfor-
tunate feature of early Christianity that is now to be rejected
or does it stand in judgment on our own attitudes? As already
noted (above pp. 179-180), the present study does not support a
view that would see in John and 1 John the canonization of a
blind conservative traditionalism. But the author(s) does believe that some views are utterly unacceptable. Brown might well
agree with this view; his displeasure is with the attitude of
the author of 1 John. But such an uncompromising stand is not
a lack of love. If a person really believes that those with whom
he disagrees are utterly alienated from God then it is not love
to leave them thus self-deceived, especially if one believes they
are leading others away from God.[302] The author'(s) strength of
feeling reflects the importance of the issue at stake, which is
the very life of God.

This central issue suggests a third topic that might be
mentioned. In 1975 N. A. Dahl wrote a brief article entitled,

"The Neglected Factor in New Testament Theology." The factor
he had in mind was the NT thought concerning God. If my analysis
of Johannine polemic is correct then theology proper does indeed
deserve even more attention than it has already received in the
study of Johannine thought (and perhaps this is even more true
for e.g. Pauline studies);[303] the assessment of the thought of
individual NT writers might need to be revised. Furthermore, if
more attention is paid to theology then at least some scholars'
versions of NT theology in general may need to be reassessed.
For example, E. Fascher has complained that O. Cullmann assumes
NT theology is almost exclusively christology.[304] What Fascher
says of Cullmann may well be true of other studies of NT theology. Finally, such attention to theology may affect our view
of the NT in general, for it has been suggested that theology is
a fundamental unifying factor among the authors of the NT.[305]
Thus it is possible that further research on theology in the NT
may produce results with wide-ranging implications.

       Such, then, are a few of the general topics the present
study has touched on. In these documents we have found an example of an uncompromising stand taken out of loyalty to that which
has been both received from tradition and experienced of God.
What is at stake in this polemic is the presence of the life of
God among mankind. As elsewhere in the NT, the concern is not
simply with various conceptions of God, various ideas, but with
events in history which demand interpretation.[306] If John is the
"spiritual Gospel" (Clement of Alexandria) it is so not in the
sense of being non-material or ahistorical, for in John there is
no sharp dichotomy between spirit and matter.[307] Rather, it is
spiritual in the sense that it interprets historical events in
the light of divine reality.[308] "The Fourth Gospel persuades and
entices the reader to venture a judgment upon history" (Hoskyns,
Riddle, 263) and this same concern with history characterizes
the Letter as well.[309] For in both documents God is revealed par
excellence in the death of the Son. The Johannine God is one
who reveals himself in this historical event and is now present
in a historical community. The opponents in each document are
represented as rejecting both the revelation of God in the death
of the Son and the presence of God in the community. Where is

God truly known and experienced?--this is the fundamental question faced in these documents. This theology which is central
to John and 1 John is theology both in the sense of an understanding of God and also in the sense of an experiential knowledge of God. This Johannine view of theology and the Johannine
practice of appealing to tradition and referring points of dispute back to their implications for theology proper have been
maintained by the Church throughout her history; they may continue
to be of value for distinguishing truth from error amidst the
present religious chaos. Now as then it is not simply obvious
where God is truly known and experienced.

NOTES

1. INTRODUCTION

[1]An attempt to do so is offered by J. C. Meagher, *The Way of the Word*, 1975.

[2]In this study I am not assuming common authorship. Indeed, I find the problem of authorship insoluble with our present tools and resources. The language I use in referring to the author(s) of John and 1 John is intended to be unbiased, neither affirming nor denying that these documents have a single common author.

[3]R. E. Brown, *The Community of the Beloved Disciple*, 1979. Cf. his remark: "the relationship between the redactor of the Gospel and the author of the Epistles is obscure, precisely because there is no scholarly agreement on how much of the present Gospel to attribute to the redactor. Were both the Gospel-redaction and the Epistles the work of the same man, and which came first? In general, in order to avoid the charge of manipulating the Gospel, I have preferred to treat the Gospel as a whole which antedated the Epistles; and thus implicitly I have worked with the thesis that even the final redaction came before I John was written" (p. 161).

[4]See "Die Fleischwerdung des Logos im Johannesevangelium," 1971-1972 and the summary statement in one of his last articles, "Präsentische und futurische Eschatologie im 4. Evangelium," 1975, 128-131. Cf. R. Kysar, *The Fourth Evangelist and His Gospel*, 1975, 157-159 for a survey of other scholars who hold a similar view.

[5]*Introduction to the New Testament*, 1975, 439.

[6]There is no generally accepted hypothesis upon which to build, nor have I found any particular theory to be satisfactory. The fundamental problem with such theories is the lack of adequate criteria for distinguishing those differences in the style and thought of a document that reflect levels of tradition in conflict with one another from differences which reflect tensions and ambiguities within a single author's thought and expression. For a survey of various major theories see Kysar, *Evangelist*, 10-81. Kysar's conclusion that a satisfactory theory has not yet been found (p. 79) is shared by Brown (cf. n.3 above) and also e.g. by R. Schnackenburg, "On the Origin of the Fourth Gospel," 1970, 226; W. Meeks, "The Divine Agent and His Counterfeit in Philo and the Fourth Gospel," 1976, 59; and D. M. Smith, "Johannine Christianity," 1975, 228-229. Earlier Kysar had taken a more positive view toward the results of source theories in "The Source Analysis of the Fourth Gospel - a Growing Consensus?" 1973, and this is still reflected in *Evangelist*, 28-29.

However, even Kysar's more qualified optimism is rightly questioned by D. A. Carson, who provides a very good statement of
the difficulties facing such theories in general as well as
the weaknesses of particular theories ("Current Source Criticism
of the Fourth Gospel: Some Methodological Questions," 1978).

[7]See the very suggestive study by S. S. Smalley, "Diversity
and Development in John," 1971.

[8]For the popularity of John among later Gnostics see E.
Pagels, *The Johannine Gospel in Gnostic Exegesis*, 1973; J. N.
Sanders, *The Fourth Gospel in the Early Church*, 1943, 47-66; and
F. -M. Braun, *Jean le théologien et son évangile dans l'église
ancienne*, 1959, 100-132, 185-209.

[9]Some variety of this hypothesis is held by e.g. J. A. T.
Robinson, "The Destination and Purpose of the Johannine Epis-
tles," 1962, 138; J. L. Houlden, *The Johannine Epistles*, 1973,
18-20; K. Wengst, *Häresie und Orthodoxie im Spiegel des ersten
Johannesbriefes*, 1976; J. Bogart, *Orthodox and Heretical
Perfectionism in the Johannine Community as Evident in the First
Epistle of John*, 1977; and R. A. Culpepper, *The Johannine School*,
1975, 283.

[10]An example will be found below, pp. 16-17.

2. JOHANNINE POLEMIC: THE GOSPEL

[11]Most scholars emphasize that "the ordinary features of a letter are missing from I John" (Kümmel, *Introduction*, 437) and conclude it is something closer to a tractate (ibid.). or a "written sermon or pastoral address" (I. H. Marshall, *The Johannine Epistles*, 1978, 14). F. O. Francis, however, has found Hellenistic letters which provide examples of the supposedly non-epistolary features of 1 John ("The Form and Function of the Opening and Closing Paragraphs of James and 1 John," 1970), so 1 John might legitimately be called a letter, albeit an unusual one. The main danger with calling it a tract is the *possible* neglect of the fact that this document is addressed to a particular group of people in a particular situation well known by the author (see Marhsall, *Epistles*, 14 and Dodd, *The Johannine Epistles*, 1946, xxi). It is not a treatise on christology so much as an interpretation and evaluation of certain events in the community's experience.

[12]C. F. D. Moule finds in John what "may be good traditions of the actual controversies of Christ's own life-time, preserved and re-set in such a way as to be entirely topical to the evangelist's own circumstances" (*The Birth of the New Testament*, 1962, 95). Cf. J. Bowman, *The Fourth Gospel and the Jews*, 1975, 32.

[13]Most scholars believe the Gospel reflects a variety of purposes. The majority of their suggestions would not be incompatible with the present hypothesis that the primary concern is to assure Christians by combating Jewish opponents. For example, the very features of the Gospel I will examine below which serve to assure Christians would also be effective for evangelism among both Jews and non-Jews. A number of scholars find a special concern for Samaritans (e.g. O. Cullmann, *The Johannine Circle*, 1976, 50-51; G. W. Buchanan, "The Samaritan Origin of the Gospel of John," 1968, 173-175). Jn. 4.31-38 probably does imply a Christian mission in Samaria, though this concern was not a dominant factor in the composition of the Gospel since there is no sensitivity to specifically Samaritan concerns and terminology (see Meeks, "Am I a *Jew*?," 1975, 177-178). Apart from these positive evangelistic concerns scholars have also detected polemic against others besides the Jewish opponents. Many scholars believe there is a polemic against disciples of John the Baptist, though not all agree (e.g. J. A. T. Robinson, "Elijah, John and Jesus," 1962, 49-50). Indeed, if there is such polemic, it is not explicit; "It is for the Evangelist a subsidiary concern, served almost automatically by his primary purpose" (W. Wink, *John the Baptist in the Gospel Tradition*, 1968, 105). The view that the Gospel is written with certain intra-Church conflicts in mind is not necessarily incompatible with the hypothesis here

followed, though this particular suggestion I find the least
probable since there is no explicit reference in the Gospel to
any such controversy, at least not over the issues that are usually mentioned such as christology, eschatology, or the sacraments. In particular, if the Gospel is written to combat a
gnosticizing tendency among some Christians then it must be
judged singularly unsuccessful since, as will be urged below, it
is so ambiguous on this matter that the Letter had to be written
later to combat these same views. Indeed, the Gospel is ambiguous
enough for some modern scholars to argue that the author himself
is a Gnostic or a Docetist. I shall return to these views below. I shall also discuss below my own view that the intra-
Church conflict most evident is the desire of some in the community to return to Judaism.

Such, then, are some of the major suggestions as to the purpose of John. Many of these suggestions are possibly or even
probably correct, but my concern in this study is with examining
the main features of the polemic of John and 1 John so I have
decided to limit my attention to those opponents that seem to be
explicitly referred to in the texts.

[14]*History and Theology in the Fourth Gospel*, 1979, 37-62.

[15]See his "Glimpses into the History of the Johannine Community," 1978, 92.

[16]The main reservation expressed by scholars has been over
Martyn's supposition that John is consciously written on two
levels, so that, for example, the street mentioned in Jn. 9.1-7
recalls the Jewish section of the author's own city. See e.g.
Schnackenburg, "Origin," 228-230 and Smith, "Christianity," 238.
For further reservations see Brown, *Community*, 174.
With regard to the acceptance of his hypothesis in general,
see Smith, "Christianity," 238; Schnackenburg, "Origin," 228-230;
Meeks, "Jew," 183; Kysar, "Community and Gospel," 1977, 364; and
Brown, *Community*, 174. Meeks and Kysar say Martyn's general
view has won wide acceptance and mention various studies which
accept and/or corroborate Martyn's work. For further evidence
of acceptance see Kysar, *Evangelist*, 150-156.

[17]*Anti-Semitism in the New Testament?*, 1978, 146-147.

[18]*The History of the Jewish People in the Age of Jesus
Christ [175 B.C. - A.D. 135]*, 1979, 2:462-463.

[19]"Die sogennate Synode von Jabne," 1975, 56-61.

[20]Ibid. 60-61. Schäfer's quote is from I. Elbogen, *Der
jüdische Gottesdienst in seiner geschichtlichen Entwicklung*,
1931, 36.

[21]A recent study suggests that within Judaism after AD 70
there may have only been followers of the Pharisees and followers
of Jesus: "If John's Gospel was written after the destruction
of the Temple and in the Diaspora, the Pharisees may very well
have been the only religious authorities recognized by the Jews.
In the period after the destruction of the Temple and in the

Diaspora, there may have been *only* the Jews who followed the
Pharisees and the Jews who followed Jesus and to the extent that
John's Gospel was a polemical work against the Jews, he was only
concerned with countering the arguments of the Pharisees, for
no other *Jewish* arguments existed in the postdestruction period"
(E. Rivkin, *A Hidden Revolution,* 1978, 102-103). If such were
the case then the *birkath ha-minim* would more likely be directed
against Christians. However, it is unclear what Rivkin means by
"religious authorities recognized by the Jews" since he first
limits this to the Pharisees and then seems to include followers
of Jesus. It is certainly debatable whether these were the only
distinctive forms of Judaism open to people at the time, whether
or not "recognized by the Jews." "It is wise to remember that
all sorts of fringe groups must have existed round the first
and second century Jewish and Christian circles that are familiar
to us. We cannot expect to be well informed about them, but
there are sufficient hints of their existence" (C. K. Barrett,
"Jews and Judaizers in the Epistles of Ignatius," 1976, 234-
235).

[22]Cf. J. Bowker, "The Origin and Purpose of St. John's
Gospel," 1965, 401.

[23]See H. L. Strack, *Jesus die Häretiker und die Christen
nach den ältesten jüdischen Angaben,* 1910, 18-34 for further
texts from the Tannaitic period. Cf. also E. Bammel, "Christian
Origins in Jewish Tradition," 1967.
There is debate about the historical value of *Sanhedrin* 43a
but even a scholar like Lauterbach who believes the story is "a
later legend about Jesus and not a contemporary report, not even
a reliable tradition" still believes that the general points of
the story may be accepted: "All it knows of him (Jesus) is that
he left Judaism, and caused others to do so and leave their true
Jewish religion. He is an enticer who led Israel astray. It
knows him as a sorcerer, or one practicing witchcraft, which was
the common opinion among the Jews even in the time of the Gospel
writers" ("Jesus in the Talmud," 1951, 490). For the last point
made Lauterbach cites Mt. 9.34; 12.24.

[24]Cf. Schürer, *History* 2:462 n.164; J. Parkes, *The Conflict
of the Church and the Synagogue,* 1934, 80-85; W. D. Davies, *The
Setting of the Sermon on the Mount,* 1964, 278-279.

[25]Cf. J. A. T. Robinson, *Redating the New Testament,* 1976,
254-285, esp. 272-275; F. L. Cribbs, "A Reassessment of the Date
of Origin and the Destination of the Gospel of John," 1970.

[26]*Der Bann in der Urkirche,* 1958, 40-42.

[27]Such local conflicts occurred throughout the second half
of the first century. Saul's trip to Damascus with letters from
Jerusalem implies a wider network of controversy (Acts 9.1-2).
For a brief survey of the conflict in the first century between
Judaism and the Church see L. Goppelt, *Apostolic and Post-
Apostolic Times,* 1970, 56-60.

[28]For the widespread contact among early Christians and the
interest various communities took in one another see J. Jervell,
"The Problem of Traditions in Acts," 1972.

[29]The author "was above all a product of the Roman Hellenistic world with its profound interest in religious syncretism
and universalism. He was well versed not only in the Bible and
its traditional Jewish interpretation nor only in the tradition
about Jesus well known to the other New Testament writers, but
also in the religious tendencies and aspirations of his contemporaries" (G. W. MacRae, *Faith in the Word*, 1973, 25), cf.
MacRae, "The Fourth Gospel and *Religionsgeschichte*, 1970, 24;
Schnackenburg, "Origin," 224-225; Smith, "Christianity," 228;
Barrett, *The Gospel according to St John*, 1978, 39; and especially Meeks, "Jew," 167-171.

[30]C. F. Burney can assert that even "the teaching of the
Prologue" would not "need time for its development" (*The Aramaic
Origin of the Fourth Gospel*, 1922, 39).

[31]J. Jocz denies that the conflict between Church and
Synagogue is evident in John on the grounds that this would call
into question the historical value which John demonstrably has
("Die Juden im Johannesevangelium," 1953, 134-135). Granted,
some scholars do indeed think that parts of the author's story
derive from his own experience rather than from traditions about
Jesus (e.g. Martyn, *History*, 81). But to hold that the author
presents his material in order to speak to a later situation is
not necessarily to say that he also composes it. Jocz's view
of the relation between history and interpretation in John is too
simple.

[32]G. Lindeskog, "Jews and Judaism in the New Testament,"
1977-1978, 64.

[33]M. de Jonge, "Jewish Expectations About the 'Messiah' According to the Fourth Gospel," 1973, 263, summarizing the position of R. Schnackenburg, "Die Messiasfrage im Johannesevangelium," 1963.

[34]The view that John is written solely for a Jewish audience
is held in particular by W. C. van Unnik, "The Purpose of St.
John's Gospel," 1959 and J. A. T. Robinson, "The Destination and
Purpose of St. John's Gospel," 1962. For criticism of this hypothesis see C. K. Barrett, *The Gospel of John and Judaism*,
1975, 1-19.

[35]Many scholars believe the references to the feasts as
Jewish (2.13; 5.1; 6.4; 7.2; 11.55) also indicate a non-Jewish
audience (e.g. Moule, *Birth*, 93-94). But it seems unlikely that
even those Gentiles who would be likely to come in contact with
John would need such information. These references are perhaps
best explained if they are seen as a part of the author's use
of the Jewish cult as a witness to Jesus (see below pp. 56-58).
If this is the case then the stress on the feasts being Jewish
is ironical; the opponents' own cherished feasts witness to
Jesus.

[36]Cf. E. F. Scott, *The Apologetic of the New Testament*, 1907, 18-19. J. N. Sevenster says Judaism's "great age" was one of the main features that was attractive to Gentiles (*The Roots of Pagan Anti-Semitism in the Ancient World*, 1975, 217). The reference to ἐν ἀρχῇ in Jn.1.1-2 might be, in part, an appeal to this concern for antiquity.

[37]See R. Lowry, "The Rejected-Suitor Syndrome," 1977, 224.

[38]"The Audience of the Fourth Evangelist," 1977, 343. As Minear hints (p. 354), the phrase is Kierkegaard's, see *Philosophical Fragments*, 1936, 74-93 (cf. Bultmann, *The Gospel of John*, 1971, 559 n.2).

[39]Cf. S. Pancaro, "'People of God' in St. John's Gospel?" 1970, 127-128.

[40]See W. Wiefel, "Die Scheidung von Gemeinde und Welt in Johannesevangelium auf dem Hintergrund der Trennung von Kirche und Synagogue," 1979, 221-223.

[41]So also W. Bauer, *Johannesevangelium*, 1912, 19; E. Grässer, "Die Antijüdische Polemik im Johannesevangelium," 1964, 83, 86-89 and "Die Juden als Teufelssöhne in Johannes 8,37-47," 1967, 169-170.

[42]Cf. F. Mussner, ZΩH, 1952, 59-60, 69-70; Blank, *Krisis*, 1964, 246-251.

[43]G. Baum, *The Jews and the Gospel*, 1961, 127.

[44]Cf. Wiefel, "Die Scheidung," 227; B. S. Easton, *Early Christianity*, 1955, 41-57; and S. L. Guterman, *Religious Toleration and Persecution in Ancient Rome*, 1951, 121-122.

[45]Cf. H. Sasse, "κοσμέω, κτλ.," 894.

[46]Cf. the comment of B. W. Bacon: "The whole object of the Appendix [i.e. Jn. 21] is to so adjust the respective claims to authoritative commission from the risen Christ that room may be left for those of 'the disciple whom Jesus loved' without detriment to the accepted claims of Peter" (*The Fourth Gospel in Research and Debate*, 1910, 200-201). So also D. J. Hawkin, "The Function of the Beloved Disciple Motif in the Johannine Redaction," 1977.

[47]"The Beloved Disciple and the date of the Gospel of John," 1979, 104.

[48]This relation between the Beloved Disciple and the Spirit is particularly evident in their witness to Jesus' death (Jn. 19.35; 1 Jn. 5.6-8), cf. Brown, *The Gospel according to John*, 1966, 1970, 952.

[49]W. C. van Unnik, "A Greek characteristic of prophecy in the Fourth Gospel," 1979, 229.

[50]C. H. Dodd, "Behind a Johannine Dialogue," 1968, 45.

[51]Dodd, "Dialogue," 43. Dodd identifies these Jewish
Christians with the Judaizers encountered by Paul. The precise
relationship, however, is obscure and this identification itself
is questionable (see Schnackenburg, "Origin," 230).

[52]See R. M. Grant, "The Origin of the Fourth Gospel," 1950,
320.

[53]This strong appeal of Judaism to some Christians is evident elsewhere in the NT, especially in Hebrews, though the
method of dealing with it there is very different from that in
John: "In the New Testament the Letter to the Hebrews proves
that in the Church of the second or third generation the hanker-
ing after the Jewish cult could be very strong, and that the
writer has to stress that the Church too has a high priest, an
altar, an oblation, and a tabernacle" (E. Schweizer, *Church
Order in the New Testament*, 1961, 17). Also see Barrett, "Judaizers," 236 for evidence in Ignatius' writings that "some
Christians were adopting a form of Judaism." So the appeal was
a temptation both to return to Judaism and, naturally, to incor-
porate aspects of Judaism into Christianity. Cf. L. Goppelt,
Christentum und Judentum im ersten und zweiten Jahrhundert,
1954, 315-318.

[54]S. Pancaro, *The Law in the Fourth Gospel*, 1975, 293, cf.
W. Gutbrod, "'Ισραήλ, κτλ.," 377-378.

[55]Many scholars find some form of interchange between the
terms οἱ 'Ιουδαῖοι and οἱ Φαρισαῖοι in the Gospel as we have it
(see e.g. Baum, *Jews*, 102; F. Gryglewicz, "Die Pharisäer und die
Johanneskirche," 1978, 148; and Meeks, "Jew," 182 n.72). Thus,
for example, D. M. Crossan comments that the tight structure of
18.28-19.16 "makes us certain that we are dealing with the same
protagonists throughout" ("Anti-Semitism and the Gospel," 1965,
198). It has been suggested, however, that the difference in
these terms reflects different sources (cf. E. Bammel, "'John
did no miracle,': John 10.41," 1965, 197-198; U. C. von Wahlde,
"The Terms for Religious Authorities in the Fourth Gospel,"
1979). That the οἱ Φαρισαῖοι material is earlier than the οἱ
'Ιουδαῖοι, at least in certain stories (e.g. 7.31-36; 8.12-22;
9.13-41), is not unreasonable. However, von Wahlde's arguments
for disentangling these hypothetical sources in 1.19-28 only con-
firm how interwoven the strands now are. In any event, the distinction in terms does pinpoint a shift in *certain* of these
stories as they now stand, as suggested by Bammel (in his course
of lectures on the Johannine literature in the Faculty of Divinity of the University of Cambridge, 1979 and previously). That
is, there is a movement from issues which might be more histor-
ically accurate to those which are most Johannine, i.e. where the
author's thought is most in control of the mode of expression.
But this feature is not limited to οἱ 'Ιουδαῖοι material. For
example, the Sabbath controversy, which is likely to reflect a
historical dispute, uses οἱ 'Ιουδαῖοι (5.10-18). So it could
be argued that in some material the term οἱ Φαρισαῖοι has been
changed to οἱ 'Ιουδαῖοι, though Baum speaks not of a change of

terms but rather a change in the sense of the one term οἱ
'Ιουδαῖοι (*Jews*, 103). Some such shift, then, need not be disputed, even by those who question the use of these terms for
distinguishing sources. But for the purposes of this dissertation
such a shift only emphasizes how interwoven the material is as
we now have it.

[56]Cf. M. H. Shepherd, "The <u>Jews</u> in the Gospel of John,"
1974, 104; Baum, *Jews*, 103, 126.

[57]Barrett, *Judaism*, 68-69, cf. K. L. Carroll, "The Fourth
Gospel and the Exclusion of Christians from the Synagogues,"
1957, 20.

[58]See I. Abrahams, *The Glory of God*, 1925, 42.

[59]Baum, *Jews*, 128, cf. J. Parkes, *Jesus, Paul and the Jews*,
1936, 71-72.

[60]See H. Gollwitzer, "Ausser Christus kein <u>Heil</u>? (Johannes
14,6)," 1967, 180; C. Maurer, "Der Exklusivanspruch des Christus
nach dem Johannesevangelium," 1970, 152-153; cf. S. Wilson,
"<u>Anti-Judaism</u> in the Fourth Gospel?" 1979, 43.

[61]Sandmel finds something of the same phenomenon in Titus
1.13-14: "My own view is that the word *Jewish* here is only an
unimportant bit of name-calling; in Christianity in the second
century, one way to denounce something was to label it Jewish"
(*Anti-Semitism*, 124). It seems that Christians also received
similar treatment, cf. Acts 11.26. This passage in Acts is
interesting in that it may refer to a point of conscious differ-
entiation between Christianity and official Judaism similar to
that which we are finding in John. Here, however, it appears
to be pagans who notice the difference. The fact that the Christians are identified with ὁ χριστός indicates concisely that
there is not only a difference but also a continuity between
Christianity and Judaism. Cf. E. Haenchen, *The Acts of the
Apostles*, 1971, 371.

[62]R. R. Reuther, *Faith and Fratricide*, 1974, 181.

[63]The reference to the Scriptures at 5.39 introduces what
might be considered to be a fourth witness in addition to the
three mentioned in 5.31-37a. Some analyses of ch. 5 divide the
section so that 5.39 goes more closely with what precedes, i.e.
the witnesses, than with the direct attack on the adversaries
which follows (e.g. Brown, *John*, 227-228). But the direct attack begins already in 5.37b, so this fourth witness is set off
from the other three. The difference would seem to be that it
is to this fourth witness that the Jewish opponents consider
themselves to be loyal. They do not receive the other three
witnesses, even when they are favorable towards them, as in the
case of the Baptist (5.35). Now the author claims that even the
witness they do respect actually testifies against them because
it witnesses to Jesus.

[64]Indeed, 5.39 is the clearest expression anywhere in the
NT of the fundamental differences between Jewish and Christian

views of Scripture. "Dieser Satz spricht kurz, ohne nähere Er-
läuterung, ohne Angabe einzelner Stellen, das Schriftverständnis
der christlichen Gemeinde aus und setzt es dem Schriftgebrauch
des Judentums entgegen. Darin spiegelt sich die Auseinander-
setzung zwischen Christentum und Judentum zur Zeit des Evangelisten und darüber hinaus wider" (Schnackenburg, Das *Johannes-*
evangelium, 1971 2:176).

[65] See B. Lindars, *The Gospel of John*, 1972, 348.

[66] For another example of the exercise of such authority in
judging messianic claims see *Sanhedrin* 93b, the judgment of Bar
Koziba (Bar Kochba).

[67] This charge is based on OT law, albeit at one remove, as
Barrett notes: "In the Old Testament it is expressly stated
that one witness is inadequate on a capital charge (Num. 35.30;
Deut. 17.6; cf. Deut. 19.15), but in the Mishnah the application
of the principle is extended (*Rosh Ha-Shanah* 3.1; *Kethuboth* 2.9:
None may be believed when he testifies of himself. . . . None
may testify of himself. These passages deal with particular
cases but appear to apply to them a general principle)" (*John*,
338).

[68] The passages containing explicit polemic in John are 5.37-
47; 6.41-58; 7.14-52; 8.12-59; 9.4; 10.22-39; and 12.37-50. Only
6.25-58 contains no mention of Moses or the Law by the opponents
(see 6.42,52 for their objections), though, as will be seen below (pp. 52-56), Moses and the Torah are certainly not absent
from this passage either.
      In addition to these appeals to Scripture to condemn Jesus,
there are various other indications of the concern of the opponents for the Law and legal purity (cf. 10.34; 12.34; 18.28,31;
19.31).

[69] See J. H. Bernard, *A Critical and Exegetical Commentary
on the Gospel according to St. John*, 1928, 271.

[70] See Pancaro, *Law*, 95-97. Cf. Braun's comment: In the
LXX "the group is used generally for transgression of the revealed
will of God and more specifically for instigation to idolatry"
("πλανάω, κτλ.," 233).

[71] On the issue of false prophecy in the OT cf. J. L. Crenshaw, *Prophetic Conflict*, 1971; F. L. Hossfeld and I. Meyer,
Prophet gegen Prophet, 1973; R. P. Carroll, *When Prophecy Failed*,
1979, esp. 184-198; and T. W. Overhold, *The Threat of Falsehood*,
1970.

[72] For further examples of Dt. 13 used of Christ see W. Horbury, "A Critical Examination of the Toledoth Jeshu," 1970,
226-227.

[73] Cf. Martyn, *History*, 75-81, 158-160. According to Martyn,
in presenting such a charge "John is not dependent on 'Jesus-
tradition,' but rather primarily on his own experience" (p. 81).
However, in view of the number and variety of references asserting

that such a charge was brought against Jesus himself (see W.
Bauer, *Das Leben Jesu im Zeitalter der neutestamentlichen Apokryphen*, 1909, 484-485, and St-B 1:1023-1024), Martyn's claim
that "Jesus-tradition" does not underlie the author's account
is, at the very least, questionable.

[74]Cf. W. F. Howard, *Christianity according to St. John*,
1943, 71.

[75]See Martyn, *History*, 72; A. F. Segal, *Two Powers in
Heaven*, 1977, 214; B. E. Schein, "Our Father Abraham," 1972,
169; J. Bergmann, *Jüdische Apologetik im neutestamentlichen
Zeitalter*, 1908, 81.

[76]W. A. Meeks, *The Prophet-King*, 1967, 56.

[77]Pancaro, *Law*, 91, cf. Meeks, *Prophet-King*, 47-61, and
D. W. Wead, "We have a Law," 1969, 185-189.

[78]"Sie verlangen, auf ihre Autorität zu hören, weil sie
sich allein zur Auslegung der Tora berufen fühlen (vgl. 9,28f).
Wer ihnen widerspricht, zeigt sich anfällig für die Worte eines
Volksverführers oder falschen Propheten. . . ." (Schnackenburg,
Johannes 2:221). Cf. Pancaro, *Law*, 87: "For the Jews and the
Pharisees Jesus is an unauthorized teacher, his teaching is
πλάνη, it is contrary to the Law; for Jesus (for Jn and Christians) is the Revealer and his teaching is the fullness of revelation—it cannot be opposed to the Law" (cf. also p. 538).

[79]Pancaro, *Law*, 503. The central issue of Jesus' identity,
his oneness with God, is brought out by W. Wilson: "Thus,
whether we affirm Jesus to have been condemned as a false Messiah, a false prophet, or a blasphemer—we are still compelled to
conclude that he was proved, in the opinion of the Jews, to be
a false Messiah, a false prophet, or a blasphemer, because he
claimed Divinity" (*An Illustration of the Method of Explaining
the New Testament by the Early Opinions of Jews and Christians
Concerning Christ*, 1838, 25).

[80]Brown describes two forms of messianic expectation:
"According to the 'normal' messianic expectations the Messiah
would be known because he would make his appearance at Bethlehem
(John vii 42; Matt ii 5). But there seems also to have been an
apocalyptic strain of messianic expectation where the Messiah's
presence on earth would be hidden until suddenly he would be
shown to his people. We have an echo of this in John vii 27"
(*John*, 53). The expectation of a hidden Messiah is found in
e.g. 4 Ezra 13.52; *Pseudo-Jonathan* on Micah 4.8; Mk. 8.27-30;
and Justin, *Dialogue with Trypho* 8.4; 90.1; 110.1. Cf. further
St-B 2:339-340; 3:315; 4:766; S. Mowinckel, *He That Cometh*,
1956, 304-308; E. Stauffer, "Agnostos Christos: Joh. ii.24 und
die Eschatologie des vierten Evangeliums," 1956; and F. -M. Braun,
*Jean le théologien. Les grandes traditions d'Israël et l'accord
des écritures selon le quatrième évangile*, 1964, 103-115.

[81]Because the author does not argue for Bethlehem as Jesus'
place of birth some have thought it possible that he did not
believe Jesus was born there. However, it is more likely that

his argument undercuts these expectations precisely because he
and his readers *do* know that Jesus comes from Bethlehem (see
Barrett, *John*, 330 and Brown, *John*, 330). That is, we perhaps
have here an example of the author's "customary ironical style"
(Barrett, ibid.).

[82]These questions concerning Jesus' origin may also allude
to a condemnation of Jesus as a bastard, a point often raised in
Jewish-Christian debate (cf. e.g. *Yebamoth* 4.13 and Origen,
Contra Celsum 1.28; for Tannaitic material see Strack, *Jesus*,
26-28). Such a charge may also lie behind the reference to being
ἐκ πορνείας in Jn. 8.41 (see Brown, *John*, 357 and Barrett,
John, 348), though such an allusion is not explicit and the primary function of the phrase is somewhat different (see Lindars,
John, 328 and below p. 71).

[83]E.g. Brown, *John*, 316 and Schnackenburg, *Johannes* 2:187.
Beside the possible reference to the Sabbath law or the law
against killing, Brown mentions that Jesus' saying could be "a
general denunciation in the style of Jer v 5, ix 4-6, etc"
(ibid.).

[84]The Rabbinic interpretation of the Sabbath law in the OT
was that healing on the Sabbath was forbidden unless life was in
danger (cf. e.g. *Mekilta* on Ex. 13.12-17; see St-B 1:623-629;
Barrett, *John*, 359-360). Jesus has a different interpretation
but this does not necessarily constitute a rejection of the OT
law itself, as some suggest (e.g. Barrett, ibid. 362).

[85]"The knowledge Jesus has of his origin and destiny is
but the result of the knowledge Jesus has of his being (and of
the Father--cf. 7,29!). It is because Jesus is the Son of God
(and knows it) that he can reveal God (by revealing himself)"
(Pancaro, *Law*, 267).

[86]Pancaro's interpretation of this passage seems the best
available but he probably goes too far when he calls the author's
position "a valid juridical argument." Rather, it is a non-
juridical use of the Law to testify to Jesus' relationship with
the Father. Pancaro seems to recognize this when he says that
"Jesus does not bear witness to himself in the ordinary sense
of the expression."

[87]Cf. R. Meyer, "περιτέμνω, κτλ.," 80-81.

[88]Opinion is divided over the identity of the ἐκείνους in
10.35 (see Pancaro, *Law*, for a survey). For the present point
the identity of these beings does not matter since the crucial
point is that they are not God.

[89]See Brown, *John*, 404, adopting the view of R. Jungkuntz,
"An Approach to the Exegesis of John 10.34-36," 1964.

[90]Only explicit references to Scripture are here considered;
many allusions that strengthen the author's case will not be
discussed. For example, for the present point about the opponents the allusion to the wicked shepherds of Ezk. 34 found in
Jn. 10.1-18 is particularly significant (see below p. 106).

[91]Dodd, *The Interpretation of the Fourth Gospel*, 1953, 379.

[92]E. C. Hoskyns, *The Fourth Gospel*, 1940, 503.

[93]"The Old Testament in Controversy with the Jews," 1955, 124.

[94]*Old Testament Quotations in the Gospel of John*, 1965, 96-98.

[95]D. M. Smith, "The Use of the Old Testament in the New," 1972, 57.

[96]"Presentación de Jesús a la luz del A. T. en el Evangelio de Juan," 1976, 520. Contrast E. F. Scott's assertion: "It is doubtful if the evangelist had any first-hand or complete acquaintance with the Old Testament" (*The Fourth Gospel*, 1908, 197), a statement that can only be regarded as a curiosity-piece among modern biblical studies.

[97]See R. Schnackenburg, *The Gospel according to St John*, 1968, 1:123.

[98]In addition to Exodus imagery which will be mentioned later, I find most interesting the possible allusions to wisdom literature (cf. Luzarraga, "Presentación," 518-520; G. Reim, *Studien zum Alttestamentlichen Hintergrund des Johannesevangelium*, 1974, 192-204; G. Ziener, "Weisheitsbuch und Johannesevangelium," 1957, 396-418; 1958, 37-60) and Genesis (Luzarraga, "Presenta-ción," 506-508; Reim, *Studien*, 98-105). As an example of the difficulties in detecting allusions consider the case of Gen. 1-3. Most scholars are agreed that Jn. 1.1 alludes to Gen. 1.1, but the extent of this allusion to Genesis in John is not clear. It has been proposed, for example, that the material concerning Jesus' mother alludes to Eve; that 19.31ff. refers to re-creation, thus alluding to the opening chapters of Genesis; that the garden mentioned in John (18.1,26; 19.41; 20.15) alludes to the garden in Gen. 2 and 3; and that Jn. 20.22 echoes Gen. 2.7 (see E. C. Hoskyns, "Genesis I-III and St. John's Gospel," 1920). While I find such possible allusions edifying, they will play no part in this study. A particularly thorough study of allusions to the OT in John is offered by A. H. Franke in *Das alte Testament bei Johannes*, 1885, though much of this study is taken up with the particular theories of the Tübingen School.

[99]One citation, that in 1.23 concerning John the Baptist, will be left for a later section of this chapter when I discuss the witness of the Baptist (pp. 92-93).

[100]For example, although Isaac is never mentioned by name in John many scholars find an Isaac typology in 3.16 and 19.17 (see Brown, *John*, 147, 917; Braun, *Traditions*, 179-180). Such an allusion may be intended, though J. E. Wood remarks that "it is somewhat surprising to find [in the NT] so few explicit references to any Isaac typology with reference to Christ's death" ("Isaac Typology in the New Testament," 1968, 586). (He notes that "the earliest reference in which Isaac on Moriah is a type of Christ

on Calvary is in Barnabas vii. 3. Thereafter the idea is frequent," ibid. n.2). While such an allusion may be intended it
is not explicit and therefore will not be considered in this
study.

[101]J. MacDonald, *The Theology of the Samaritans*, 1964, 16.

[102]H. Odeberg, "'Ιακώβ," 191-192.

[103]See H. Odeberg, *The Fourth Gospel Interpreted in Its Relation to Contemporaneous Religious Currents in Palestine and the
Hellenistic-Oriental World*, 1968, 152-169.

[104]This reference to the spring/well of ὕδωρ ζῶν and the
internal work of the Spirit may include a polemic against the
Samaritan view of Moses. Cf. this passage from *Memar Marqah*
6.3: "The Divine One planted it ["a fine garden"] and the Glory
tended it and the True One covered it over until Moses came.
This is a well of living water dug by a prophet whose like has
not arisen from mankind. The water in it is from the mouth
of the Divine One. Let us eat to the full of the fruit which is
in this garden and drink of the waters that are in this well. We
do not need to seek it in a place which we are unable to reach.
It is not in heaven; it is not in the crossing of the sea. It is
made in the mouth and in the heart" (J. MacDonald, *Memar Marqah*,
1963, 2:222). On contemporary evaluations of Moses see further
below, pp. 51-56.

[105]*Essais sur la christologie de saint Jean*, 1951, 269-273.

[106]"Joh 12,39-41 Zur christologischen Schriftauslegung des
vierten Evangelisten," 1972, 176; cf. *Johannes* 2:520.

[107]*Jesus Christ in the Old Testament*, 1965, 106.

[108]*Die Erhöhung und Verherrlichung Jesu im Johannesevangelium*,
1970, 219.

[109]Though Schnackenburg says this δόξα is that of the pre-
existent Christ, nevertheless he also admits it is related to
Jesus' earthly ministry: "Jesaja hat nicht unmittelbar die
σημεῖα im Erdenleben Jesu gesehen, sondern den präexistenten
Christus in seiner Herrlichkeit, allerdings als den zu seinem
irdischen Werk Bestimmten" (*Johannes* 2:520).

[110]N. A. Dahl, "The Johannine Church and History," 1976, 108.

[111]F. W. Young has made the point that "when John makes the
statement, ταῦτα εἶπεν ᾿Ησαΐας ὅτι εἶδεν τὴν δόξαν αὐτοῦ, he did
it against the background of considerable previous Jewish speculation concerning Isaiah's vision" ("A Study of the Relation of
Isaiah to the Fourth Gospel," 1955, 221). Dahl has made the
same point, adding to the material given by Young, but he has
also indicated concisely the distinctness of the author's view:
"Within Jewish 'Merkabah mysticism' the vision of the prophet
must have been thought to imply a visionary ascent to heaven.
Traditions of this type are taken over by the Christian apocryphon

'The Ascension of Isaiah,' where they are combined with specifically Christian elements: in his heavenly vision Isaiah also saw the hidden descent and the triumphant ascent of the Savior. In the Fourth Gospel there is no mythological imagery of this type, but the basic idea in 12.41 is akin to that of "The Ascension of Isaiah.' The prophet is supposed to have seen not simply the glory of the pre-existent *Logos asarkos*, but the glory of Christ incarnate and crucified. In the context of John 12 there can be no doubt that this is the meaning" ("Church," 107-108).

[112] Hanson suggests, like Lindars, that the first reference to joy might be a vision of the future, perhaps referring to Gen. 17.17, but unlike Lindars he takes the second rejoicing as a vision of the pre-existent Christ, perhaps "when he recognizes the pre-existent Word in one of the three angels" in Gen. 18 (*Jesus*, 126).

[113] For such views, and the picture of Abraham in general, see, along with the commentaries: St-B 2:525-526; J. Bowker, "Origin," 402 n.1; Braun, *Traditions*, 177-178; Dahl, "Church," 110; J. Jeremias, "'Αβραάμ," 8; F. Manns, "*La vérité vous fera libres*", 1976, 107-146, esp. 143-145; H. Lona, Abraham in *Johannes 8*, 1976, 295-304.

[114] Ἑώρακας is superior to ἑώρακέν σε because it has stronger manuscript support, is more in keeping with the character of the Jewish opponents who would assume the superiority of Abraham, and because the shift to ἑώρακέν σε is easily explained as a harmonization with 8.56. See B. M. Metzger, A Textual Commentary on the Greek New Testament, 1971, 226-227.

[115] G. Delling, "ἡμέρα," 951.

[116] Cf. H. Leroy, Rätsel und Missverständnis, 1968, 84-87. Lindars rejects this interpretation: "But this interpretation (in spite of its wide support among modern critics) is excluded, if Abraham has already had the joy of seeing the vision fulfilled, as argued above. Hence we must take it to mean 'my time (era)' (so AG, p. 348a) [= BAGD 4.a., 347c]" (*John*, 335). As has been noted, this view that the author has in mind Abraham rejoicing in Paradise in the time of Jesus seems inappropriate to the point at issue in 8.56-58, namely, Jesus' own pre-existence.

[117] Cf. St-B 2:561 and Meeks, Prophet-King, 294-295.

[118] See e.g. P. Borgen, "God's Agent in the Fourth Gospel," 1968; E. R. Goodenough, By Light, Light, 1969; Meeks, Prophet-King, and "Moses as God and King," 1968; J. Jeremias, "Μωυσῆς," 850-864; and M. R. D'Angelo, Moses in the Letter to the Hebrews, 1979, 95-149.

[119] Bread from Heaven, 1965, 61-67.

[120] "Jew," 176. Meeks' observation applies more widely than the possible homiletical pattern in Jn. 6; e.g. the a fortiori arguments would be included.

[121]With the exception, which I share, that John is not written against Docetism (*History*, 127 n.188).

[122]This concern with the present call of God is evident in the change of tense from δέδωκεν to δίδωσιν (see Borgen, *Bread*, 61-67, 172-173), and by the shift from αὐτοῖς to ὑμῖν (see Reim, *Studien*, 14). "By these changes Jesus indicates that the OT is being fulfilled now in his own work" (Brown, *John*, 262).

[123]Martyn does believe midrash is used in John to testify to Jesus but he attributes this to the Signs Source (*History*, 118).

[124]Somewhat analogous is von Campenhausen's assertion that, in presenting his opponents' appeal to Scripture, the author is attempting to show that Scripture itself is ambiguous. It cannot, therefore, be an unambiguous 'sign' used to gain criteria by which one can be certain of recognizing revelation and evaluating it correctly (*The Formation of the Christian Bible*, 1972, 57; cf. Bultmann, *John*, 228). Like Martyn, von Campenhausen thinks the author is using Scripture to neutralize the appeal to Scripture. As we have seen, the appeal to Scripture for criteria to judge religious claims is an important feature in the description of the opponents (pp. 29-33). But the author does not deny that Scripture provides such criteria. Rather, he thinks his opponents have missed them. The author is more favorably disposed toward objective criteria than is compatible with the existentialism of von Campenhausen and Bultmann. But this is not to say that these scholars are entirely wide of the mark. For the author, the signs, including Scripture *are* ambiguous in the sense that they are open to various interpretations. But they do testify to Jesus, at least for those who have a heart that wills God's will (7.18) and who are illuminated by the Spirit. Thus, the author appeals to objective criteria, in particular the tradition he holds in common with his opponents. Whether or not they are able to appreciate his appeal to Scripture depends, in his eyes, on their internal disposition. I will return to this matter, since a very important aspect of the author's polemic is his attack against the inner disposition of the opponents. This inner disposition is characterized by a self-assurance that is related to their belief that they have unambiguous criteria. The author's attack on this attitude, however, is not a rejection of objective criteria.

[125]Cf. J.-N. Aletti, "Le discours sur le pain de vie (Jean 6). Problèms de composition et fonction des citations de l'Ancien Testament," 1974.

[126]Cf. J. P. Miranda, *Der Vater, der mich gesandt hat*, 1972, 308-388.

[127]J. J. Enz suggests John is modeled on the whole of Exodus ("The Book of Exodus as a Literary Type for the Gospel of John," 1957) while R. H. Smith concentrates on the first twelve chapters of Exodus, comparing Jesus' signs with those of YHWH/Moses ("Exodus Typology in the Fourth Gospel," 1962). See further, A. Piper, "Unchanging Promises," 1957, esp. 12-13, 20-21,

and R. E. Nixon, *The Exodus in the New Testament*, 1963. H.
Sahlin devotes the larger part of his work *Zur Typologie des
Johannesevangelium*, 1950, 8-73 to going through John chapter by
chapter suggesting elements of Exodus typology. Of the books
dealing with Moses, that by T. F. Glasson (*Moses in the Fourth
Gospel*, 1963) is particularly rich in suggestions of Exodus motifs in John. See also Luzarraga, "Presentación," 508-515.

[128]Cf. Brown, *John*, 32-34; Glasson, *Moses*, 65-73.

[129]Cf. Glasson, *Moses*, 48-59; Hoskyns, *Gospel*, 367-368;
Brown, *John*, 322. It is not certain, however, that there is a
quotation here from the OT. St. Chrysostom, for example, puts
a full stop after γραφή (*John*, Hom. 51.1), although he is not
followed by modern commentators (see Lindars, *John*, 299). Cf.
Reim, *Studien*, 56-88.

[130]R. Morgan, "Fulfillment in the Fourth Gospel," 1957, 161-
162. The symbol of the vine is so general that it is impossible
to limit it to its use in Exodus imagery, see Brown, *John*, 669-
672.

[131]Glasson, *Moses*, 95-96; Meeks, *Prophet-King*, 307-313.
Like the vine image, the shepherd image is very rich, see J. G.
S. S. Thomson, "The Shepherd-Ruler Concept in the Old Testament
and Its Application in the New Testament," 1955; Schnackenburg,
Johannes 2:371-372; S. Amsler, *L'ancien testament dans l'église*,
1960, 42.

[132]Glasson, *Moses*, 96-98; Brown, *John*, 61-63. This image is
left vague by the author and he probably intends to allude to a
number of the OT uses of the lamb image, cf. Amsler, *L'ancien*,
41-42 and Barrett, "The Interpretation of the Old Testament in
the New," 1970, 406.

[133]The light would be a reference to the pillar of fire, cf.
R. A. Henderson, *The Gospel of Fulfilment*, 1936, 101.

[134]See Ziener, "Weisheitsbuch" for the suggestion of direct
links between John, Exodus and the Wisdom of Solomon.

[135]*Biblical Exegesis in the Apostolic Period*, 1975, 152.

[136]*God Who Acts*, 1952, 63.

[137]Cf. R. V. G. Tasker, *The Old Testament in the New Testament*, 1954, 56-58; L. Morris, *The New Testament and the Jewish
Lectionaries*, 1964, 64-72; Morgan, "Fulfillment," 155-156; F.
Mussner, "'Kultische' Aspeckte im Johanneischen Christusbild,"
1967; J. T. Williams, "Cultic Elements in the Fourth Gospel,"
1980; Bowman, *Jews*, 41-43.

[138]My inclusion of these verses from ch. 12 at this point reflects a well known feature of the Gospel. Certain events associated in the Synoptics with the Passion are found elsewhere in
John, the most obvious example being the cleansing of the Temple.
A further example might be Jesus' trial. E. Bammel suggests

Jn. 11.45-54 represents the trial of Jesus ("'Ex illa itaque die
consilium fecerunt . . .'," 1970) while A. E. Harvey believes
Jesus' trial is the subject of the entire Gospel (*Jesus on Trial*,
1976). Cf. A. Trites' suggestion that in Jn. 1-12 Jesus' ministry
is presented as a lawsuit and in Jn. 13-17 a post-resurrection
lawsuit is evident (*The New Testament Concept of Witness*, 1977,
78-122).

[139]Zeph. 3.15-20 mentions the King gathering Israel together
and thus the reference a few verses earlier in John to Jesus'
death gathering "into one the children of God who are scattered
abroad" (11.52) may also be a part of the author's presentation
of Jesus as King. Cf. D. Marzotto, *L'unità degli uomini nel vangelo di Giovanni*, 1977, 37-96 for other Jewish material concerning the gathering of Israel.

[140]See B. Lindars, *New Testament Apologetic*, 1961, 99 n.2.
J. Beutler believes the quote comes from Ps. 42 ("Psalm 42/43
im Johannesevangelium," 1978, 35-38). He suggests that a midrash on Pss. 42,43 lies behind Jn. 11.33,35,38; 14.1-9,27. Such
a non-explicit use of the OT is outside the scope of this present
study, but if Beutler's suggestion were accepted it would add
another form of the author's use of Jewish exegesis to that already noted with regard to Jn. 6.

[141]See e.g. A. Dauer, *Die Passionsgeschichte im Johannesevangelium*, 1972, 300.

[142]The lack of reference to ἵνα πληρωθῇ makes it uncertain
whether the author considers the Psalm material in 12.27 as
actually spoken about Christ, let alone by him.

[143]Cf. V. C. Pfitzner, "The Coronation of the King - Passion
Narrative and Passion Theology in the Gospel of St. John," 1976,
6-7.

[144]If Ps. 22 (21) were regarded as messianic among the Jews
then obviously its use by Christians would more directly testify
to Jesus' identity as Messiah. However, according to Freed
(*Quotations*, 102 n.1) this Psalm was not so used apart from the
Rabbis. Thus it must remain uncertain whether its use here would
be understood by Jewish opponents as a *direct* affirmation that
Jesus is the Messiah. If not, then the witness to Jesus' identity is more indirect, i.e. this appeal to the OT indicates that
all that Jesus suffered was in fulfillment of Scripture and in
his suffering he is like the righteous sufferer of the Psalms.

[145]G. Bampfylde has argued at length that the ἵνα clause
should be taken with what precedes instead of what follows
("John XIX 28," 1969). However, the grammar does not necessarily
support this interpretation (BDF 478 suggests the ἵνα clause is
subordinant to what follows it) and the use of the singular ἡ
γραφή is evidence against Bampfylde's interpretation (see Barrett,
John, 553). Since a text from the OT is ready to hand it does
seem best to take the ἵνα clause with what follows it. However,
we may follow Brown's suggestion that the two interpretations
should not be too sharply separated (*John*, 908). His translation

is intended to be sufficiently ambiguous to include both suggested meanings: "in order to bring the Scripture to its complete fulfillment."
     If this word διψῶ had not explicitly been referred to as a
fulfillment of Scripture then an allusion at this point would
have been evident, but the author's own intention would have been
far less clear. This text may legitimate the search for OT allusions in John, even if such a search is not a part of this
dissertation.

[146]For other possible passages, all of them from the Psalms,
see Hoskyns, *Gospel*, 632.

[147]The Exodus passage is the more likely reference rather
than Num. 9.12, even though they are very close (see Freed,
Quotations, 113).

[148]These allusions to the Passover include the reference to
hyssop (19.29) and the flow of blood (19.34), see J. M. Ford,
"'Mingled Blood' from the Side of Christ (John xix. 34)," 1969,
338.

[149]Some scholars think the original reference was to the
Psalm, which was later overlaid with the Exodus theme, see Bultmann, *John*, 677 n.1; Lindars, *John*, 590; *Apologetic*, 96; Schacken-
burg, *Das Johannesevangelium*, 1975, 3:342.

[150]The actual form of Zech. 12.10 used is unclear, see Barrett, *John*, 559.

[151]Schnackenburg offers a number of observations concerning
the significance of ὄψονται which suggest that "scheint bei den
'Aufschauenden' doch zuerst an die Glaubenden gedacht zu sein.
Die Juden sind davon nicht ausgenommen, wenn auch nicht allein
gemeint" (*Johannes* 3:344).

[152]Most scholars follow P. Gardner-Smith in rejecting the
view that John is directly dependent on the Synoptics (*Saint
John and the Synoptic Gospels*, 1938), the most notable exception
being Barrett (see *John*, 42-54). Cf. Kysar, *Evangelist*, 54-66
for a survey of opinion concerning the nature of the traditions
the four Gospels may have shared.

[153]Cf. Amsler, *L'ancien*, 44 and Barrett, "The Old Testament
in the Fourth Gospel," 1947.

[154]A. Sand, "'Wie geschrieben steht. . . .' Zur Auslegung
der jüdischen Schriften in den urchristlichen Gemeinden," 1972,
354.

[155]See Gollwitzer, "Heil," 179 for a list of 13 contrasts
between Jesus and Torah/Judaism (e.g. he begins by saying that
for the author, "Nicht die Tora ist präexistent, sondern Jesus;
nicht die Tora ist μονογενής, aus Gott gezeugt, sondern
Jesus. . . .).

[156]Meeks, *Prophet-King*, 288. Parkes notes that this feature
is common to the Synoptics as well: "there is in every source

[i.e. in each of the four Gospels] a contradiction. The main-
tainance of the *Law* and its abrogation stand side by side"
(*Jesus*, 55).

[157]E.g. J. Jeremias, "Μωυσῆς," 873; Lindars, *John*, 98.

[158]*Interpretation*, 82. J. E. Carpenter, for example, assumes
Jesus brings an entirely new truth from heaven, (*The Johannine
Writings*, 1927, 261-262). See further e.g. Amsler, *L'ancien*,
36; Dahl, "Church," 107; Dauer, *Passionsgeschichte*, 302-303;
Lindeskog, "Anfänge des jüdisch-christlichen Problems," 1978,
269; J. Painter, <u>John</u>: *Witness and Theologian*, 1975, 32-33;
Howard, *Christianity*, 30; R. H. Smith, "Typology," 341 n.32.
An interpretation of the entire Gospel in the light of 1.17 is
provided by K. Haacker in *Die Stiftung des Heils*, 1972. He
characterizes the relation between Jesus and Moses as both a
contrast and a similarity: "das Werk Moses (genauer: die Frucht
seines Wirkens) steht im Gegensatz zum Werk Jesu, aber die Funktion Moses und die Funktion Jesu sind vergleichbar. . . . Jesus
ist ein Stifter (wie Mose), aber er bringt die neue Stiftung"
(p. 35).

[159]"Moses," 641.

[160]Cf. Smith, "Use," 57 and Bultmann, *John*, 78-79.

[161]Cf. above (pp. 27-28) concerning the view of the Temple
in Jn. 2.14-18. The other major reference to the Temple (ὁ
τόπος, 11.48) refers to Jesus' popularity as a threat to the
existence of the Temple. There is no charge made that Jesus opposes the Temple. Rather, the Temple is God's house and Jesus
is zealous of it.

[162]Various suggestions have been made as to the nature of
this Samaritan ignorance. Bernard, for example, says: "The
Athenian inscription 'Αγνώστῳ θεῷ quoted in Acts 17.23 provides
no parallel to the ignorance of the Samaritans. The Samaritans
knew, as the Athenians professedly did not know, the Name of the
God to whom they erected their altar on Mount Gerizim; but their
ignorance was an ignorance of His cháracter and purposes" (*John*,
147). Schnackenburg suggests: "The Samaritans . . . do not
possess true knowledge of God; their worship rather grew out of
national and political ambitions" (*John* 1:435). Neither of
these suggestions is satisfactory. Perhaps Barrett is to be
followed when he says simply that the Samaritans were outside the
main stream of revelation (*John*, 237).

[163]For explicit references to Paul in this regard see Baum,
Jews, 267; Brown, *John*, 225; Bultmann, *John*, 79, 268 n.4.

[164]Cf. Cribbs, "Reassessment," 47-48; Wilson, "Anti-Judaism,"
36; Enz, "Exodus," 212 n.19; Luzarraga, "Presentación," 498.

[165]"The Fathers of the Church and the Old Testament," 1975,
31.

[166]Cf. A. T. Hanson, *The New Testament Interpretation of
Scripture*, 1980, 97-109, a response to de la Potterie's suggestion

("Χάρις paulinienne et χάρις johannique," 1975) that χάρις means
the gift of revelation in Christ rather than a description of
the substance of that revelation. To agree with Hanson that the
OT is "a genuine revelation of God's character as full of mercy
and truth" (p. 104) is not necessarily to agree with him that
for the author of John all revelation in the OT was of Jesus the
λόγος (pp. 103-104). Cf. M. D. Hooker, "The Johannine Prologue
and the Messianic Secret," 1975, 53; Lindars, *John*, 95; A. M.
Ramsey, *The Glory of God and the Transfiguration of Christ*, 1949,
61.

[167]There are, of course, others in the OT who are said to
have seen and/or heard God (see e.g. Gen. 12.7; 18.1; 32.30;
Ex. 6.3; Is. 6.1; Amos 7.7; 9.1, Ezk. 10.18-19; 11.22-23; 43.4,7;
Job 42.5), but Moses was considered exceptional. For example,
according to Num. 12.6-8 Moses' experience of hearing the voice
and seeing the form of YHWH was a repeated occurrence and different from the experience of the prophets (cf. Dt. 34.10).
So this unique place of Moses in the traditions about theophanies, along with the reference to Moses in Jn. 5.45-47, and the
place of the Law in this controversy (5.16-18) indicate a probable reference here to the witness at Sinai.

[168]Jn. 5.37 may also include a denial of the very possibility
"that there could be *direct* sight or hearing of God" (Lindars,
John, 229; cf. Brown, *John*, 225; against Pancaro, *Law*, 230).
The main argument in favor of this interpretation is the clear
expression of such a belief elsewhere in the Gospel (1.18; 6.46),
though these texts are modified by others which affirm that God
is visible in Jesus (12.45; 14.9; 15.24; 17.24). But even if
there is such a denial, for the author's argument to be sound
at 5.37 he must assume that, while God was not literally, directly visible at Sinai, nevertheless, he did reveal himself
there in some sense. The author's point in this passage is
not to reject the view that God revealed himself to Moses and
in the Scripture, but rather to reject the claim of the opponents that they are the heirs of this revelation.

[169]The literary aspect of Jn. 8.31-59 has been the subject
of two full-scale works. Lona (*Abraham*) has applied structur-
alist theory, while G. L. Bartholomew ("An Early Christian
Sermon-Drama: John 8:31-59," 1974) analyzes the story as a
drama designed to provoke the Jews within the Christian community (p. 119) by depicting their alienation from Jesus.

[170]Other editions number this text 5.19. Charles notes that
the Rabbis compare Jesus to Balaam, in which case the Rabbis
would be bringing the same charges against Jesus and his followers as John brings against his Jewish opponents. Another such
connection would be present in 5.22 when the disciples of Balaam
are referred to as men of "blood and deceit" (cf. Ps. 55.23),
if, as Charles suggests, this text is used elsewhere of Balaam,
who perhaps represents Jesus (ibid.). That Balaam is used by
the Rabbis to refer to Jesus is affirmed by Bammel ("Origins,"
323) and denied by Lauterbach ("Jesus," 503-510).

[171]Cf. Schnackenburg's comment: "Der Gedanke, dass Israel
als Bundesvolk der (erstgeborene) Sohn Gottes ist, begegnet
häufig im AT (vgl. Ex 4,22; Dt 14,1; 32,6; Jr 3,4.19; 31,9;
Is 63,16; 64,7)" (*Johannes* 2:285).

[172]Some interpreters would question whether the author accuses the opponents of being children of the devil in that they
think the phrase ἐκ τοῦ πατρὸς τοῦ διαβόλου refers to the father
of the devil (cf. e.g. Conzelmann, "ψεῦδος, κτλ.," 602; Bultmann,
John, 318). There is no doubt that this is the proper translation of the phrase according to its grammar (see BDF 268.2).
However, to speak of the devil's father is to introduce a concept
found nowhere else in either OT or NT, although it is found in
later Gnosticism. The uniqueness of the idea would argue caution in accepting such an interpretation. As always, the most
important consideration in interpretation is the larger context.
Conzelmann appeals to the context as follows: "The Jews do
not descend from the devil but from the devil's father. This is
obviously an *ad hoc* construction designed to work out the analogy.
On the one side we find God, His Son, and the children of God,
while on the other side we have the father of the devil, the
devil as antichrist rather than antigod, and the children.
Naturally the father of the devil has no concrete function"
(ibid.). Conzelmann here admits that the idea of the devil's
father is a bolt of lightning from a clear sky that strikes nothing, but he attempts to find the reason for its introduction
here from the shape of the analogy. It is possible, however, to
understand the analogy differently and more in keeping with the
author's thought in general and the present context in particular. This alternative interpretation would find, first, on the
one side God, the father of children, and on the other side the
devil who is also the father of children. Secondly, on the one
side there is Christ the speaker of truth, and on the other side
there is the devil, the liar. Thus, the devil stands over
against both the Father and the Son, a notion that harmonizes
well with the Johannine view of the unity of the Father and the
Son. This unity is even evident in the immediate context in that
the Jews are seen as standing over against both God (8.42,47)
and Jesus (8.42-43,45-46). This interpretation would take τοῦ
διαβόλου as an appositive, in spite of the inappropriate article
before πατρός (cf. Acts 12.12 for an example of double articles
in an appositive). This would serve the context better since
the topic is the opponents' father, not the devil's (8.38,41).
Such an interpretation is followed by most commentators. Barrett thinks that 1 Jn. 3.8 "puts the interpretation beyond doubt"
and suggests that "the awkwardness is probably due to the fact
that John is forcing the negative parallel with Jesus and his
Father" (*John*, 349).

[173]De la Potterie, *La vérité dans saint Jean*, 1977, 919.
Similarly, W. Kern, "Der symmetrische Gesamtaufbau von Jo 8,12-
58," 1956, 452.

[174]The ἀρχή seems to be different for the two. Jesus is the
agent of creation (1.3) while the devil's nature, as it is here
described, does not go back before mankind's existence since he
is called ἀνπρωποκτόνος. Most commentators see a reference here

to the Fall (e.g. Barrett, *John*, 349; Schnackenburg, *Johannes* 2:287), but some (e.g. Brown, *John*, 349; Dahl, "Der Erstgeborene Satans und der Vater des Teufels (Polyk. 7.1 und Joh 8.44)," 1964) see a reference to Cain's slaying of Abel. This is less likely, however, since it requires an emended text (see Lona, *Abraham*, 281-284) and, as de la Potterie notes, "de telles spéculations sont certainement étrangères au texte actuel, qui concentre toute son attention sur l'action néfaste (et intérieure) du *diable* sur les Juifs. Quand Jean parle de Caïn (1 Jn 3,12), c'est pour montrer qu'il était sous l'empire du Mauvais" (*La vérité*, 923 n.43). Furthermore, the death in view is primarily spiritual death. Since in John life is defined as knowledge of God and Jesus (17.3), the falling away from God at the beginning is a more appropriate reference than a particular action later (Cain murdering Abel) which was itself a result of the Fall. In rejecting Jesus the opponents show themselves to be alienated from God, in the realm of death, the realm of the devil.

[175]Hoskyns, *Gospel*, 394. A reference to the fall of the devil is probably not in view here, cf. Hoskyns, ibid.; G. Stemberger, *La symbolique du bien et du mal selon saint Jean*, 1970, 95 n.20; 128 n.8; de la Potterie, *La vérité*, 927.

[176]Cf. Bultmann, "ἀλήθεια, κτλ.," 245-246; *John*, 321 *et passim*; Schnackenburg, *Johannes* 2:288; J. M. Boice, *Witness and Revelation in the Gospel of John*, 1970, 151-152; Stemberger, *La symbolique*, 119.

[177]De la Potterie, *La vérité*, 925, 926 n.47 *et passim*; Pancaro, *Law*, 99-100; Beutler, *Martyria*, 1972, 323-324.

[178]There is no agreement as to the significance of ἐκ τῶν ἰδίων. De la Potterie seems to provide the most satisfactory interpretation when, after a survey of the use of ἴδιος and ἐκ in John he concludes, "ἐκ τῶν ἰδίων signifie donc que le mensonge est ce qu'il y a de plus 'propre' (ἴδιος) au diable; quand il 'ment', il tire ce mensonge *de lui-même*; ἐκ τῶν ἰδίων est l'équivalent de ἐξ ἑαυτοῦ (cf. le v.44e: ἐν αὐτῷ)" (*La vérité*, 929 n.63).

[179]Cf. Westcott, *The Gospel according to St. John*, 1908, 2: 21-22.

[180]However, to take αὐτοῦ as masculine is also somewhat harsh since one would have expected, if not ὁ πατήρ τῶν ψεύστων, at least a plural (αὐτῶν) to go along with the ἐστέ at the beginning of the verse.

[181]Cf. A. Feuillet, *Le mystère de l'amour divin dans la théologie johannique*, 1972, 35-38, and below pp. 174-176.

[182]Cf. M. Vellanickal, *The Divine Sonship of Christians in the Johannine Writings*, 1977, 260.

[183]G. Schrenk, "πατήρ, κτλ.," 1002.

[184]Cf. Walter, *L'incroyance des croyants selon saint Jean*, 1976, 94.

[185]The motif of the opponents' questioning is closely related to the motif of the enigmatic saying. By presenting
Jesus' revelation as incomprehensible the author shows the distance between Jesus and mankind, as well as the superiority of
the community which now, through the Spirit, understands. Cf.
Leroy, *Rätsel*, esp. 171-188 and Meeks, "Man from Heaven," 1972.
The enigmatic sayings in John are comparable to the parables in
the Synoptics, especially in their characteristic paradox and
the need for humble openness before them. Cf. J. D. Crossan,
In Parables, 1973, e.g. 119-120.

[186]Cf. F. J. Moloney, "From Cana to Cana (John 2:1-4:54) and
the Fourth Evangelist's Concept of Correct (and Incorrect)
Faith," 1980.

[187]Cf. Brown, *John*, 87 and R. F. Collins, "The Representative
Figures of the Fourth Gospel - I," 1976, 36.

[188]Bultmann (*John*, 103-104) and Schnackenburg (*John* 1:315)
understand Nathanael's difficulty over Jesus' association with
Nazareth as due to that village's obscurity and insignificance.
It is more likely that his problem was the same as that of the
opponents', namely, the Messiah was not expected to come from
Nazareth. Such a concern for the Scriptures is indicated in
1.45, even if it is not implied in the reference to the fig tree
in 1.48 ("There is no basis for the common view that Nathanael
was sitting under the fig-tree to study Scripture (a supposed
practice of the scribes)," C.-H. Hunzinger, "συκῆ, κτλ.," 753
n.25, cf. J. R. Michaels, "Nathanael under the Fig Tree," 1966,
183).
     It is difficult to know how Nathanael's question, "Can any-
thing good come out of Nazareth?" should be read. Often it is
simply assumed that it has a pejorative tone. But this is not
necessarily the case. According to Westcott (*John* 1:55), some
of the Fathers took it as affirmative, as meaning something good
could come from Nazareth. It is perhaps best to see it as indicating indecision. He has reason to question whether Jesus is
the Messiah, but he is open to the possibility, as his subsequent
action and its resulting confession show. It is this openness
and docility which distinguishes Nathanael; it may be evident
even in his initial question.

[189]Against Gutbrod, "'Ισραήλ," 385: "At 1:47 Nathanael is
called an ἀληθῶς 'Ισραηλίτης, ἐν ᾧ δόλος οὐκ ἔστιν. Why he is
described thus is unimportant."

[190]Many commentators take ἀληθῶς as an attributive and trans-
late: true Israelite (e.g. Bultmann, *John*, 104 n.4). This interpretation has been challenged by J. Painter in "Christ and
the Church in John 1,45-51," 1977, 360 (reversing his position
in *John*, 48). He says "what is said about (περί) Nathanael is
that 'Truly *he is* (implied) an Israelite in whom there is no
guile.'" Furthermore, Painter says, "There is no evidence that
John regards Nathanael as the true Israelite and therefore as
the model of the true Israel (believers). Rather he is really a
blunt and guileless Israelite." Painter's rejection of Nathanael's function as a representative figure ignores the use of

the term Ἰσραήλ in John, the context of the Nathanael story,
and most of all his character in distinction to that of the
Jews. Nevertheless, he may well be correct that ἀληθῶς must be
taken adverbially. But even if this is the case, the difference
between taking ἀληθῶς as an attributive or as an adverb is
"negligible" (Pancaro, Law, 293 n.19).

[191]"If δόλος is given the sense of ψεῦδος, the designation
of Nathanael as 'Israel' in whom there is no δόλος can perhaps
be related to Jn 8,44.55, where the Jews are denied the right to
call themselves children of Abraham or of God because they are
characterized by ψεῦδος (unbelief and hatred for Jesus and his
revelation) like their father, the devil. The characteristic of
the new Israel is its love for the ἀλήθεια Jesus is and brings"
(Pancaro, Law, 304). Cf. also the suggestion of M.-E. Boismard
that δόλος might have the sense of religious idolatry (Du
baptême à Cana (Jean 1.19-2,11), 1956, 96-97).

[192]Cf. e.g. Bultmann, John, 69 n.2; W. Michaelis, "ὁράω,
κτλ.," 361-366.

[193]So e.g. Barrett, John, 185; Brown, John, 88; S. S. Smalley,
John - Evangelist and Interpreter, 1978, 218.

[194]See Schnackenburg, John 1:426 and cf. A. Jaubert, Ap-
proches de l'Evangile de Jean, 1976, 140-146.

[195]Cf. F. F. Bruce, The Time is Fulfilled, 1978, 39; Mac-
Donald, Theology, 205; H. G. Kippenberg, Garizim und Synagoge,
1971, 312-313.

[196]Ἀναγγελεῖ is better rendered "explain," cf. 16.13,14,15,
25.

[197]The Samaritan Taheb was primarily a lawgiver and teacher,
a restorer. Cf. MacDonald, Theology, 362-371, esp. 364-365.

[198]Μήτι usually indicates a negative answer but it can also
indicate indecision, cf. BDF 427.2.

[199]The docility presented in the characterization of the
disciples in the first chapters of the Gospel is evident throughout the Gospel, e.g. in such texts as 7.17-18; 10.4; 15.4.

[200]In the second half of the first century there was a sudden
change of opinion in Judaism concerning the value and authority
of the bath qol which may have been due at least in part to the
Christian appeal to divine revelation (see Davies, Paul and
Rabbinic Judaism, 1955, 363-364). In one of the most important
of the texts concerning this change of opinion, Baba Metzia
59b, R. Eliezer b. Hyrkanos is disputing with R. Joshua b.
Hananiah (AD 80-120). The Rabbis do not accept R. Eliezer's
arguments so he performs a series of miracles, but they do not
accept these as proving anything. The story concludes: "Again
he said to them: 'If the halachah agrees with me, let it be
proved from Heaven!' Whereupon a Heavenly Voice cried out: 'Why
do ye dispute with R. Eliezer, seeing that in all matters the

halachah agrees with him!' But R. Joshua arose and exclaimed:
'It is not in heaven' [Dt. 30.12]. What did he mean by this?--
Said R. Jeremiah: That the Torah had already been given at Mount
Sinai; we pay no attention to a Heavenly Voice, because Thou
hast long since written in the Torah at Mount Sinai, *After the
majority must one incline* [Ex. 23.2]." By such stories "the
sources make it abundantly clear that no deliverance of a *bath
qôl* could supersede the authority of the Torah" (Davies, ibid.
214). This text is of interest for its striking testimony to
the importance of the Torah in Judaism (cf. above pp. 25-26).
It is also significantly different from the text in Jn. 12. In
John the issue is the inability to understand the Voice, while
in *Baba Metzia* the Voice is understood, but as a matter of principle it is not accepted. In John there is no indication that
the people would not have accepted if they had understood.
Rather, they do not understand because they have not accepted
Jesus' revelation.

[201]Cf. above n. 13. For the existence of these later
followers see Acts 18.25; 19.1-7; Justin, *Dialogue with Trypho*,
80; and especially *Clementine Recognitions* 1.54.60.

[202]Cf. Mt. 3.1-12; 11.7; 14.5; Mk. 1.5; Lk. 1.14,16; 3.7,15;
7.24-35; Jn. 5.35; Acts 13.24 and Josephus, *Jewish Antiquities*
18.116-119.

[203]Cf. B. Olsson, *Structure and Meaning in the Fourth Gospel*,
1974, 266-272.

[204]Πατήρ: Mt. 64x, Mk. 18x, Lk. 56x, Jn. 137x, Johannine
Letters 18x.

[205]Cf. F. Mussner, *The Historical Jesus in the Gospel of
St John*, 1967.

[206]E. Schweizer (*Ego Eimi*, 1965) and Bultmann (*John*, 225 n.3)
suggest a non-Jewish background, but the use of ἐγώ εἰμι is almost certainly dependent on Jewish usage instead, cf. e.g. P. B.
Harner, *The "I Am" of the Fourth Gospel*, 1970, 6-36, esp. 26-30;
Schnackenburg, *Johannes* 2:62-67, esp. 63-64, and the literature
there cited. There is considerable agreement among scholars
that the closest parallel to the author's use of the absolute
ἐγώ εἰμι is to be found in Isaiah, see Vanderlip, *Christianity
according to John*, 1975, 67.

[207]Harner, *I Am*, 60-61. Harner is here referring only to
the Isaiah passages but his remarks are not inappropriate when
applied to Ex. 3.14 as well.

[208]The textual evidence for the words πρὸ ἐμοῦ is finely
balanced, as implied by the use of brackets (see Metzger, *Commentary*, 230). Their omission would not affect the present discussion.

[209]Bernard (*John*, 353) finds here a reference to messianic
claimants, an interpretation not unlikely nor incompatible with
that which I am suggesting. Bultmann says it refers to "all

pretended revealers of all ages" (*John*, 377), though he admits
"Moses and the other authorities of the OT" would not be in mind
(ibid. 376). Brown (*John*, 393-394), Schnackenburg (*Johannes*
2:366-367), Lindars (*John*, 359), and Robinson ("The Parable of
the Shepherd (John 10.1-5)," 1962) come closest to the view here
offered when they find a reference in this text to the Pharisees,
though the three commentators do not fit this text into the larger framework of the polemic and Robinson is mainly concerned
with sorting out levels of tradition.

[210]Cf. P. W. Meyer, "A Note on John 10.1-18," 1956. Indeed,
Jesus' death is closely related to the ἐγώ εἰμι formula in general for, as J. E. Morgan-Wynne has shown, in John "the cross is
the proof that Jesus is ἐγώ εἰμι" ("The Cross and the Revelation
of Jesus as ἐγώ εἰμι in the Fourth Gospel (Joh. 8.28)," 1980,
223).

[211]Cf. Thüsing, *Die Erhöhung*, esp. 226-233; E. Haenchen,
"Der Vater, der mich gesandt hat," 1963, 215-216.

[212]Cf. C.-J. Pinto de Oliveira, "Le verbe *Didônai* comme expression des rapports du Père et du Fils dans le IVe évangile,"
1965 and O. Battaglia, *La teologia del dono*, 1971.

[213]Cf. 10.38; 12.37; 14.11; 20.30-31. Σημεῖον and ἔργον are
functionally equivalent, see Brown, *John*, 528-529.

[214]Cf. C. Charlier, "L'évangile de l'amour dans la mort,"
1956.

[215]R. T. Fortna, "Christology in the Fourth Gospel," 1975,
504.

[216]The motif of Jesus' origin is closely related to that of
Jesus as the one sent by the Father and the focal point of this
sending is Jesus' death, cf. Miranda, *Der Vater*, 132-147.

[217]The emphasis on the death is evident apart from 19.35 but
obviously this verse makes it all the stronger. While I am not
convinced by the efforts of scholars to find material from the
later controversies interpolated into the Gospel (cf. pp. 189-190
n.13), nevertheless, 19.35 does seem to be such. It is the most
convincing instance because it explicitly represents itself as an
interpolation and it is totally in keeping with what I believe
to have been the nature of the later difficulty. I will argue
in the next chapter that the later opponents were not Docetists,
but they did deny that Jesus, the Christ, the Son of God, died.
These later opponents also appear to have claimed to be true to
the Johannine tradition. If so, then 19.35 would possibly represent the later community underlining the key text of the Gospel
that belies this claim by the later opponents.

[218]Cf. the comment by B. Childs: "The revelation of God is
in terms of his attributes rather than his appearance. Usually
in the Old Testament the goodness of God signifies his benefits
which are experienced by Israel. . . . Of course the usage in
v. 19 is unique and without an exact parallel, but the concern

is clearly to define God's revelation in terms of his activity
toward Israel. Thus along with the display of goodness is the
proclamation of the name. The name of God, which like his glory
and his face are vehicles of his essential nature, is defined in
terms of his compassionate acts of mercy" (*Exodus*, 1974, 596).

[219]H. Conzelmann, "φῶς, κτλ.," 353.

[220]Cf. O. Michel, "μισέω, κτλ.," 691 and Painter, *John*, 73.

[221]Cf. J. Schneider, "ἔρχομαι, κτλ.," 672.

[222]Cf. R. Bultmann, "πιστεύω, κτλ.," 223.

3. JOHANNINE POLEMIC: THE LETTER

[223]"The Idea of Incarnation in First John," 1970, 219-302.

[224]E.g. Kümmel, *Introduction*, 440; cf. Miranda, *Being and the Messiah*, 1977, 196.

[225]Cf. R. Schnackenburg, *Die Johannesbriefe*, 1975, 11: "Er gibt am Beginn (1,1-4) seine Absicht kund, die grundlegende Heilsbotschaft von der Gemeinschaft mit Gott auf Grund der Verbindung mit Jesus Christus zu künden; aber er lässt sich dabei durch die Abwehr der Irrehrer und das Bemühen um innere Festigung der christlichen Gemeinde treiben."

[226]For such material from a somewhat later period see E. Pagels, *The Gnostic Gospels*, 1979, esp. 102-118.

[227]This list is a modified version of that given by H. S. Songer, "The Life Situation of the Johannine Epistles," 1970, 400-402.

[228]"Gedankengang und Grundgedanke des ersten Johannesbriefs," 1892, 171ff. The following is an abbreviated form of this outline, following that presented by Schnackenburg (*Briefe*, 10):

Introduction 1.1-4.
A. 1. Ethical thesis: walking in the light as the true sign
        of fellowship with God 1.5-2.17.
    2. Christological thesis: faith in Jesus as the Christ as
        the basis of fellowship with God 2.18-27.
B. 1. Ethical thesis: doing righteousness as the sign of being
        born of God 2.28-3.24.
    2. Christological thesis: the Spirit which is of God con-
        fesses that Jesus Christ has come in the flesh 4.1-6.
C. Both theses bound together:
    1. Love based on faith 4.7-21.
    2. Faith as the basis for love 5.1-12.
Conclusion 5.13-21.

The strength of this outline lies in its concentration on the themes of belief and behavior. As will emerge from the present study, the relation between these two aspects of Christianity is a central concern in 1 John and thus provides the ground for a good outline.

[229]Cf. e.g. 5.1 with 5.5, and see de Jonge, "The Use of the Word ΧΡΙΣΤΟΣ in the Johannine Epistles," 1970, 67.

[230]Cf. A. Wurm, *Die Irrlehrer im ersten Johannesbrief*, 1903, 9, and Wengst, *Spiegel*, 17.

[231]"ΧΡΙΣΤΟΣ," 71, cf. de Jonge, "Variety and Development in Johannine Christology," 1977, 200-205.

[232]Cf. Wurm, *Die Irrlehrer* for the best presentation of such a hypothesis concerning the false teaching combated in 1 John.

[233]To find people saying "Jesus is not the Christ" within a Christian community is not really so much more peculiar than some saying "Jesus be cursed" (1 Cor. 12.3). So, if we are to envision people actually standing up in Corinth and saying "Jesus be cursed," the possibility of people saying "Jesus is not the Christ" should not be entirely ruled out. It is very unlikely, however, that this was occurring at Corinth. W. C. van Unnik has proposed a more satisfactory interpretation of 1 Cor. 12.3 when he suggests that to say 'Ανάθεμα 'Ιησοῦς is to say something that is true of "a certain phase in Jesus' work of salvation" but is not true as "a pronouncement of what Jesus really *is*" ("Jesus: Anathema or Kyrios (1 Cor. 12.3)?" 1973, 121). Thus it is as improbable in Corinth as it is in the Johannine community(s) that someone is getting up and saying something very obviously unchristian. In both cases the error is probably more subtle.

[234]So Wurm, *Die Irrlehrer*, 24, 53ff. Cf. also C. Clemen, "Beiträge zum geschichtlichen Verständnis der Johannesbriefe," 1905, 275.

[235]*A Critical and Exegetical Commentary on the Johannine Epistles*, 1912, xliv.

[236]*Christ in Christian Tradition*, I, 1975, 79.

[237]Cf. S. de Ausejo, "El concepto de 'carne' aplicado a Cristo en el IV Evangelio," 1958.

[238]Cf. E. Käsemann, "Aufbau und Anliegen des Johanneischen Prologs," 1957, 93.

[239]Cf. E. Käsemann, *The Testament of Jesus*, 1968, 26.

[240]Cf. the comment by Schanz in *Kommentar über das Evangelium des hl. Johannes*, 1885, 41 as quoted by Wurm, *Die Irrlehrer*, 58: "Der Evangelist setzt die menschliche Natur als selbstverständlich voraus und beweist, dass Jesus nicht blosser Mensch war."

[241]Cf. R. Hamerton-Kelly, *Pre-existence, Wisdom, and the Son of Man*, 1973, 202-203, 207.

[242]*Community*, 166 n.230. De la Potterie rejects both Docetism and Monophysitism (*La vérité*, 990 n.254).

[243]If σάρξ here refers to the Eucharist as well as to Jesus' death then this passage would function in the author's polemic by not only declaring life to be found in Jesus' death, but also by emphasizing that this Jesus is present in the Christian community. Thus, it would make more emphatic the claim that the

Christians are the children of God, as opposed to their Jewish
opponents. On the relation between Jesus' death and the Eucharist in this passage see esp. H. Schürmann, "Joh. 6,51c--ein
Schlüssel zur johanneischen Brotrede," 1958.

[244]See e.g. Schnackenburg, *Briefe*, 19-20; Kümmel, *Introduction*, 441-442; Songer, "Situation," 404-405; Wurm, *Die Irrlehrer*,
80-81; Clemen, "Beiträge," 272; and Robinson, *Redating*, 286
n.154 (reversing his earlier position in "Destination," 62-64).

[245]Wengst, *Spiegel*, esp. 24-34. It should be stressed that
only Cerinthus' christological teaching as described in Irenaeus,
Against Heresies 1.26.1 is under consideration. One of the
elements in Cerinthus' position which is not found reflected in
1 John will be mentioned below (n.268).

[246]*The Johannine Epistles*, 1973, 50.

[247]"νόμος, κτλ.," 1086.

[248]"νόμος, κτλ.," 1086, so also de la Potterie, "'Le péché,
c'est l'iniquité' (I Joh., III,4)," 1956.

[249]Ibid. 34. See also Wengst, *Spiegel*, 38ff. and his summary: "Sündlosigkeit ist hier eine Seinsbestimmung und keine
Tatbestimmung" (p. 45).

[250]Ibid. 45, referring to N. Turner, *Grammatical Insights
into the New Testament*, 1965, 151.

[251]See E. M. Yamauchi, "The Descent of Ishtar, the Fall of
Sophia, and the Jewish Roots of Gnosticism," 1978, 170. Yamauchi suggests that "Hellenistic philosophy and astrology provided
Gnosticism with its *anthropology*," (ibid.) which in turn "led
intellectuals, who were not necessarily Gnostics, to reject the
doctrines of the incarnation, the crucifixion, and the resurrection of Jesus in favour of a docetic Christology" (ibid. 171).
Hengel has suggested the same when he says, "the gnostic 'docetism' which did away with the scandal of the death of Jesus on
the cross in the interest of the impassibility of the God of the
philosophers demonstrates that the gnostic systems are secondary
attempts at an 'acute Hellenization' of the Christian creed,
i.e. necessary consequences of a popular influence" (*Crucifixion*,
1977, 16). These suggestions seem to be applicable to the opponents in 1 John in that they are not yet Gnostics in the later
developed sense but are moving in that direction, quite possibly
through the influence of certain aspects of Hellenistic thought.
See K. Weiss, "Die 'Gnosis' im Hintergrund und im Spiegel der
Johannesbriefe," 1973, and cf. A. H. Armstrong, "Gnosis and
Greek Philosophy," 1978, esp. 94-99 and B. Aland, "Gnosis und
Philosophie," 1977.

[252]Cf. C. F. D. Moule, "The Individualism of the Fourth Gospel," 1962; E. Schweizer, "The concept of the church in the gospel and epistles of St. John," 1959, 235-237; J. F. O'Grady,
Individual and Community in John, 1978.

[253]Even a certain elitism may be present in the Gospel itself, see B. Rigaux, "Les destinataires du IVe évangile à la
lumière de Jn 17," 1970, 317-318.

[254]If the same opponents are in view in 2 Jn. as most schol-
ars believe then the opponents did indeed claim to be 'advanced'
Christians (2 Jn. 9). Cf. Robinson, *Redating*, 286 and Marshall,
Epistles, 16.

[255]This recognition of sin is a major contrast between the
author and his opponents for they are *saying* they are sinless
(1.8,10). It may be possible to be sinless in the sense of
keeping the commandments, but to *claim* to be sinless is great
self-deception and pride. So, St. Paul could say his conscience
was clear (1 Cor. 4.4) and yet also say that he had not reached
the goal (Phil. 3.12-14) and, indeed, could call himself the
foremost of sinners (1 Tim. 1.15-16, a Pauline sentiment whether
or not 1 Timothy was written by Paul, see J. N. D. Kelly, *Pastoral Epistles*, 1963, 54-55).

[256]Others holding such a view include A. Klöpper, "Aur Lehrer
von der Sünde im 1. Johannesbrief, Erläuterung von 5,16 - fin,"
1900, 589-590 and G. Forkman, *The Limits of the Religious Community*, 1972, 174.

[257]In 1 John τέλειος/τελειοῦν occurs at 2.5; 4.12,17,18
(twice). It is only used with reference to ἀγάπη/ἀγαπᾶν.

[258]Cf. Jn. 17.11,12,15; 10.28; 6.39.

[259]"Sins Within and Sins Without," 1975.

[260]Scholer, "Sins," 244. Alternatively, it could be evidence
of a particularly clumsy redactor. Actually, 5.17 may of itself
indicate that the author understands sin in more than one sense.

[261]Such a juxtaposition of statements indicating maturity
with those indicating immaturity is not uncommon in early Christian literature, 1 Corinthians being a striking example.

[262]Cf. I. de la Potterie, "La notion de '_commencement_' dans
les écrits johanniques," 1978, 399: "A diverses reprises, face
aux doctrines hétérodoxes, Jean emploie la formule ἀπ' ἀρχῆς pour
rappeler aux chrétiens le début de leur foi: 'depuis le commencement', ils ont entendu le message (2,24 [bis: avec inver-
sion]; 3,11; 2 Jn 6); 'depuis le commencement' ils avaient le
commandement nouveau, celui de s'aimer les uns les autres (2,7;
2 Jn 5)."

[263]This reference to the χρῖσμα might be parallel to the idea
that the λόγος indwells believers. For example, in 2.14 it is
said of the young men: ὁ λόγος τοῦ θεοῦ ἐν ὑμῖν μένει καὶ
νενικήκατε τὸν πονηρόν, and the opposite is said of the opponents:
ψεύστην ποιοῦμεν αὐτὸν καὶ ὁ λόγος αὐτοῦ οὐκ ἔστιν ἐν ἡμῖν
(1.10). But this reference to the λόγος complicates the picture
since it is possible that in 1 John λόγος refers both to the
message they have received and to Jesus himself (see p. 149).

[264]"L'onction du chrétien par la foi," 1959, 44,cf. *La
vérité*, 584-585 and "Commencement," 400-401. So also Marshall,
Epistles, 153-155; E. Malatesta, *Interiority and Covenant*,

1978, 220-225; Brown, *Community*, 140 n.270; and H. Conzelmann,
"'Was von Anfang war'," 1954, 201 n.22. Brown and Conzelmann
are rejecting Käsemann's suggestion that 1 Jn. 2.27 is evidence
that in 1 John religious tradition is in conflict with "die
durch den Geist vermittelte und im Wort des Kerygmas erfolgende
praesentia Christi" ("Ketzer und Zeuge," 1951, 309).

[265]Marshall, *Epistles*, 209 n.19. He also quotes Dodd,
Epistles, 100: "the Church as a whole, speaking through its responsible teachers." Note especially the change to the first
person singular in 2.1-14; 5.13, and cf. 3 Jn. 12 for a similar
claim.

[266]These criteria for discernment were common among early
Christians. They may be characterized as a concern for past
revelation, present conduct, and community benefit. Cf. J. D. G.
Dunn, "Prophetic 'I' - sayings and the Jesus Tradition," 1978,
188-193.

[267]Cf. Houlden, *Epistles*, 13-14. Wengst was of this opinion
also before he wrote *Spiegel*, cf. *Spiegel*, 9-10.

[268]See Wurm, *Die Irrlehrer*, 3. This interpretation has very
important implications for the identity of the false teaching in
view. Above (p. 130) the common view was accepted that 5.6 refutes a christology similar to that represented by Cerinthus in
Irenaeus, *Against Heresies*, 1.26.1. In the same passage, however, St. Irenaeus says Cerinthus, "taught that the world was
not made by the primary God, but by a certain power far separated
from him, and at a distance from that Principality who is supreme
over the universe, and ignorant of him who is above all." There
is no indication that the opponents in 1 John held any such view.
This does not mean that they did not, since the author may have
reasons of his own for not attacking them on such an issue. However, it is improbable that he would not refute such views if
they were held. It would seem best, therefore, to assume such
views were not held by the opponents and, consequently, there is
no exegetical data to suggest that the opponents should be called
Cerinthians. We lack the information necessary to say who they
were or how they were related to Cerinthus, if at all, so the
most that can be said is that they represent a position somewhere
between the author's and that of Cerinthus (cf. esp. Wengst,
Spiegel, 34).
  Aside from Cerinthus, the other major group which might hold
views similar to those of the opponents in 1 John are the
"Docetists" in the letters of Ignatius. Schnackenburg considers
the parallels to be closest between 1 John and the opponents in
Ignatius' letters, but not all that close (*Briefe*, 20-22). He
concludes: "Nach allem müssen wir feststellen, dass sich die
in 1 und 2 Joh abgewehrte Irrlehre mit keiner der uns sonst aus
jener Zeit bekannten häretischen Erscheinungsformen gleichsetzen
lässt, wohl aber mit mehr als einer verwandte Züge aufweist"
(p. 22). So also Brown, *Community*, 105-106 and cf. Hoskyns,
Gospel, 118.

[269]For interpreting αὐτοῦ as referring to the Son see Marshall, *Epistles*, 108 n.1.

[270]Cf. J. E. Weir, "The Identity of the Logos in the First Epistle of John," 1975.

[271]This interpretation of οὗτος as referring to Jesus is followed by a majority of commentators, cf. Marshall, *Epistles*, 254.

NOTES

4. JOHN AND 1 JOHN COMPARED

[272] E.g. Dodd, "The First Epistle of John and the Fourth Gospel," 1937, and H. J. Holtzmann, "Das Problem des ersten johanneischen Briefes in seinem Verhältniss zum Evangelium," 1881-1882, esp. 151-152, believe such evidence indicates there are different authors, while e.g. W. F. Howard, "The Common Authorship of the Johannine Gospel and Epistles," 1947; A. P. Salom, "Some Aspects of the Grammatical Style of 1 John," 1955; R. Law, The Tests of Life, 1909, 339-363; and Brooke, Epistles, i-xxvii, believe it indicates unity of authorship.

[273] The most complete list of such differences known to me is that of J. Moffatt, An Introduction to the Literature of the New Testament, 1918, 590-593. Moffatt's list also appears in a modified form in Marshall, Epistles, 34. I will mention all the differences Moffatt notes and will supplement his discussion with that of other scholars.

[274] Such a lack of appeal to the OT is also characteristic of the letters of Ignatius and Polycarp, in contrast to the practice of Clement of Rome and Barnabas (of Alexandria?) (cf. H. B. Swete, An Introduction to the Old Testament in Greek, 1902, 413-414). If the Johannine literature is to be associated with Asia Minor then this difference among the Apostolic Fathers is particularly interesting.

[275] The Word of the Cross, 1974, 9.

[276] Jn. 16.26-27 refers to the Father hearing the prayer of the disciples, thus nullifying the force of Moffatt's assertion: "There are other indications of a transference to God, in the ep., of functions which the gospel reserves for Christ (e.g. the hearing of prayer, 3.22; 5.14f., cp. Jn. 14.13f.)" (Introduction, 591).

[277] Cf. K. Wengst, Der erste, zweite und dritte Brief des Johannes, 1978, 54; cf. Bultmann, Epistles, 20.

[278] N. Lazure also contrasts the depiction of the Spirit as personal in John but in 1 John as "une puissance divine faissant part au croyant de la communion de vie avec le Père et le Fils" (Les valeurs morales de la théologie johannique, 1965, 117, cf. 93-118). G. Johnston appears to go further and deny that in John πνεῦμα is used as a person; he says it refers to "the power of God in the life and teaching of Jesus, and the power of God and of Christ in the life and doctrine of the Church" (The Spirit-Paraclete in the Gospel of John, 1970, 151). The exact nature of Johnston's view, however, is unclear since he also

says, "the distinction between the paraclete as a person and the
spirit as a power or force seriously distorts the issues from the
beginning" (ibid. 87).

[279]Cf. the remarks of E. F. Scott: "The Spirit is known by
this--that it testifies to the reality of Jesus' earthly life."
The author'(s) thought "all turns on the conviction that the
Spirit which works now is linked with the earthly life of Jesus,
and interprets its meaning" (*The Spirit in the New Testament*,
1923, 210,211).

[280]Dodd, "First Epistle," 142-144; Conzelmann, "Anfang"; G.
Klein, "Das wahre Licht scheint schon," 1971; cf. Marshall,
Epistles, 35-38 and P. Vielhauer, *Geschichte der urchristlichen
Literatur*, 1975, 467-470.

[281]For further elements of future eschatology in John see
Howard, *Christianity*, 109-115.

[282]M. D. Hooker, "John the Baptist and the Johannine Prologue," 1970, 358.

[283]For further criticism of Klein see Kümmel, *Introduction*,
444-445.

[284]See W. E. Sproston, "Satan in the Fourth Gospel," 1980,
309-310.

[285]"A Neglected Factor in the Interpretation of Johannine
Eschatology," 1970, 158.

[286]*Der Glaubende und die feindliche Welt*, 1970, esp. 228-296.

[287]L. Erdozáin comes to a similar conclusion from his study
of σημεῖα in John. Because the σημεῖα can either reveal or con-
ceal it is evident that the author is concerned with the human
heart and his dualism "no es de ninguna manera metafísico y ob-
jetivo, sino moral y subjetivo" (*La función del signo en la fe
según el cuarto evangelio*, 1968, 49). A similar emphasis on
salvation history and morality is found in Lazure, *Les valeurs*,
13-62.

[288]*Weltferner Gott oder Gott der Liebe*, 1977, 84-121, esp.
191-194 on dualism.

[289]O. Böcher has shown that Johannine dualism is most closely
parallel to that found in intertestamental Judaism, including
Qumran, which in turn is building on aspects of OT thought (*Der
johanneische Dualismus im Zusammenhang des nachbiblischen Judentums*, 1965). So also de la Potterie, *La vérité*, 911 and "L'arrière-fond du thème johannique de vérité," 1959, 293-294; J. L.
Price, "Light from Qumran upon Some Aspects of Johannine Theology," 1972, 13-25; J. H. Charlesworth, "A Critical Comparison of
the Dualism in 1QS 3:13-4:26 and the 'Dualism' Contained in the
Gospel of John," 1972; Mussner, ΖΩΗ, 185-186. Y. Ibuki, however,
has added an important qualification when he notes that the
reference to Jesus as the truth can be called a fulfillment of the

OT but it does not exactly parallel Jewish or Gnostic thought;
it is Christian (*Die Wahrheit im Johannesevangelium*, 1972, 360).
The same can be said of the dualism; it is not exactly Jewish
or Gnostic. However, the fact that it can be seen as a development from Jewish thought calls in question the appeal to Gnosticism by those like Schottroff and Langbrandtner, especially as
they must exclude texts from the Gospel that do not agree with
their hypotheses.

[290] The terms are Böcher's (*Dualismus*, 72,76), following B.
Otzen, "Die neugefundenen hebräischen Sektenschriften und die
Testamente der zwölf Patriarchen," 1953, 135.

[291] "Nicodemus and Jesus: Some Observations on Misunderstanding and Understanding in the Fourth Gospel," 1971.

[292] See Böcher, *Dualismus*, 74; D. G. Vanderlip, *Christianity*,
144-145; and Schnackenburg, *Johannes* 2:342.

[293] Much has been written on the relation between divine
sovereignty and human responsibility in Johannine thought. The
best brief discussion known to me is the excursus by Schnackenburg in *Johannes* 2:328-346. Noteworthy is D. A. Carson's conclusion after a major study of the tension between these two
aspects of Johannine thought: "The FG maximizes God's sovereignty in salvation history and in election while simultaneously
demanding that men believe. And supremely, it presents Jesus as
the final demonstration of the way divine predestination and
human freedom under God are joined, not set antithetically
against each other" ("Predestination and Responsibility. Elements of Tension-Theology in the Fourth Gospel against Jewish
Background," 1975, 279--soon to be published).

[294] Cf. G. Panikulam, *Koinōnia in the New Testament*, 1979,
134-135; Vellanickal, *Sonship*, 224-225.

[295] Cf. de la Potterie, *La vérité*; Ibuki, *Die Wahrheit*; and
J. Blank, "Der johanneische Wahrheits-Begriff," 1963.

[296] It is interesting that Qumran, which had a dualistic
framework close to that of the Johannine community, was also
separated from its opponents on the social level, though voluntarily. On Johannine Christianity and sectarianism see Meeks,
"Man from Heaven," and Bogart, *Perfectionism*, 136-141, and cf.
R. Scroggs, "The Earliest Christian Communities as Sectarian
Movement," 1975, 1-23.

[297] Cf. Barrett's comment that "John intended to bind the
church to the apostolic witness; but in other respects he meant
to leave it free" (*Judaism*, 75).

[298] Cf. e.g. E. Käsemann, "The Canon of the New Testament and
the Unity of the Church," 1964, and J. D. G. Dunn, *Unity and
Diversity in the New Testament*, 1977, esp. 372-388.

[299] Dunn finds the unifying factor to be Jesus Christ, more
particularly, the "*unity between Jesus the man and Jesus the*

exalted one" (Unity, 371). He further suggests that this *"centre also determined the circumference"* (ibid. 379). If one single point is to be found which is common to the whole NT then Dunn may have found it. It is questionable, however, whether all of the doctrinal boundaries drawn in ther NT are so closely related to christology. Also, Dunn's suggestion leaves out the matter of ethical boundaries, which in some documents, e.g. 1 John, are inseparable from the doctrinal issues. An alternative way of viewing the unity is to find it in a larger Faith or Vision which consists in a constellation of points which no document represents but which each document reflects to some extent. This alternative view does not view the NT as a collection of different documents that have some specific point in common. Nor does it approach the NT as an entity in itself apart from the Church which is responsible for its existence. Rather, it approaches the NT as a collection of different kinds of documents, none of which attempts to represent its author's thought in any complete or systematic way. It recognizes that for each document there is far more that we do not know about it and its context than that which we do know. On this view, that which unifies the canon is the Faith of the Church that formed the canon. A 'motto,' suggested to me by William Horbury, which is fundamental to this Faith and is also a unifying factor in the canon is "faith in *God* through Christ."

[300] Lofthouse poses a question similar to Brown's but responds to it by noting that love, in Johannine thought, is not an emotion but a matter of the will, the character of which is seen in the laying down of one's life (*The Father and the Son*, 1934, 207-221).

[301] Indeed, this characteristic is not limited to the Fourth Gospel. Cf. Marmorstein's comment after rejecting Christian claims to have first introduced the notion of God's love (!): "There are in the Gospels glowing passages of God's love; but many more, spoken or written with greater force and power, which show a very uncompromising attitude towards all those who do not agree, whether in thoughts or in·deeds, with the teachings of Christianity" (*The Old Rabbinic Doctrine of God*, 1927, 202).

[302] Cf. A. Perego, "Verità e carità," 1964.

[303] Cf. H. Moxnes, "Theology in Conflict. Studies in Paul's Understanding of God in Romans," 1977, 1-13, soon to be published.

[304] "Christologie oder Theologie? Bemerkungen zu O. Cullmanns *Christologie des Neuen Testaments*," 1962.

[305] See B. Ramm, "The Apologetic of the Old Testament," 1958, 15. According to the survey of G. Hasel in *New Testament Theology*, 1978, 144-170 it appears such a proposal has not yet been developed.

[306] See E. C. Hoskyns and F. N. Davey, *The Riddle of the New Testament*, 1931, 259-264.

[307]Cf. C. F. D. Moule, "The Meaning of 'Life' in the Gospel and Epistles of St John," 1975, 123.

[308]Such would seem to be the meaning of St. Clement's comment as well: "But John, last of all, conscious that the outward facts (τὰ σωματικά) had been set forth in the Gospels, was urged on by his disciples, and, divinely moved by the Spirit (πνεύματι θεοφορηθείς), composed a spiritual Gospel (πνευματικὸν εὐαγγέλιον)" (Eusebius, *Ecclesiastical History*, 6.14.7).

[309]Cf. Scott, *Spirit*, 211 and Miranda, *Being*, 158,160,168-194.

BIBLIOGRAPHY

Aalen, S., "Glory, Honour," *DNTT* 2:44-52

————, "'Truth', a Key Word in St. John's Gospel," *SE* 2:3-24

Abrahams, I., *The Glory of God. Three Lectures* (Oxford: University Press, 1925)

Ackerman, J. S., "The Rabbinic Interpretation of Psalm 82 and the Gospel of John: John 10:34," *HTR* 59 (1966): 186-191

Agourides, S., "Peter and John in the Fourth Gospel," *SE* 4:3-7

Aland, B., "Gnosis und Philosophie," in *Proceedings of the International Colloquium on Gnosticism. Stockholm August 20-25, 1973*, ed. G. Widengren (Stockholm: Almqvist and Wiksell, 1977), pp. 34-73

Aletti, J.-N., "Le discours sur le pain de vie (Jean 6). Problèmes de composition et fonction des citations de l'Ancien Testament," *RSR* 62 (1974): 169-197

Allen, E. L. "The Jewish Christian Church in the Fourth Gospel," *JBL* 74 (1955): 88-92

Alonso Díaz, J., "El discernimiento entre el verdadero y falso profeta según la Bíblia," *Estudios Eclesiásticos* 49 (1974): 5-17

Amos, H. P., "The Gnostic Background of the First Epistle of John," PhD, Southern Baptist Theological Seminary, 1934

Amsler, S., *L'ancien testament dans l'église. Essai d'herméneutique chrétienne* (Neuchatel: Delachaux and Niestlé, 1960)

Appold, M. L., *The Oneness Motif in the Fourth Gospel: Motif Analysis and Exegetical Probe into the Theology of John*, Wissenschaftliche Untersuchungen zum Neuen Testament 2/1 (Tübingen: Mohr, 1976)

Armstrong, A. H., "Gnosis and Greek Philosophy," in *Gnosis. Festschrift für Hans Jonas*, ed. B. Aland (Göttingen: Vandenhoeck and Ruprecht, 1978), pp. 87-124

Aune, D. E., "Orthodoxy in First Century Judaism? A Response to N. J. McEleney," *JSJ* 7 (1976): 1-10

de Ausejo, S., "El concepto de 'carne' aplicado a Cristo en el IV Evangelio," *EstBib* 17 (1958): 411-427

227

Bacon, B. W., *The Fourth Gospel in Research and Debate. A Series of Essays on Problems Concerning the Origin and Value of the Anonymous Writings Attributed to the Apostle John* (New York: Moffat, Yard, 1910)

Bächli, O., "'Was habe ich mit Dir zu schaffen?' Eine formelhafte Frage im A.T. und N.T.," *TZ* 33 (1977): 69-80

Bammel, E., "The Baptist in Early Christian Thought," *NTS* 18 (1971): 95-128

————, "Christian Origins in Jewish Tradition," *NTS* 13 (1967): 317-335

————, "'Ex illa itaque die consilium fecerunt . . .'," in *The Trial of Jesus. Cambridge Studies in honour of C. F. D. Moule*, ed. E. Bammel, SBT 13 (London: SCM, 1970), pp. 11-40

————, "'John did no miracle': John 10.41," in *Miracles. Cambridge Studies in their Philosophy and History*, ed. C. F. D. Moule (London: Mowbray, 1965), pp. 179-202

Bampfylde, G., "John XIX 28. A Case for a different translation," *NovT* 11 (1969): 247-260

Bardy, G., "Cérinthe," *RB* 30 (1921): 344-373

Barrett, C. K. "The Dialectical Theology of St John," in *New Testament Essays* (London: SPCK, 1972), pp. 49-69

————, *The Gospel according to St John. An Introduction with Commentary and Notes on the Greek Text*, 2d ed. (London: SPCK, 1978)

————, *The Gospel of John and Judaism*, tr. D. M. Smith (London: SPCK, 1975)

————, "The Interpretation of the Old Testament in the New," in *The Cambridge History of the Bible. 1. From the Beginnings to Jerome*, eds. P. R. Ackroyd and C. F. Evans (Cambridge: University Press, 1970): 377-411

————, "Jews and Judaizers in the Epistles of Ignatius," in *Jews, Greeks and Christians, Religious Cultures in Late Antiquity*, eds. R. Hamerton-Kelly and R. Scroggs (Leiden: Brill, 1976), pp. 220-244

————, "John and the Synoptic Gospels," *ExpT* 85 (1974): 228-233

————, "The Old Testament in the Fourth Gospel," *JTS* 48 (1947): 155-169

Bartholomew, G. L., "An Early Christian Sermon-Drama: John 8:31-59," PhD, Union Theological Seminary, 1974

Battaglia, O., *La teologia del dono. Ricerca di teologia biblica sul tema del dono di Dio nel Vangelo e nella I Lettera di Giovanni*, Collectio Assisiensis 7 (Assisi: Porziùncola, 1971)

Bauer, W., *Johannesevangelium*, HNT 2 (Tübingen: Mohr-Siebeck, 1912)

————, *Das Leben Jesu im Zeitalter der neutestamentlichen Apokryphen* (Tübingen: Mohr-Siebeck 1909)

————, *Orthodoxy and Heresy in Earliest Christianity*, with Appendices by G. Strecker, tr. the Philadelphia Seminar on Christian Origins (London: SCM, 1972)

Baum, G., *The Jews and the Gospel. A Re-examination of the New Testament* (Westminster, MD: Newman, 1961)

Baumeister, T., "Der Tod Jesu und die Leidensnachfolge des Jüngers nach dem Johannesevangelium und dem Ersten Johannesbrief," *Wissenschaft und Weisheit* 40 (1977): 81-99

Becker, J., "Beobachtungen zum Dualismus im Johannesevangelium," *ZNW* 65 (1974): 71-87

Bell, H. I., "Search the Scriptures (Joh 5,39)," *ZNW* 37 (1938): 10-13

Beltz, W., "Gnosis und Altes Testament - Überlegungen zur Frage nach dem jüdischen Ursprung der Gnosis," *ZRGG* 28 (1976): 353-357

Berger, K., "Zu 'Das Wort ward Fleisch' Joh. I 14a," *NovT* 16 (1974): 161-166

Bergmann, J., *Jüdische Apologetik im neutestamentlichen Zeitalter* (Berlin : Reimer, 1908)

Bernard, J. H., *A Critical and Exegetical Commentary on the Gospel according to St. John*, ed. A. H. McNeile, ICC (Edinburgh: Clark, 1928)

Betz, H. D., "Orthodoxy and Heresy in Primitive Christianity. Some Critical Remarks on Georg Strecker's Republication of Walter Bauer's *Rechtgläubigkeit und Ketzerei im ältesten Christentum*," *Int* 19 (1965): 299-311

Betz, O., "The Eschatological Interpretation of the Sinai-Tradition in Qumran and in the New Testament," *RQ* 6 (1967): 89-107

————, *Der Paraklet. Fürsprecher im häretischen Spätjudentum, im Johannes-Evangelium und in neu gefundenen gnostischen Schriften*, Arbeiten zur Geschichte des Spätjudentums und Urchristentums 2 (Leiden: Brill, 1963)

Beutler, J., *Martyria: traditionsgeschichtliche Untersuchungen zum Zeugnisthema bei Johannes*, Frankfurter theologische Studien 10 (Frankfurt: Knecht, 1972)

————, "Psalm 42/43 im Johannesevangelium," *NTS* 25 (1978): 33-57

Bianchi, Ugo, ed., *Le origini dello gnosticismo, colloquio di Messina, 13-18 aprile 1966*, Studies in the History of Religions 12 (Leiden: Brill, 1967)

Black, M., "The Christological Use of the Old Testament in the New Testament," *NTS* 18 (1971): 1-14

Blank, J., "Der johanneische Wahrheits-Begriff," *BZ* 7 (1963): 163-173

————, *Krisis: Untersuchungen zur johanneischen Christologie und Eschatologie* (Freiburg: Lambertus, 1964)

Böcher, O., *Der johanneische Dualismus im Zusammenhang des nach-biblischen Judentums* (Gütersloh: Mohn, 1965)

Bogart, J., *Orthodox and Heretical Perfectionism in the Johannine Community as Evident in the First Epistle of John,* SBLDS 33 (Missoula: Scholars, 1977)

Boice, J. M., *Witness and Revelation in the Gospel of John* (Exeter: Paternoster, 1970)

Boismard, M.-E., *Du baptême à Cana (Jean 1,19-2,11)* (Paris: Cerf, 1956)

Borgen, P., *Bread from Heaven. An Exegetical Study of the Concept of Manna in the Gospel of John and the Writings of Philo,* NovTSup 10 (Leiden: Brill, 1965)

————, "God's Agent in the Fourth Gospel," in *Religions in Antiquity. Essays in Memory of Erwin Ramsdell Goodenough,* ed. J. Neusner (Leiden: Brill, 1968), pp. 137-148

————, "The Use of Tradition in John 12.44-50," *NTS* 26 (1979): 18-35

Borig, R., *Der Wahre Weinstock. Untersuchungen zu Jo 15, 1-10,* StANT 16 (Munich: Kösel, 1967)

Boring, M. E., "The Influence of Christian Prophecy on the Johannine Portrayal of the Paraclete and Jesus," *NTS* 25 (1978): 113-123

Bornhäuser, K., *Das Johannesevangelium, eine Missionsschrift für Israel,* Beiträge zur Förderung christlicher Theologie 2/15 (Gütersloh: Bertelsmann, 1928)

Bowker, J., *Jesus and the Pharisees* (Cambridge: University Press, 1973)

————, "The Origin and Purpose of St John's Gospel," *NTS* 11 (1965): 398-408

Bowman, J., *The Fourth Gospel and the Jews. A Study in R. Akiba, Esther and the Gospel of John,* Pittsburgh Theological Monograph Series 8 (Pittsburgh: Pickwick, 1975)

Bratcher, R. J., "'The Jews' in the Gospel of John," *BT* 26 (1975): 401-409

Braumann, G., Brown, C., "ἡμέρα," *DNTT* 2:886-895

Braun, F.-M., "Le don de Dieu et l'initiation chrétienne (Jn, 2-4)," *NRT* 86 (1964): 1025-1048

————, *Jean le théologien et son évangile dans l'église ancienne*, EBib (Paris: Gabalda, 1959)

————, *Jean le théologien. Les grandes traditions d'Israël et l'accord des écritures selon le quatrième évangile*, EBib (Paris: Gabalda, 1964)

————, *Jean le théologien, sa théologie: le mystère de Jésus-Christ*, EBib (Paris: Gabalda, 1966)

————, *Jean le théologien, sa théologie: le Christ, notre Seigneur heir, aujourd'hui, toujours*, EBib (Paris: Gabalda, 1972)

Braun, H., "πλανάω, κτλ.," *TDNT* 6:228-253

Bream, H. N., "No Need to Be Asked Questions: A Study of Jn. 16:30," in *Search the Scriptures. New Testament Studies in Honor of Raymond T. Stamm*, eds. J. M. Myers, O. Reimherr, H. N. Bream, Gettysburg Theological Series 3 (Leiden: Brill, 1969), pp. 49-74

Brooke, A. E., *A Critical and Exegetical Commentary on the Johannine Epistles*, ICC (Edinburgh: Clark, 1912)

Brown, R. E., *The Community of the Beloved Disciple. The Life, Loves, and Hates of an Individual Church in New Testament Times* (New York: Paulist, 1979)

————, *The Gospel according to John*, AB 29,30 (Garden City: Doubleday, 1966, 1970)

————, "The Unity and Diversity in New Testament Ecclesiology," *NovT* 6 (1963): 298-308

Bruce, F. F., *The Defense of the Gospel in the New Testament*, rev. ed. (Grand Rapids: Eerdmans, 1977)

————, *This Is That. The New Testament Development of Some Old Testament Themes* (Exeter: Paternoster, 1968)

————, *The Time is Fulfilled. Five Aspects of the Fulfillment of the Old Testament in the New* (Exeter: Paternoster, 1978)

Buchanan, G. W., "The Samaritan Origin of the Gospel of John," in *Religions in Antiquity: Essays in Memory of Erwin Ramsdell Goodenough*, ed. J. Neusner (Leiden: Brill, 1968), pp. 148-175

Bultmann, R., "ἀλήθεια, κτλ.," *TDNT* 1:232-251

————, *The Gospel of John, A Commentary*, eds. R. W. N. Hoare and J. K. Riches, tr. G. R. Beasley-Murray (Oxford: Blackwell, 1971)

Bultmann, R., *The Johannine Epistles*, tr. R. P. O'Hara, L. C. McGaughy, and R. W. Funk, Hermeneia (Philadelphia: Fortress, 1973)

————, *Theology of the New Testament*, tr. K. Grobel, 2 Vols. (London: SCM, 1952,1955)

————, Weiser, A., "πιστεύω, κτλ.," *TDNT* 6:174-228

Burney, C. F., *The Aramaic Origin of the Fourth Gospel* (Oxford: Clarendon, 1922)

Cadman, W. H., *The Open Heaven. The Revelation of God in the Johannine Sayings of Jesus*, ed. G. B. Caird (New York: Herder and Herder, 1969)

Caird, G. B., "The Glory of God in the Fourth Gospel: An Exercise in Biblical Semantics," *NTS* 15 (1969): 265-277

————, "The Will of God. II. In the Fourth Gospel," *ExpT* 72 (1961): 115-117

von Campenhausen, H., "Das Bekenntnis im Urchristentum," *ZNW* 63 (1972): 210-253

————, *The Formation of the Christian Bible*, tr. J. A. Baker (London: Black, 1972)

Carpenter, J. E., *The Johannine Writings. A Study of the Apocalypse and the Fourth Gospel* (London: Constable, 1927)

Carroll, K. L., "The Fourth Gospel and the Exclusion of Christians from the Synagogues," *BJRL* 40 (1957): 19-32

Carroll, R. P., *When Prophecy Failed. Reactions and responses to failure in the Old Testament prophetic traditions* (London: SCM, 1979)

Carson, D. A., "Current Source Criticism of the Fourth Gospel: Some Methodological Questions," *JBL* 97 (1978): 411-429

————, "Predestination and Responsibility. Elements of Tension-Theology in the Fourth Gospel against Jewish Background," PhD, Cambridge, 1975

Cassem, N. H., "A Grammatical and Contextual Inventory of the Use of κόσμος in the Johannine Corpus with Some Implications for a Johannine Cosmic Theology," *NTS* 19 (1972): 81-91

Charlesworth, J. H., "A Critical Comparison of the Dualism in 1QS 3:13-4:26 and the 'Dualism' Contained in the Gospel of John," *JQ*, pp. 76-106

Charlier, C., "L'évangile de l'amour dans la mort," *BVC* 14 (1956): 7-16

Childs, B., *Exodus. A Commentary* (London: SCM, 1974)

Chrysostom, St. John, *Homilies on the Gospel of St. John and The Epistle to the Hebrews*, ed. P. Schaff, Nicene and Post-Nicene Fathers of the Christian Church 1/14 (Grand Rapids: Eerdmans, n.d.)

Clark, F., "Tension and Tide in St. John's Gospel," *Irish Theological Quarterly* 24 (1957): 154-165

Clemen, C., "Beiträge zum geschichtlichen Verständnis der Johannesbriefe," 6 (1905): 271-281

Coggins, R. J., *Samaritans and Jews. The Origins of Samaritanism Reconsidered* (Oxford: Blackwell, 1975)

Collins, R. F., "The Representative Figures of the Fourth Gospel," *DowR* 94 (1976): 26-46, 118-132

Colwell, E. C., *John Defends the Gospel* (Chicago: Willett, Clark, 1936)

————, Titus, E. L., *The Gospel of the Spirit: A Study in the Fourth Gospel* (New York: Harper, 1953)

Conzelmann, H., "Was von Anfang war," in *Neutestamentliche Studien für Rudolf Bultmann zu seinem siebzigsten Geburtstag am 20. August 1954*, BZNW 21 (Berlin: Töpelmann, 1957), pp. 194-201

————, "φῶς, κτλ.," *TDNT* 9:310-358

————, "ψεῦδος, κτλ.," *TDNT* 9:594-603

Corell, A., *Consummatum Est: Eschatology and Church in the Gospel of St John* (London: SPCK, 1958)

Crehan, J., *The Theology of St. John* (London: Darton, Longman, Todd, 1965)

Crenshaw, J. L., *Prophetic Conflict. Its Effect Upon Israelite Religion*, BZAW 124 (Berlin: de Gruyter, 1971)

Cribbs, F. L., "A Reassessment of the Date of Origin and the Destination of the Gospel of John," *JBL* 89 (1970): 38-55

de la Croix, P.-M., *The Biblical Spirituality of St. John* (Staten Island, N.Y.: Alba House, 1966)

Crossan, D. M., "Anti-Semitism and the Gospel," *TS* 26 (1965): 189-214

Crossan, J. D., *In Parables. The Challenge of the Historical Jesus* (New York: Harper and Row, 1973)

Cullmann, O., "L'évangile johannique et l'histoire du salut," *NTS* 11 (1965): 111-122

————, *The Johannine Circle, It's place in Judaism, among the disciples of Jesus and in early christianity*, tr. J. Bowden (London: SCM, 1976)

Culpepper, R. A., *The Johannine School: An Evaluation of the Johannine-school Hypothesis Based on an Investigation of the Nature of Ancient Schools*, SBLDS 26 (Missoula: Scholars, 1975)

Cuming, G. J., "The Jews in the Fourth Gospel," *ExpT* 60 (1949): 290-292

Dahl, N. A., "Der Erstgeborene Satans und der Vater des Teufels (Polyk. 7.1 und Joh 8.44)," in *Apophoreta. Festschrift für Ernst Haenchen zu seinem siebzigsten Geburtstag am 10. Dezember 1964*, ed. W. Eltester, BZNW 30 (Berlin: Töpelmann, 1964): 70-84

————, "The Johannine Church and History" in *Jesus in the Memory of the Early Church. Essays by Nils Alstrup Dahl* (Minneapolis: Augsburg, 1976), pp. 99-119

————, "The Neglected Factor in New Testament Theology," *Reflection* 73 (1975): 5-8

Dammers, A. H., "Hard Sayings - II. I John 5.16ff.," *Theology* 66 (1963): 370-372

D'Angelo, M. R., *Moses in the Letter to the Hebrews*, SBLDS 42 (Missoula: Scholars, 1979)

Dauer, A., *Die Passionsgeschichte im Johannesevangelium. Eine traditionsgeschichtliche und theologische Untersuchung zu Joh 18,1-19,30*, StANT 30 (Munich: Kösel, 1972)

Davies, W. D., *Paul and Rabbinic Judaism. Some Rabbinic Elements in Pauline Theology*, 2d ed. (London: SPCK, 1955)

————, *The Setting of the Sermon on the Mount* (Cambridge: University Press, 1964)

Debrunner, A., Kleinknecht, H., Procksch, O., Kittel, G., "λέγω, κτλ.," *TDNT* 4:69-143

Delling, G., "ἐρευνάω, κτλ.," *TDNT* 2:655-657

Delling, G., von Rad, G., "ἡμέρα, κτλ.," *TDNT* 2:943-953

Derrett, J. D. M., "The Zeal of the House and the Cleansing of the Temple," *DowR* 95 (1977): 79-94

Dillon, R. J., "Wisdom Tradition and Sacramental Retrospect in the Cana Account (Jn 2,1-11)," *CBQ* 24 (1962): 268-296

Dodd, C. H., "Behind a Johannine Dialogue" in *More New Testament Essays* (Manchester: University Press, 1968), pp. 41-57

————, "The First Epistle of John and the Fourth Gospel," *BJRL* 21 (1937): 129-156

————, *Historical Tradition in the Fourth Gospel* (Cambridge: University Press, 1963)

————, *The Interpretation of the Fourth Gospel* (Cambridge: University Press, 1953)

Dodd, C. H., *The Johannine Epistles*, MNTC (London: Hodder and Stoughton, 1946)

――――, *The Old Testament in the New* (London: Athlone, 1952)

Doskocil, W., *Der Bann in der Urkirche. Eine Rechtesgeschicht-liche Untersuchung*, Münchener Theologische Studien, 3. Kanonistische Abteilung 11 (Munich: Zink, 1958)

Douglas, M., "Social Preconditions of Enthusiasm and Heterodoxy," in *Forms of Symbolic Action. Proceedings of the 1969 Annual Spring Meeting of the American Ethnological Society*, ed. R. F. Spencer (Seattle: University Press, 1969), pp. 69-80

Dulière, W. L., *La haute terminologie de la rédaction johannique; les vocables qu'elle a introduits chez les Gréco-Romains: le Logos-Verbe, le Paraclet-Esprit-Saint et le Messias-Messie*, Collection Latomus 117 (Brussels: Latomus, 1970)

Dunlop, L., "The Pierced Side. Focal Point of Johannine Theology," *TBT* 86 (1976): 960-965

Dunn, J. D. G., "Prophetic 'I'-sayings and the Jesus Tradition: The Importance of Testing Prophetic Utterances within Early Christianity," *NTS* 24 (1978): 175-198

――――, *Unity and Diversity in the New Testament. An Inquiry into the Character of Earliest Christianity* (London: SCM, 1977)

Dupont, J., *Essais sur la christologie de saint Jean. Le Christ, Parole, Lumière et Vie, La Gloire du Christ* (Bruges: Éditions de l'Abbaye de Saint-André, 1951)

Easton, B. S., *Early Christianity: The Purpose of Acts and Other Papers*, ed. F. C. Grant (London: SPCK, 1955)

Ehrhardt, A., "Christianity Before the Apostles' Creed," *HTR* 55 (1962): 74-119

Eichholz, G., "Der 1. Johannesbriefe als Trostbrief und die Einheit der Schrift," *EvT* 5 (1938): 73-83

Elbogen, I., *Der jüdische Gottesdienst in seiner geschichtlichen Entwicklung* 3d ed. (Frankfurt: Kauffmann, 1931)

Ellis, E. E., "Midrash, Targum and New Testament Quotations," in *Neotestamentica et Semitica. Studies in Honour of Matthew Black*, eds. E. E. Ellis and M. Wilcox (Edinburgh: Clark, 1969), pp. 61-69

Ely, M. R., *Knowledge of God in Johannine Thought* (New York: Macmillan, 1925)

Emerton, J. A., "Melchizedek and the Gods: Fresh Evidence for the Jewish Background of John X.34-36," *JTS* 17 (1966): 399-401

Enz, J. J., "The Book of Exodus as a Literary Type for the Gospel of John," *JBL* 76 (1957): 208-215

Erdozáin, L., *La función del signo en la fe según el cuarto evangelio. Estudio crítico exegético de las perícopas Jn IV,
46-54 y Jn XX, 24-29*, AnBib 33 (Rome: Pontifical Biblical
Institute, 1968)

Eusebius, *The Ecclesiastical History*, trs. J. E. L. Oulton and
H. J. Lawlor, Loeb Classical Library (London: Heinemann,
1942)

Evans, E., "The Verb 'ΑΓΑΠΑιΝ in the Fourth Gospel" in *Studies
in the Fourth Gospel*, ed. F. L. Cross (London: Mowbray,
1957), pp. 64-71

Fascher, E., "Christologie oder Theologie? Bemerkungen zu O.
Cullmanns *Christologie des Neuen Testaments*," *TLZ* 87
(1962): 881-910

————, "Christologie und Gnosis im vierten Evangelium," *TLZ*
93 (1968): 721-730

Fee, G. D., "Once More - John 7:37-39," *ExpT* 89 (1978): 116-118

Fensham, F. C., "I am the Way, the Truth and the Life," *Neotestamentica* 2 (1968): 81-88

Feuillet, A., "Les *Ego Eimi* christologiques du quatrième évangile," *RSR* 54 (1966): 5-22, 213-240

————, "Étude structurale de la première épître de saint Jean,"
in *Neues Testament und Geschichte. Historisches Geschehen
und Deutung im Neuen Testament. Oscar Cullmann zum 70.
Geburtstag*, eds. H. Baltensweiler and B. Reicke (Zürich:
Theologischer, 1972), pp. 307-327

————, *Johannine Studies*, tr. T. E. Crane (Staten Island, N.Y.:
Alba House, 1965)

————, "Man's Participation in God's Life: A Key·Concept in
John," *ComJn*, pp. 141-151

————, *Le mystère de l'amour divin dans la théologie johannique*,
EBib (Paris: Gabalda, 1972)

Filson, F. V., "First John: Purpose and Message," *Int* 23 (1969):
259-276

Findlay, G. G., *Fellowship in the Life Eternal. An Exposition
of the Epistles of St. John* (London: Hodder and Stoughton,
1909)

Fiorenza, E. S., ed. *Aspects of Religious Propaganda in Judaism
and Early Christianity*, University of Notre Dame Center for
the Study of Judaism and Christianity in Antiquity 2 (Notre
Dame: University Press, 1976)

Fischel, H. A. "Jewish Gnosticism in the Fourth Gospel," *JBL* 65 (1946): 157-174

Fitch, W. O., "The Interpretation of St. John 5,6," *SE* 4:194-197

Florovsky, G., "The Fathers of the Church and the Old Testament," in *Aspects of Church History, The Collected Works of Georges Florovsky*, Vol. 4 (Belmont, Mass.: Nordland, 1979): 31-38

Foerster, W., "σατανᾶς," *TDNT* 7:151-163

Ford, J. M., "'Mingled Blood' from the Side of Christ (John xix. 34)," *NTS* 15 (1969): 337-338

Forestell, J. T., *The Word of the Cross. Salvation as Revelation in the Fourth Gospel*, AnBib 57 (Rome: Pontifical Biblical Institute, 1974)

Forkman, G., *The Limits of the Religious Community. Expulsion from the Religious Community within the Qumran Sect, within Rabbinic Judaism, and within Primitive Christianity*, tr. P. Sjölander, Coniectanea Biblica. New Testament Series 5 (Lund: Gleerup, 1972)

Fortna, R. T., "Christology in the Fourth Gospel: Redaction-Critical Perspectives," *NTS* 21 (1975): 489-504

————, "From Christology to Soteriology. A Redaction-Critical Study of Salvation in the Fourth Gospel," *Int* 27 (1973): 31-47

Francis, F. O., "The Form and Function of the Opening and Closing Paragraphs of James and 1 John," *ZNW* 61 (1970): 110-126

Franke, A. H., *Das alte Testament bei Johannes. Ein Beitrag zur Erklärung und Beurtheilung der johanneischen Schriften* (Göttingen: Vandenhoeck and Ruprecht, 1885)

Freed, E. D., "Did John Write His Gospel Partly to Win Samaritan Converts?" *NovT* 12 (1970): 241-256·

————, *Old Testament Quotations in the Gospel of John*, NovTSup 11 (Leiden: Brill, 1965)

Freedman, H., Simon, M., eds., *Midrash Rabbah*, 10 Vols. (London: Soncino, 1939)

Fuller, R., "The 'Jews' in the Fourth Gospel," *Dialog* 16 (1977): 31-37

Furnish, V. P., *The Love Command in the New Testament* (London: SCM, 1973)

Galot, J., *Etre né de Dieu. Jean 1,13*, AnBib 37 (Rome: Pontifical Biblical Institute, 1969)

Gardner-Smith, P., *Saint John and the Synoptic Gospels* (Cambridge: University Press, 1938)

Giblin, C. H., "Suggestion, Negative Response, and Positive Action in St John's Portrayal of Jesus (John 2.1-11; 4.46-54;
7.12-14; 11.1-44)," *NTS* 26 (1980): 197-211

Glasson, T. F., *Moses in the Fourth Gospel*, SBT 40 (London: SCM,
1963)

Gollwitzer, H., "Ausser Christus kein Heil? (Johannes 14,6),"
Antijudaismus, pp. 171-194

Goodenough, E. R., *By Light, Light. The Mystic Gospel of Hellenistic Judaism* (Amsterdam: Philo, 1969)

Goppelt, L., *Apostolic and Post-Apostolic Times*, tr. R. A. Gue-
lich (London: Black, 1970)

————, *Christentum und Judentum im ersten und zweiten Jahrhundert. Ein Aufriss der Urgeschichte der Kirche*, Beiträge zur
Förderung christlicher Theologie 2/55 (Gütersloh: Bertelsmann, 1954)

Grabbe, L. L., "Orthodoxy in First Century Judaism? What Are the
Issues?" *JSJ* 8 (1977): 149-153

Grässer, E., "Die Antijüdische Polemik im Johannesevangelium,"
NTS 11 (1964): 74-90

————, "Die Juden als Teufelssöhne in Johannes 8,37-47," *Antijudaismus*, pp. 157-170

Grant, R. M., *Gnosticism and Early Christianity* (New York: Co-
lumbia University Press, 1959)

————, "The Origin of the Fourth Gospel," *JBL* 69 (1950): 305-322

Grillmeier, A., *Christ in Christian Tradition. Vol. 1: From the
Apostolic Age to Chalcedon (451)*, tr. J. Bowden, 2d ed.
(London: Mowbrays, 1975)

Grossouw, W. K., "Christian Spirituality in John," *ComJn*, pp.
205-224

Gryglewicz, F., "Die Pharisäer und die Johanneskirche," in
Probleme der Forschung, eds. A. Fuchs and L. Herold, Studien
zum Neuen Testament und seiner Umwelt A/3 (Munich: Wien,
1978): 144-158

Guilding, A., *The Fourth Gospel and Jewish Worship. A Study of
the Relation of St. John's Gospel to the Ancient Jewish
Lectionary System* (Oxford: Clarendon, 1960)

Gutbrod, W., von Rad, G., Kuhn, K. G., "Ισραήλ, κτλ.," *TDNT*
3:356-391

————, Kleinknecht, H., "νόμος, κτλ.," *TDNT* 4:1022-1091

Guterman, S. L., *Religious Toleration and Persecution in Ancient
Rome* (London: Aiglon, 1951)

Haacker, K., "Samaritan, etc.," *DNTT* 3:449-467

————, *Die Stiftung des Heils. Untersuchungen zur Strucktur der johanneischen Theologie* (Stuttgart: Calwer, 1972)

Haarbeck, H., Fries, G., Klappert, B., Brown, C., Betz, O., Thiselton, A. C., "Word, Tongue, Utterance," *DNTT* 3:1078-1146

Haas, C., de Jonge, M., Swellengrebel, J. L. *A Translator's Handbook on the Letters of John,* Helps for Translators 13 (London: United Bible Societies, 1972)

Haenchen, E., *The Acts of the Apostles. A Commentary,* tr. B. Noble, G. Shinn, H. Anderson, rev. and updated R. McL. Wilson (Oxford: Blackwell, 1971)

————, "'Der Vater, der mich gesandt hat,'" *NTS* 9 (1963): 208-216

Häring, T., "Gedankengang und Grundgedanke des ersten Johannesbriefs," in *Theologische Abhandlungen. Carl von Weizsäcker zu seinem siebzigsten Geburtstag 11. Dezember 1892 gewidmet* (Freiburg: Mohr-Siebeck, 1892), pp. 171-200

Hagner, D. A., "The Vision of God in Philo and John: A Comparative Study," *Journal of the Evangelical Theological Society* 14 (1971): 81-93

Haible, E., "Das Gottesbild der Hochzeit von Kana. Zur biblischen Grundlegung der Eingottlehre," *MTZ* 10 (1959): 189-199

Hamerton-Kelly, R., *God the Father. Theology and Patriarchy in the Teaching of Jesus,* Overtures to Biblical Theology (Philadelphia: Fortress, 1979)

————, *Pre-existence, Wisdom, and the Son of Man. A Study of the Idea of Pre-existence in the New Testament,* NTSMS 21 (Cambridge: University Press, 1973)

Hanson, A. T., *Jesus Christ in the Old Testament* (London: SPCK, 1965)

————, "John's Citation of Psalm lxxxii. John x.33-6," *NTS* 11 (1965): 158-162

————, "John's Citation of Psalm lxxxii Reconsidered," *NTS* 13 (1967): 363-367

————, *The New Testament Interpretation of Scripture* (London: SPCK, 1980)

Harner, P. B., *The "I Am" of the Fourth Gospel: A Study in Johannine Usage and Thought,* Facet Books, Biblical Series 26 (Philadelphia: Fortress, 1970)

Harrington, D. J., *God's People in Christ. New Testament Perspectives on the Church and Judaism,* Overtures to Biblical Theology (Philadelphia: Fortress, 1980)

Harvey, A. E., *Jesus on Trial: A Study in the Fourth Gospel*
(London: SPCK, 1976)

Hasel, G., *New Testament Theology: Basic Issues in the Current
Debate* (Grand Rapids: Eerdmans, 1978)

Hauck, F., "μένω, κτλ.," *TDNT* 4:574-588

Hawkin, D. J., "The Function of the Beloved Disciple Motif in
the Johannine Redaction," *Laval Théologique et Philosophique*
33 (1977): 135-150

————, "Orthodoxy and Heresy in John 10:1-21 and 15:1-17,"
EvQ 47 (1975): 208-213

————, "A Reflective Look at the Recent Debate on Orthodoxy and
Heresy in Earliest Christianity," *Église et Théologie* 7
(1976): 367-378

Hayward, C. T. R., "The Holy Name of the God of Moses and the
Prologue of St John's Gospel," *NTS* 25 (1978): 16-32

Henderson, R. A., *The Gospel of Fulfilment. A Study of St.
John's Gospel* (London: SPCK, 1936)

Hengel, M., *Crucifixion in the ancient world and the folly of
the message of the cross* (London: SCM, 1977)

Hickling, C. J. A., "Attitudes to Judaism in the Fourth Gospel,"
EvJean, pp. 347-354

Hilgenfeld, A., *Judentum und Judenchristentum. Eine Nachlese zu
der Ketzergeschichte des Urchristentums, zur Ältesten
Kirchengeschichte* (Leipzig: Fues-Reisland, 1886)

————, *Die Ketzergeschichte des Urchristentums* (Leipzig: Fues-
Riesland, 1884)

Hindley, J. C., "Witness in the Fourth Gospel," *SJT* 18 (1965):
319-337

Hodges, Z. C., "Grace after Grace - John 1:16. Part 1 of Problem Passages in the Gospel of John," *BS* 135 (1978): 34-45

Holtzmann, H. J., "Das Problem des ersten johanneischen Briefes
in seinem Verhältniss zum Evangelium," *Jahrbuch für protes-
tantische Theologie* 7 (1881): 690-712; 8 (1882): 128-152,
316-342; 460-485

Hooker, M. D., "The Johannine *Prologue* and the Messianic Secret,"
NTS 21 (1974): 40-58

————, "John the Baptist and the Johannine Prologue," *NTS* 16
(1970): 354-358

Horbury, W., "A Critical Examination of the Toledoth Jeshu,"
PhD, Cambridge, 1970

Horbury, W., "Tertullian on the Jews in the Light of *De Spectaculis* xxx.5-6," *JTS* 23 (1972): 455-459

Hoskyns, E. C., *The Fourth Gospel*, ed. F. N. Davey, 2 Vols. (London: Faber and Faber, 1940)

————, "Genesis I-III and St. John's Gospel," *JTS* 21 (1920): 210-218

————, "The Johannine Epistles," in *A New Commentary on Holy Scripture Including the Apocrypha*, ed. C. Gore, et al. (New York: Macmillan, 1928) 3:658-673

————, Davey, N., *The Riddle of the New Testament* (London: Faber and Faber, 1931)

Hossfeld, F. L., Meyer, I., *Prophet gegen Prophet. Eine Analyse der alttestamentlichen Texte zum Thema: Wahre und falsche Propheten*, Biblische Beiträge 9 (Freiburg: Schweizerisches Katholisches Bibelwerk, 1973)

Houlden, J. L., *The Johannine Epistles*, BNTC (London: Black, 1973)

Howard, W. F., *Christianity according to St. John* (London: Duckworth, 1943)

————, "The Common Authorship of the Johannine Gospel and Epistles," *JTS* 48 (1947): 12-25

————, *The Fourth Gospel in Recent Criticism and Interpretation*, rev. C. K. Barrett (London: Epworth, 1955)

Howton, J., "'Son of God' in the Fourth Gospel," *NTS* 10 (1964): 227-237

Hulen, A. B., "The Call of the Four Disciples in John 1," *JBL* 67 (1948): 153-158

Hunter, A. M., *According to John* (London: SCM, 1968)

Hunzinger, C.-H., "συκῆ, κτλ.," *TDNT* 7:751-759

Ibuki, Y., *Die Wahrheit im Johannesevangelium*, BBB 39 (Bonn: Hanstein, 1972)

Irenaeus, *Against Heresies*, trs. A. Roberts and W. H. Rambaut, Ante-Nicene Christian Library 5/1 (Edinburgh: Clark, 1868)

Jacobs, L., "Greater Love Hath No Man . . . The Jewish Point of View of Self-Sacrifice," *Judaism* 6 (1957): 41-47

Jaubert, A., *Approaches de l'Évangile de Jean* (Paris: Seuil, 1976)

Jeremias, J., "᾽Αβραάμ," *TDNT* 1:8-9

————, "Μωυσῆς," *TDNT* 4:848-873

Jervell, J., "'Er kam in sein Eigentum.' Zum Joh. 1,11," *ST* 10
     (1956): 14-27

———, "The Problem of Traditions in Acts," in *Luke and the
     People of God. A New Look at Luke-Acts* (Minneapolis: Augs-
     burg, 1972), pp. 19-39

Jocz, J., *The Jewish People and Jesus Christ. A Study in the
     Relationship between the Jewish People and Jesus Christ*
     (London: SPCK, 1949)

———, "Die Juden im Johannesevangelium," *Jud* 9 (1953): 129-142

Johnston, G., *The Spirit-Paraclete in the Gospel of John*, NTSMS
     12 (Cambridge: University Press, 1970)

Jonas, H., *The Gnostic Religion. The Message of the Alien God
     and the Beginnings of Christianity* (Boston: Beacon, 1958)

Jones, P. R., "A Structural Analysis of I John," *RevExp* 67 (1970):
     433-444

de Jonge, M., "The Beloved Disciple and the date of the Gospel
     of John," *Text*, pp. 99-114

———, "Jewish Expectations about the 'Messiah' according to
     the Fourth Gospel," *NTS* 19 (1973): 246-270

———, "Nicodemus and Jesus: Some Observations on Misunder-
     standing and Understanding in the Fourth Gospel," *BJRL*
     53 (1971): 337-359

———, "The Use of the Word ΧΡΙΣΤΟΣ in the Johannine Epistles,"
     StJn, pp. 66-74

———, "Variety and Development in Johannine Christology," in
     *Jesus: Stranger from Heaven and Son of God. Jesus Christ
     and the Christians in Johannine Perspective*, ed. and tr. J.
     E. Steely, Society of Biblical Literature Sources for Bib-
     lical Study 11 (Missoula: Scholars, 1977): 193-213

Josephus, *Jewish Antiquities*, tr. H. St. J. Thackeray, et al.,
     6 Vols., Loeb Classical Library (London: Heinemann, 1930-
     1945)

———, *The Jewish War*, ed. H. St. J. Thackeray, et al., 2 Vols.,
     Loeb Classical Library (London: Heinemann, 1927,1957)

Jungkuntz, R. "An Approach to the Exegesis of John 10:34-36,"
     Concordia Theological Monthly 35 (1964): 556-565

Käsemann, E., "Aufbau und Anliegen des Johanneischen Prologs,"
     in *Libertas Christiana. Friedrich Delekat zum 65. Geburts-
     tag*, eds. E. Wolf and W. Matthias, BEvT 26 (Munich: Kaiser,
     1957): 75-99

———, "The Canon of the New Testament and the Unity of the
     Church," in *Essays on New Testament Themes*, SBT 41 (London:
     SCM, 1964): 95-107

Käsemann, E., "Ketzer und Zeuge. Zum johanneischen Verfasser-problem," *ZTK* 48 (1951): 292-311

————, *The Testament of Jesus. A Study of the Gospel of John in the Light of Chapter 17*, tr. G. Krodel (Philadelphia: Fortress, 1968)

————, "Unity and Diversity in New Testament Ecclesiology," *NovT* 6 (1963): 290-297

Kelly, J. N. D., *A Commentary on the Pastoral Epistles. I Timothy, II Timothy, Titus*, BNTC (London: Black, 1963)

Kern, W., "Der symmetrische Gesamtaufbau von Jo 8,12-58," *ZKT* 78 (1956): 451-454

Kierkegaard, S., *Philosophical Fragments or A Fragment of Philosophy by Johannes Climacus*, tr. D. F. Swenson (Princeton: University Press, 1936)

Kippenberg, H. G., *Garizim und Synagoge. Traditionsgeschichtliche Untersuchungen zur samaritanischen Religion der aramäischen Periode*, Religionsgeschichtliche Versuche und Vorarbeiten 30 (Berlin: de Gruyter, 1971)

Kirk, K. E., *The Vision of God. The Christian Doctrine of the Summum Bonum*, 2d ed. (London: Longmans, Green, 1932)

Kittel, G., von Rad, G., "δοκέω, κτλ.," *TDNT* 2:232-255

Klassen, W., "Humility in the NT," *IDB, Supplementary Volume*, pp. 422-423

Klein, G., "'Das wahre Licht scheint schon.' Beobachtungen zur Zeit- und Geschichtserfahrung einer urchristlichen Schule," *ZTK* 68 (1971): 261-326

Klijn, A. F. J., Reinink, G. J., *Patristic Evidence for Jewish-Christian Sects*, NovTSup 36 (Leiden: Brill, 1973)

Klöpper, A., "Zur Lehre von der Sünde im 1. Johannesbrief, Er-läuterung von 5,16 - fin.," *ZWT* 43 (1900): 585-602

Knight, G. A. F., "Antisemitism in the Fourth Gospel," *Reformed Theological Review* 27 (1968): 81-88

Köster, H., "Geschichte und Kultus im Johannesevangelium und bei Ignatius von Antiochien," *ZTK* 54 (1957): 56-69

————, "GNOMAI DIAPHOROI. The Origin and Nature of Diversification in the History of Early Christianity," *HTR* 58 (1965): 279-318

————, "Häretiker im Urchristentum," *RGG* 3:17-21

————, "One Jesus and Four Primitive Gospels," *HTR* 61 (1968): 203-247

Kossen, H. B., "Who were the Greeks of John xii 20?" *StJn*, pp. 97-110

Kraft, R. A., "The Multiform Jewish Heritage of Early Christianity," *CJG-RC* 3:175-199

Kruijf, Th. C., "The Glory of the Only Son (John i 14)," *StJn*, pp. 111-123

Kümmel, W. G., *Introduction* to the New Testament, tr. H. C. Kee, rev. ed. (London: SCM, 1975)

Kuhn, P., *Gottes Selbsterniedrigung in der Theologie der Rabbinen*, StANT 17 (Munich: Kösel, 1968)

Kuyper, L. J., "Grace and Truth. An Old Testament Description of God and Its Use in the Johannine Gospel," *Int* 18 (1964): 3-19

Kysar, R., "Community and Gospel: Vectors in Fourth Gospel Criticism," *Int* 31 (1977): 355-366

————, The Fourth *Evangelist* and His Gospel. *An Examination of Contemporary Scholarship* (Minneapolis: Augsburg, 1975)

————, *John, the Maverick Gospel* (Atlanta: John Knox, 1976)

————, "The Source Analysis of the Fourth Gospel - A Growing Consensus?" *NovT* 15 (1973): 134-152

Langbrandtner, W., *Weltferner Gott oder Gott der Liebe. Der Ketzerstreit in der johanneischen Kirche. Eine exegetisch-religionsgeschichtliche Untersuchung mit Berücksichtigung der koptisch-gnostischen Texte aus Nag-Hammadi*, Beiträge zur biblischen Exegese und Theologie 6 (Frankfurt: Lang, 1977)

Lattke, M., "Einheit im Wort. Die spezifische Bedeutung von ἀγάπη, ἀγαπᾶν und φιλεῖν im Johannesevangelium," PhD, Freiburg im Breisgau, 1973

Lauterbach, J. Z., "*Jesus* in the Talmud," in *Rabbinic Essays* (Cincinnati: Hebrew Union College, 1951), pp. 473-570

————, *Mekilta de-Rabbi Ishmael*, 3 Vols., The JPS Library of Jewish Classics (Philadelphia: Jewish Publication Socity of America, 1961)

Law, R., The *Tests* of Life. A Study of the First Epistle of St. *John*, 2d ed. (Edinburgh: Clark, 1909)

Lazure, N., *Les valeurs morales de la théologie johannique (Evangile et Épitres)*, EBib (Paris: Gabalda, 1965)

Leaney, A. R. C., "The Gospels as Evidence for First-Century Judaism," in *Historicity and Chronology in the New Testament*, Theological Collections 6 (London: SPCK, 1965)

Le Déaut, R., "Apropos a Definition of Midrash," *Int* 25 (1971): 259-282

Lee, E. K., *The Religious Thought of St. John* (London: SPCK, 1950)

Lefévre, A., "Die Seitenwunde Jesu," *Geist und Leben* 33 (1960): 86-96

Leistner, R., *Antijudaismus im Johannesevangelium? Darstellung des Problems in der neueren Auslegungsgeschichte und Untersuchung der Leidengeschichte*, Theologie und Wirklichkeit 3 (Bern: Lang, 1974)

Leroy, H., *Rätsel und Missverständnis. Ein Beitrag zur Formgeschichte des Johannesevangeliums*, BBB 30 (Bonn: Hanstein, 1968)

Lightfoot, R. H., *St. John's Gospel, A Commentary*, ed. C. F. Evans (Oxford: Clarendon, 1956)

Lindars, B., *Behind the Fourth Gospel* (London: SPCK, 1971)

———, *The Gospel of John*, New Century Bible (London: Oliphants, 1972)

———, "Jesus and the Pharisees," in *Donum Gentilicium. New Testament Essays in Honour of David Daube*, eds. E. Bammel, C. K. Barrett, and W. D. Davies (Oxford: Clarendon, 1978), pp. 51-67

———, *New Testament Apologetic. The Doctrinal Significance of the Old Testament Quotations* (London: SCM, 1961)

———, "The Passion in the Fourth Gospel," in *God's Christ and His People. Studies in Honour of Nils Alstrup Dahl*, eds. J. Jervell and W. A. Meeks (Oslo: Universitetsforlaget, 1977), pp. 71-86

———, Borgen, P., "The Place of the Old Testament in the Formation of New Testament Theology: Prolegomena and Response," *NTS* 23 (1976): 59-75

Lindeskog, G., "Anfänge des jüdisch-christlichen Problems. Ein programmatischer Entwurf, " in *Donum Gentilicium. New Testament Essays in Honour of David Daube*, eds. E. Bammel, C. K. Barrett, and W. D. Davies (Oxford: Clarendon, 1978), pp. 255-275

———, "Jews and Judaism in the New Testament. Four Theses," *Annual of the Swedish Theological Institute* 11 (1977-1978): 63-67

Lofthouse, W. F., *The Father and the Son. A Study in Johannine Thought* (London: SCM, 1934)

Lona, H. E., *Abraham in Johannes 8. Ein Beitrag zur Methodenfrage*, Europäische Hochschulschriften, Reihe 23: Theologie 65 (Bern: Lang, 1976)

Longenecker, R., *Biblical Exegesis in the Apostolic Period* (Grand Rapids: Eerdmans, 1975)

Louw, J. P., "Narrator of the Father - ΕΞΗΓΕΙΣΘΑΙ and Related
Terms in Johannine Christology," in *The Christ of John:
Essays on the Christology of the Fourth Gospel*, Neotestamen-
tica 2 (Potchefstroom, SA: Pro Rege, 1971): 32-40

Lowry, R., "The Rejected-Suitor Syndrome: Human Sources of New
Testament 'Antisemitism,'" *Journal of Ecumenical Studies*
14 (1977): 219-232

Lütgert, W., "Die Juden im Johannesevangelium," in *Neutestamentliche Studien für Georg Heinrici zu seinem 70. Geburtstag
(14. März 1914) dargebracht von Fachgenossen, Freunden und
Schülern*, eds. A. Deissmann and H. Windisch, Untersuchungen
zum Neuen Testament 6 (Leipzig: Hinrichs, 1914): 147-154

Lussier, E., *God is Love. According to Saint John* (New York:
Alba House, 1977)

Luzarraga, J., "Presentación de Jesús a la luz del A. T. en el
Evangelio de Juan," *Estudios Eclesiásticos* 51 (1976): 497-520

MacDonald, J., *Memar Marqah. The Teaching of Marqah*, 2 Vols.,
BZAW 84 (Berlin: Töpelmann, 1963)

————, *The Theology of the Samaritans* (London: SCM, 1964)

MacGregor, J., *Studies in the History of Christian Apologetics:
New Testament and Post-Apostolic* (Edinburgh: Clark, 1894)

MacRae, G. W., "The Ego-Proclamation in Gnostic Sources," in
*The Trial of Jesus: Cambridge Studies in Honour of C. F. D.
Moule*, ed. E. Bammel, STB 2/13 (London: SCM, 1970): 122-134

————, *Faith in the Word. The Fourth Gospel*, Herald Biblical
Booklets (Chicago: Franciscan Herald, 1973)

————, "The Fourth Gospel and *Religionsgeschichte*," CBQ 32
(1970): 13-24

Mahoney, R., *Two Disciples at the Tomb. The Background and Message of John 20.1-10*, Theologie und Wirklichkeit 6 (Bern:
Lang, 1974)

Malatesta, E., *Interiority and Covenant. A Study of εἶναι and
μένειν ἐν In the First Letter of Saint John*, AnBib 69 (Rome:
Pontifical Biblical Institute, 1978)

Manns, F., *"La vérité vous fera libres." Étude exégétique de
Jean 8/31-59*, Studium Biblicum Franciscanum, Analecta 11
(Jerusalem: Franciscan, 1976)

Manson, T. W., "The Old Testament in the Teaching of Jesus,"
BJRL 34 (1952): 312-332

Marmorstein, A., *The Old Rabbinic Doctrine of God 1. The Names
and Attributes of God*, Jews' College Publications 10 (Oxford: University Press, 1927)

Marshall, I. H., *The Johannine Epistles*, NICNT (Grand Rapids: Eerdmans, 1978)

————, "Orthodoxy and heresy in earlier Christianity," *Themelios* 2 (1976): 5-14

Martyn, J. L., "Clementine Recognitions 1,33-71, Jewish Christianity, and the Fourth Gospel," in *God's Christ and His People. Studies in Honour of Nils Alstrup Dahl*, eds. J. Jervell and W. A. Meeks (Oslo: Universitetsforlaget, 1977), pp. 265-295

————, "Glimpses into the History of the Johannine Community. From its Origin through the Period of Its Life in Which the Fourth Gospel Was Composed," in *The Gospel of John in Christian History. Essays for Interpreters*, Theological Inquiries (New York: Paulist, 1978), pp. 90-121

————, *History and Theology in the Fourth Gospel*, rev. and enl. (Nashville: Abingdon, 1979)

————, "Persecution and Martyrdom. A Dark and Difficult Chapter in the History of Johannine Christianity," in *The Gospel of John in Christian History. Essays for Interpreters*, Theological Inquiries (New York: Paulist, 1978), pp. 55-89

————, "Source Criticism and Religionsgeschichte in the Fourth Gospel," in *Jesus and Man's Hope, Vol. 1*, ed. D. G. Buttrick, A Perspective Book (Pittsburgh: Pittsburgh Theological Seminary, 1970), pp. 247-273

Marzotto, D., *L'unità degli uomini nel vangelo di Giovanni*, Supplementi alla *Revista Biblia* 9 (Brescia: Paideia, 1977)

Mattill, A. J., "Johannine Communities behind the Fourth Gospel: Georg Richter's Analysis," *TS* 38 (1977): 294-315

Maurer, C., "Der Exklusivanspruch des Christus nach dem Johannesevangelium," *StJn*, pp. 143-154

Mayer, R., "Israel, etc.," *DNTT* 2:304-323

McComiskey, T., "Israel ['Ιακώβ]," *DNTT* 2:316-319

McEleney, N. J., "Orthodoxy in Judaism of the First Christian Century," *JSJ* 4 (1973): 19-42

————, "Orthodoxy in Judaism of the First Christian Century. Replies to David E. Aune and Lester L. Grabbe," *JSJ* 9 (1978): 83-88

McGiffert, A. C., *A History of Christianity in the Apostolic Age*, International Theological Library (Edinburgh: Clark, 1897)

McNeil, B., "The Quotation at John XII 34," *NovT* 19 (1977): 22-33

Meagher, J. C., *The Way of the Word. The Beginning and the Establishing of Christian Understanding* (New York: Seabury, 1975)

Meeks, W. A., "'Am I a Jew?'": Johannine Christianity and Judaism,"
    CJG-RC 1:163-186

————, "The Divine Agent and His Counterfeit in Philo and the
    Fourth Gospel," in Aspects of Religious Propaganda in
    Judaism and Early Christianity, ed. E. S. Fiorenza, Univer-
    sity of Notre Dame Center for the Study of Judaism and Chris-
    tianity in Antiquity 2 (Notre Dame: University Press, 1976):
    43-67

————, "The Man From Heaven in Johannine Sectarianism," JBL
    91 (1972): 44-72

————, "Moses as God and King," in Religions in Antiquity. Es-
    says in Memory of Erwin Ramsdell Goodenough, ed. J. Neusner
    (Leiden: Brill, 1968), pp. 354-371

————, The Prophet-King. Moses Traditions and the Johannine
    Christology, NovTSup 14 (Leiden: Brill, 1967)

Metzger, B. M., A Textual Commentary on the Greek New Testament
    (London: United Bible Societies, 1971)

Meyer, P. W., "A Note on John 10:1-18," JBL 75 (1956): 232-235

Meyer, R., "περιτέμνω, κτλ.," TDNT 6:72-84

Michaelis, W., "ὁράω, κτλ.," TDNT 5:315-382

Michaels, J. R., "Alleged Anti-Semitism in the Fourth Gospel,"
    Gordon Review 11 (1968): 12-24

————, "Nathanael under the Fig Tree," ExpT 78 (1966): 182-183

Michel, O., "μισέω," TDNT 4:683-694

Miller, M. P., "Targum, Midrash and the Use of the Old Testament
    in the New Testament," JSJ 2 (1971): 29-82

Minear, P. S., "The Audience of the Fourth Gospel," Int 31
    (1977): 339-354

————, "The Beloved Disciple in the Gospel of John. Some Clues
    and Conjectures," NovT 19 (1977): 105-123

————, "The Idea of Incarnation in First John," Int 24 (1970):
    291-302

————, "'We don't know where . . .' John 20:2," Int 30 (1976):
    125-139

Miranda, Jose P., Being and the Messiah. The Message of St.
    John, tr. J. Eagleson (Maryknoll: Orbis, 1977)

Miranda, Juan P., Der Vater, der mich gesandt hat: Religions-
    geschichtliche Untersuchungen zu den johanneischen Sendungs-
    formeln, Zugleich ein Beitrag zur johanneischen Christologie
    und Ekklesiologie, Europäische Hochschulschriften Reihe 23,
    Band 7 (Bern: Land, 1972)

Moffatt, J., *An Introduction to the Literature of the New Testament*, 3d ed., International Theological Library (Edinburgh: Clark, 1918)

Mol, H. J., *Identity and the Sacred: A Sketch for a New Social-Scientific Theory of Religion*, (New York: Free Press, 1977)

Moloney, F. J., "From Cana to Cana (John 2:1-4:54) and the Fourth Evangelist's Concept of Correct (and Incorrect) Faith," *StBib*, pp. 184-213

————, *The Johannine Son of Man*, Biblioteca di scienza religiose 14 (Rome: Libreria Ateneo Salesiano, 1976)

Momigliano, A., *Alien Wisdom. The Limits of Hellenization* (Cambridge: University Press, 1976)

Moore, G. F., *Judaism in the First Centuries of the Christian Era, the Age of the Tannaim*, 3 Vols. (Cambridge, Mass.: Harvard, 1927-1930)

Morgan, R., "Fulfillment in the Fourth Gospel," *Int* 11 (1957): 155-165

Morgan-Wynne, J. E., "The Cross and the Revelation of Jesus as ἐγώ εἰμι in the Fourth Gospel (Joh. 8.28)," *StBib*, pp. 219-226

Morris, L., *The Gospel according to John. The English Text with Introduction, Exposition and Notes*, NICNT (Grand Rapids: Eerdmans, 1971)

————, *The New Testament and the Jewish Lectionaries* (London: Tyndale, 1964)

Moule, C. F. D., *The Birth of the New Testament* (London: Black, 1962)

————, "The Fulfilment Theme in the New Testament," *Journal of Theology for Southern Africa* 14 (1976): 6-16

————, "Fulfilment-Words in the New Testament: Use and Abuse," *NTS* 14 (1968): 293-320

————, "The Individualism of the Fourth Gospel," *NovT* 5 (1962): 171-190

————, The Intention of the Evangelists," in *New Testament Essays*, ed. A. J. B. Higgins (Manchester: University Press, 1959), pp. 165-179

————, "The Meaning of 'Life' in the Gospel and Epistles of St John. A Study in the Story of Lazarus, John 11:1-44," *Theology* 78 (1975): 114-125

————, "A Neglected Factor in the Interpretation of Johannine Eschatology," *StJn*, pp. 155-160

Mowinckel, S., *He That Cometh*, tr. G. W. Anderson (Oxford: Blackwell, 1956)

Moxnes, H., "Theology in Conflict. Studies in Paul's Understanding of God in Romans," Phd, Oslo, 1977

Müller, U. B., "Die Bedeutung des Kreuzestodes Jesu im Johannesevangelium Erwägungen zur Kreuzestheologie im Neuen Testament," *Kerygma und Dogma* 21 (1975): 49-71

————, *Die Geschichte der Christologie in der johanneischen Gemeinde*, Stuttgarter Bibelstudien 77 (Stuttgart: Katholisches Bibelwerk, 1975)

Mulder, H., "Ontstaan en Doel van het vierde Evangelist," *Gereformeerd Theologisch Tijdschrift* 69 (1969): 233-258

Mussner, F., *The Historical Jesus in the Gospel of St John*, tr. W. J. O'Hara, Quaestiones Disputatae 19 (New York: Herder and Herder, 1967)

————, "'Kultische' Aspeckte im Johanneischen Christusbild," in *Praesentia Salutis. Gesammelte Studien zu Fragen und Themen des Neuen Testament* (Düsseldorf: Patmos, 1967)

————, ΖΩΗ: *Die Anschauung vom 'Leben' im 4. Evangelium unter Berücksichtigung der Johannesbriefe. Ein Beitrag zur biblischen Theologie*, Münchener Theologische Studien 1/5 (Munich: Zink, 1952)

Neusner, J., "History and Purity in First-Century Judaism," *History of Religions* 18 (1978): 1-17

————, "The Idea of Purity in Ancient Judaism," *JAAR* 43 (1975): 15-26

————, "Judaism in a Time of Crisis. Four Responses to the Destruction of the Second Temple," *Judaism* 21 (1972): 313-327

Newman, B. M., "Some observations regarding the argument, structure, and literary characteristics of the Gospel of John," *TBT* 26 (1975): 234-239

Nixon, R. E., *The Exodus in the New Testament* (London: Tyndale, 1963)

O'Collins, G. C., "Anti-Semitism in the Gospel," *TS* 26 (1965): 663-666

Odeberg, H., *The Fourth Gospel Interpreted in Its Relation to Contemporaneous Religious Currents in Palestine and the Hellenistic-Oriental World* (Chicago: Argonaut, 1968)

————, "'Ιακώβ," *TDNT* 3:191-192

Oepke, A., "ἀπατάω, κτλ.," *TDNT* 1:384-385

O'Grady, J. F., *Individual and Community in John* (Rome: Pontifical Biblical Institute, 1978)

O'Grady, J. F., "Individual and Johannine Ecclesiology," *BTB*
5 (1975): 227-261

Olsson, B., *Structure and Meaning in the Fourth Gospel: A Text-
Linguistic Analysis of John 2:1-11 and 4:1-42*, Coniectanea
Biblica New Testament Series 6 (Lund: Gleerup, 1974)

O'Neill, J. C., "The Prologue to St. John's Gospel," *JTS* 20
(1969): 41-52

_____, *The Puzzle of 1 John. A New Examination of Origins*
(London: SPCK, 1966)

O'Rourke, J., "John's Fulfilment Texts," *Sciences Ecclésiastiques*
19 (1967): 433-443

Otzen, B., "Die neugefundenen hebräischen Sektenschriften und
die Testamente der zwölf Patriarchen," *ST* 7 (1953): 125-157

Overholt, T. W., *The Threat of Falsehood: A Study in the Theology of the Book of Jeremiah*, SBT 2/16 (London: SCM, 1970)

Pagels, E., *The Gnostic Gospels* (London: Weidenfeld and Nicolson,
1979)

————, *The Johannine Gospel in Gnostic Exegesis. Heracleon's
Commentary on John*, Society of Biblical Literature Monograph
Series 17 (Nashville: Abingdon, 1973)

Painter, J., "Christ and the Church in John 1,45-51," *EvJean*,
pp. 359-362

_____, "The Church and Israel in the Gospel of John: A Re-
sponse," *NTS* 25 (1978): 103-112

————, *John: Witness and Theologian* (London: SPCK, 1975)

Pancaro, S., *The Law in the Fourth Gospel. The Torah and the
Gospel, Moses and Jesus, Judaism and Christianity according
to John*, NovTSup 42 (Leiden: Brill, 1975)

————, "'People of God' in St John's Gospel?" *NTS* 16 (1970):
114-129

————, "The Relationship of the Church to Israel in the Gospel
of St. John," *NTS* 21 (1975): 396-405

Panikulam, G., *Koinōnia in the New Testament. A Dynamic Expression of Christian Life*, AnBib 85 (Rome: Pontifical Biblical
Institute, 1979)

Parkes, J., *The Conflict of the Church and the Synagogue. A
Study in the Origins of Antisemitism* (London: Soncino, 1934)

————, *Jesus, Paul and the Jews* (London: SCM, 1963)

Perego, A., "Verità e carità," *Divus Thomas* 67 (1964): 22-31

Pfitzner, V. C., "The Coronation of the King - Passion Narrative
and Passion Theology in the Gospel of St John," *Lutheran
Theological Journal* 10 (1976): 1-12

Phillips, G. L., "Faith and Vision in the Fourth Gospel," in
Studies in the Fourth Gospel, ed. F. L. Cross (London: Mowbrays, 1957), pp. 83-96

Pinto de Oliveira, C.-J., "Le verbe *Didōnai* comme expression des
rapports du Père et du Fils dans le IVe évangile," *Revue des
Sciences Philosophiques et Théologiques* 49 (1965): 81-104

Piper, A., "Unchanging Promises. Exodus in the New Testament,"
Int 11 (1957): 3-22

Pollard, T. E., "The Father-Son and God-Believer Relationships
according to St. John: A Brief Study," *EvJean*, pp. 363-369

de la Potterie, I., "L'arrière-fond du thème johannique de
vérité," *SE* 1:277-294

————, "La notion de 'commencement' dans les écrits johanniques," in *Die Kirche des Angangs. Für Heinz Schürmann*,
eds. R. Schnackenburg, J. Ernst, and J. Wanke (Freiburg:
Herder, 1978), pp. 379-403

————, "L'onction du chrétien pour la foi," *Bib* 40 (1959): 12-
69

————, "'Le péché, c'est l'iniquité' (I Jn III:4)," *NRT* 78
(1956): 785-797

————, *La vérité dans Saint Jean*, 2 Vols., AnBib 73,74 (Rome:
Pontifical Biblical Institute, 1977)

————, "Χάρις paulinienne et χάρις johannique," in *Jesus und
Paulus. Festschrift für Werner Georg Kümmel zum 70. Geburtstag*, eds. E. E. Ellis and E. Grässer (Göttingen: Vandenhoeck
and Ruprecht, 1975), pp. 256-282

du Preez, J., "'Sperma autou' in 1 John 3:9," *Neotestamentica*
9 (1975): 105-112

Price, J. L., "Light from Qumran upon Some Aspects of Johannine
Theology," *JQ*, pp. 9-37

————, "The Search for the Theology of the Fourth Evangelist,"
JAAR 35 (1967): 3-15

Quelle, G., Bertram, G., Stahlin, G., Grundmann, W., "ἁμαρτάνω,
κτλ.," *TDNT* 1:267-316

von Rad, G., Bertram, G., Bultmann, R., "ζάω, κτλ.," *TDNT*
2:832-875

Ramm, B., "The Apologetic of the Old Testament: The Basis of a
Biblical and Christian Apologetic," *BETS* 1 (1958): 15-20

Ramsey, A. M., *The Glory of God and the Transfiguration of Christ* (London: Longmans, Green, 1949)

Reim, G., *Studien zum Alttestamentlichen Hintergrund des Johannesevangelium*, NTSMS 22 (Cambridge: University Press, 1974)

Richardson, P., *Israel in the Apostolic Church*, NTSMS 10 (Cambridge, University Press, 1969)

Richter, G., "Die Fleischwerdung des Logos im Johannesevangelium," *NovT* 13 (1971): 81-126; 14 (1972): 257-276

————, "Präsentische und futurische Eschatologie im 4. Evangelium," in *Gegenwart und kommendes Reich. Schülergabe Anton Vögtle zum 65. Geburtstag*, eds. P. Fiedler and D. Zeller (Stuttgart: Katholisches, Bibelwerk, 1975), pp. 117-152

Riga, P., "Signs of Glory. The Use of 'Sēmeion' in St. John's Gospel," *Int* 17 (1963): 402-424

Rigaux, B., "Les destinataires du IVᵉ évangile à la lumière de Jn 17," *Revue Théologique de Louvain* 1 (1970): 289-319

Rivkin, E., *A Hidden Revolution. The Pharisees' Search for the Kingdom Within* (Nashville: Abingdon, 1978)

Robinson, J. A. T., "The Destination and Purpose of St. John's Gospel," *TNTS*, pp. 107-125

————, "The Destination and Purpose of the Johannine Epistles," *TNTS*, pp. 126-138

————, "Elijah, John and Jesus, An Essay in Detection," *TNTS*, pp. 28-52

————, "The New Look on the Fourth Gospel," *TNTS*, pp. 94-106

————, "The Parable of the Shepherd (John 10.1-5)," *TNTS*, pp. 67-75

————, *Redating the New Testament* (London: SCM, 1976)

————, "The Relation of the Prologue to the Gospel of St John," *NTS* 9 (1963): 120-129

Rowland, C., "The Visions of God in Apocalyptic Literature," *JSJ* 10 (1979): 137-154

Ruether, R. R., *Faith and Fratricide: The Theological Roots of Anti-Semitism* (New York: Seabury, 1974)

Rusche, H., "Der neue Exodus (Hinweise zur Interpretation des Johannesevangeliums)," *Bibel und Kirche* 14 (1959): 74-76

Russell, J. B., *The Devil. Perceptions of Evil from Antiquity to Primitive Christianity* (Ithica: Cornell, 1977)

Ryrie, C. C., "Apostasy in the Church," *BS* 121 (1964): 44-53

Sahlin, H., *Zur Typologie des Johannesevangeliums*, Uppsala Universitets Årsskrift 1950:4 (Uppsala: Lundequistaska, 1950)

Salom, A. P., "Some Aspects of the Grammatical Style of 1 John," *JBL* 74 (1955): 96-102

Sand, A., "'Wie geschrieben steht . . .' Zur Auslegung der jüdischen Schriften in den urchristlichen Gemeinden," in *Schriftauslegung. Beiträge zur Hermeneutik des Neuen Testamentes und im Neuen Testament*, ed. J. Ernst (Munich: Schöningh, 1972), pp. 331-357

Sanders, J., "Hermeneutics of True and False Prophecy," in *Canon and Authority. Essays in Old Testament Religion and Theology*, eds. G. W. Coats and B. O. Long (Philadelphia: Fortress, 1977), pp. 21-41

Sanders, J. N., *The Fourth Gospel in the Early Church: Its Origin and Influence on Christian Theology up to Irenaeus* (Cambridge: University Press, 1943)

Sandmel, S., *Anti-Semitism in the New Testament?* (Philadelphia: Fortress, 1978)

Sasse, H., "κοσμέω, κτλ.," *TDNT* 3:867-898

de Satgé, J., "The Human Integrity of St John's Jesus," *StBib*, pp. 75-78

Schäfer, P., "Die sogenannte Synode von Jabne. Zur Trennung von Juden und Christen im ersten/zweiten Jh. n. Chr.," *Jud* 31 (1975): 54-64, 116-124

Schein, B. E., "Our Father Abraham," PhD, Yale, 1972

Schelkle, K., "John's Theology of Man and the World," *ComJn*, pp. 127-140

Schnackenburg, R., *The Gospel according to St John, Vol. 1*, tr. K. Smyth (London: Burns and Oates, 1968)

————, "Joh 12,39-41 Zur christologischen Schriftauslegung des vierten Evangelisten," in *Neues Testament und Geschichte. Historisches Geschehen und Deutung im Neuen Testament. Oscar Cullmann zum 70. Geburtstag*, eds. H. Baltensweiler and B. Reicke (Zürich: Theologischer, 1972), pp. 167-177

————, *Die Johannesbriefe*, 5th ed., HTKNT 13/3 (Freiburg: Herder, 1975)

————, *Das Johannesevangelium, II Teil*, HTKNT 4/2 (Freiburg: Herder, 1971)

————, *Das Johannesevangelium, III Teil*, HTKNT 4/3 (Freiburg: Herder, 1975)

Schnackenburg, R., "Das Messiasfrage im Johannesevangelium," in
*Neutestamentliche Aufsätze. Festschrift für Prof. Josef
Schmid zum 70. Geburtstag*, eds. J. Blinzler, O. Kuss, and
F. Mussner (Regensburg: Pustet, 1963), pp. 240-264

————, "On the Origin of the Fourth Gospel," in *Jesus and Man's
Hope, Vol. 1*, ed. D. G. Buttrick, A Perspective Book (Pittsburgh: Pittsburgh Theological Seminary, 1970), pp. 223-246

Schneider, C., "Ursprung und Ursachen der christlichen Intoler-
anz," *ZRGG* 30 (1978): 193-218

Schneider, J., "ἔρχομαι, κτλ.," *TDNT* 2:666-684

Scholer, D. M., "Sins Within and Sins Without: An Interpretation
of 1 John 5:16-17," in *Current Issues in Biblical and Patristic Interpretation. Studies in Honor of Merrill C. Tenny
Presented by his Former Students*, ed. G. Hawthorne (Grand
Rapids: Eerdmans, 1975), pp. 230-246

Schottroff, L., *Der Glaubende und die feindliche Welt. Beobach-
tungen zum gnostischen Dualismus und seiner Bedeutung für
Paulus und das Johannesevangelium*, WMANT 37 (Neukirchen-
Vluyn: Neukirchen, 1970)

Schrenk, G., Quell, G., "πατήρ, κτλ.," *TDNT* 5:945-1022

Schürer, E., *The History of the Jewish People in the Age of
Jesus Christ (175 B.C. - A.D. 135)*, eds. G. Vermes, F.
Millar, and M. Black, rev. ed., 2 Vols. (Edinburgh: Clark,
1973, 1979)

Schürmann, H., "Joh. 6,51c - ein Schlüssel zur johanneischen
Brotrede," *BZ* 2 (1958): 244-262

Schweizer, E., *Church Order in the New Testament*, tr. F. Clarke,
SBT 32 (London: SMC, 1961)

————, "The concept of the church in the gospel and epistles of
St. John," in *New Testament Essays. Studies in Memory of
Thomas Walter Manson, 1893-1958*, ed. A. J. B. Higgins (Man-
chester: University Press, 1959), pp. 230-245

————, *Ego Eimi. Die religionsgeschichtliche Herkunft und
theologische Bedeutung der johanneischen Bildreden, zugleich
ein Beitrag zur Quellenfrage des vierten Evangeliums*, 2d ed.,
Forschungen zur Religion und Literatur des Alten und Neuen
Testaments 38/56 (Göttingen: Vandenhoeck and Ruprecht, 1965)

Scott, E. F., *The Apologetic of the New Testament*, Crown Theological Library 22 (London: Williams and Norgate, 1907)

————, *The Fourth Gospel: Its Purpose and Theology*, 2d ed.
(Edinburgh: Clark, 1908)

————, *The Spirit in the New Testament* (London: Hodder and
Stoughton, 1923)

Scroggs, R., "The Earliest Christian Communities as Sectarian
    Movement," *CJR-RC* 2:1-23

Seebass, H., "'Αβραάμ," *DNTT* 1:76-80

————, Brown, C., "Moses," *DNTT* 2:635-643

Segal, A. F., *Two Powers* in Heaven. *Early Rabbinic Reports about
    Christianity and Gnosticism*, Studies in Judaism and Late
    Antiquity 25 (Leiden: Brill, 1977)

Sevenster, J. N., *The Roots of Pagan Anti-Semitism in the An-
    cient World*, NovTSup 41 (Leiden: Brill, 1975)

Shepherd, M. H., "The First Letter of John," in *The Interpreter's
    One-Volume Commentary on the Bible*, ed. C. M. Laymon (New
    York: Abingdon, 1971), pp. 935-939

————, "The Jews in the Gospel of John. Another Level of
    Meaning," *ATR Supplement Series 3* (1974): 95-112

Sikes, W. W., "The Anti-Semitism of the Fourth Gospel," *JR* 21
    (1941): 23-30

Simonis, A. J., *Die Hirtenrede im Johannes-evangelium. Versuch
    einer Analyse von Johannes 10.1-18 nach Entstehung, Hinter-
    grund und Inhalt*, AnBib 29 (Rome: Pontifical Biblical Insti-
    tute, 1967)

Smalley, S. S., "Diversity and Development in John," *NTS* 17
    (1971): 276-292

————, *John: Evangelist and Interpreter* (Exeter: Paternoster,
    1978)

Smith, D. M., "Johannine Christianity: Some Reflections on its
    Character and Delineation," *NTS* 21 (1975): 222-248

————, *John*, Proclamation Commentaries (Philadelphia: Fortress,
    1976)

————, "The Use of the Old Testament in the New," in *The Use
    of the Old Testament in the New and Other Essays. Studies
    in Honor of William Franklin Stinespring*, ed. J. M. Efird
    (Durham, N.C.: Duke University, 1972), pp. 3-65

Smith, M., *Jesus the Magician* (London: Gollancz, 1978)

Smith, R. H., "Exodus Typology in the Fourth Gospel," *JBL* 81
    (1962): 329-342

Songer, H. S., "The Life Situation of the Johannine Epistles,"
    RevExp 67 (1970): 399-409

Sproston, W. E., "Satan in the Fourth Gospel," *StBib*, pp. 307-311

Stagg, F., "Orthodoxy and Orthopraxy in the Johannine Epistles,"
    RevExp 67 (1970): 423-432

Stanley, D. M., "Authority in the Church: A New Testament Reality," *CBQ* 29 (1967): 555-573

Stauffer, E., "Agnostos Christos: Joh. ii.24 und die Eschatologie
des vierten Evangeliums," in *The Background of the New Testament and Its Eschatology*, eds. W. D. Davies and D. Daube
(Cambridge: University Press, 1956), pp. 281-299

Stemberger, G., *La symbolique du bien et du mal selon saint Jean*
(Paris: Seuil, 1970)

Stevens, G. B., *The Johannine Theology. A Study of the Doctrinal
Contents of the Gospel and Epistles of the Apostle John*
(London: Dickinson, 1894)

Strack, H. L., *Jesus die Häretiker und die Christen nach den
ältesten jüdischen Angaben. Texte, Übersetzung und Erläu-
terungen* (Leipzig: Hinrichs, 1910)

Sturch, R. L., "The πατρίς of Jesus," *JTS* 28 (1977): 94-96

Swete, H. B., *An Introduction to the Old Testament in Greek*,
2d ed. (Cambridge: University Press, 1902)

Talbert, C. H., "Artistry and Theology: An Analysis of the
Architecture of Jn 1,19-5,47," *CBQ* 32 (1970): 341-366

Tasker, R. V. G., *The Old Testament in the New Testament*, 2d
ed. (Grand Rapids: Eerdmans, 1954)

Tavard, G. H., "Christianity and Israel: How did Christ Fulfill
the Law?" *DowR* 75 (1957): 55-68

Teeple, H. M., *The Mosaic Eschatological Prophet*, *JBL* Monograph
10 (Philadelphia: Society of Biblical Literature, 1957)

Thomas, R. W., "The Meaning of the Terms 'Life' and 'Death' in
the Fourth Gospel and in Paul," *SJT* 21 (1968): 199-212

Thomson, J. G. S. S., "The Shepherd-Ruler Concept in the Old
Testament and its Application in the New Testament," *SJT*
8 (1955): 406-418

Thüsing, W., *Die Erhöhung und Verherrlichung Jesu im Johannesevangelium*, 2d ed., NTAbh 21, 1/2 (Munich: Aschendorffsche,
1970)

Trites, A. A., *The New Testament Concept of Witness*, NTSMS 31
(Cambridge: University Press, 1977)

Trudinger, P., "Concerning Sins, Mortal and Otherwise. A Note on
1 John 5,16-17," *Bib* 52 (1972): 541-542

————, "The Meaning of 'Life' in St. John. Some Further Reflections," *BTB* 6 (1976): 258-263

Turner, H. E. W., *The Pattern of Christian Truth. A Study in the
Relations between Orthodoxy and Heresy in the Early Church*
(London: Mowbray, 1954)

Turner, N., *Grammatical Insights into the New Testament* (Edinburgh: Clark, 1965)

van Unnik, W. C., "A Greek characteristic of prophecy in the
Fourth Gospel," *Text*, pp. 211-229

————, "Jesus: Anathema or Kyrios (1 Cor. 12.3)," in *Christ and
Spirit in the New Testament*, eds. B. Lindars and S. S. Smalley (Cambridge: University Press, 1973), pp. 113-126

————, "The Purpose of St John's Gospel," *SE* 1:382-411

————, "The Quotation from the Old Testament in John 12:34,"
NovT 3 (1959): 174-179

Untergassmair, F. G., *Im Namen Jesu. Der Namensbegriff im Johannesevangelium. Eine exegetisch-religionsgeschichtliche
Studie zu den johanneischen Namensaussagen*, 2d ed., Forschung
zur Bibel 13 (Stuttgart: Katholisches Bibelwerk, 1977)

Vanderlip, D. G., *Christianity according to John* (Philadelphia:
Westminster, 1975)

Vellanickal, M., *The Divine Sonship of Christians in the Johannine Writings*, AnBib 72 (Rome: Pontifical Biblical Institute,
1977)

Vielhauer, P., *Geschichte der urchristlichen Literatur. Ein-
leitung in das Neue Testament, die Apokryphen und die Apo-
stolischen Väter* (Berlin: de Gruyter, 1975)

Vorster, W. S., "Heterodoxy in 1 John," *Neotestamentica* 9 (1975):
87-97

Vriezen, T. C., Lohse, E., Georgi, D., Conzelmann, H., Althaus,
P., "Ewiges Leben," *RGG* 2:799-809

van der Waal, C., "The Gospel according to John and the Old
Testament," *Neotestamentica* 6 (1972): 28-47

von Wahlde, U. C., "The Terms for Religious Authorities in the
Fourth Gospel: A Key to Literary Strata?" *JBL* 98 (1979):
231-253

Walter, L., *L'incroyance des croyants selon saint Jean*, Lire la
Bible 43 (Paris: Cerf, 1976)

Wead, D. W., *The Literary Devices in John's Gospel*, Theologischen
Dissertationen 4 (Basil: Reinhardt, 1970)

————, "We have a Law," *NovT* 11 (1969): 185-189

Weir, J. E., "The Identity of the Logos in the First Epistle of
John," *Expt* 86 (1975): 118-120

Weisengoff, J. P., "Light and Its Relation to Life in Saint
John," *CBQ* 8 (1946): 448-451

Weiss, K., "Die 'Gnosis' im Hintergrund und im Spiegel der
Johannesbriefe," in *Gnosis und Neues Testament. Studien aus
Religionswissenschaft und Theologie*, ed. K.-W. Tröger (Berlin:
Evangelische, 1973), pp. 341-356

Weiss, K., "Orthodoxie und Heterodoxie im 1 Johannesbrief," *ZNW*
58 (1967): 247-255

Wengst, K., *Der erste, zweite und dritte Brief des Johannes*,
Ökumenischer Taschenbuchkommentar zum Neuen Testament 16
(Gütersloh: Mohn, 1978)

—————, *Häresie und Orthodoxie im Spiegel des ersten Johannes-*
briefes (Gütersloh: Mohn, 1976)

Westcott, A., "The Divisions of the First Epistle of St. John.
Correspondence between Drs. Westcott and Hort," *Expositor*
3 (1907): 481-493

Westcott, B. F., *The Gospel according to St. John, The Greek*
Text with Introduction and Notes, 2 Vols. (London: Murray,
1908)

—————, *The Revelation of the Father: Short Lectures on the*
Titles of the Lord in the Gospel of St John (London: Murray,
1884)

Wiefel, W., "Die Scheidung von Gemeinde und Welt im Johannesevangelium auf dem Hintergrund der Trennung von Kirche und
Synagoge," *TZ* 35 (1979): 213-227

Wilcox, M., "On investigating the use of the Old Testament in
the New Testament," *Text*, pp. 231-243

Wiles, M. F., "The Old Testament in Controversy with the Jews,"
SJT 8 (1955): 113-126

Wilkens, W., *Die Entstehungsgeschichte des vierten Evangeliums*
(Zollikon: Evangelischer, 1958)

—————, *Zeichen und Werke: Ein Beitrag zur Theologie des 4.*
Evangeliums in Erzählungsung Redestoff, ATANT 55 (Zürich:
Zwingli, 1969)

Williams, J. T., "Cultic Elements in the Fourth Gospel," *StBib*,
pp. 339-350

Wilson, R. McL., *Gnosis and the New Testament* (Oxford: Blackwell,
1968)

Wilson, S., "Anti-Judaism in the Fourth Gospel? Some Considerations," *Irish Biblical Studies* 1 (1979): 28-50

Wilson, W., *An Illustration of the Method of Explaining the New*
Testament by the Early Opinions of Jews and Christians Con-
cerning Christ, rev. ed. (Cambridge: Parker, 1838)

Wind, A., "Destination and Purpose of the Gospel of John," *NovT*
14 (1972): 26-69

Windisch, H., *Die Katholischen Briefe*, rev. H. Preisker, HNT 15
(Tübingen: Mohr-Siebeck, 1951)

Wink, W., *John the Baptist in the Gospel Tradition*, NTSMS 7
    (Cambridge: University Press, 1968)

Wood, A. S., "Unity and Schism: Determinative Biblical Princi-
    ples," *Theological Students Fellowship Bulletin* 67 (1973):
    9-15; 68 (1974): 1-6

Wood, J. E., "Isaac Typology in the New Testament," *NTS* 14
    (1968): 583-589

Wright, G. E., *God Who Acts. Biblical Theology as Recital*,
    SBT 8 (London: SCM, 1952)

Wülfing von Martitz, P., Fohrer, G., Schweizer, E., Lohse, E.,
    Schneemelcher, W., "υἱός, υἱοθεσία," *TDNT* 8:334-399

Wurm, A., *Die Irrlehrer im ersten Johannesbrief*, BSt 8/1 (Frei-
    burg: Herder, 1903)

Yamauchi, E. M., "The Descent of Ishtar, the Fall of Sophia, and
    the Jewish Roots of Gnosticism," *Tyndale Bulletin* 29 (1978):
    143-175

Yates, R., "The Antichrist," *EvQ* 46 (1974): 42-50

Young, F. W., "A Study of the Relation of Isaiah to the Fourth
    Gospel," *ZNW* 64 (1955): 215-232

Ziener, G., "Weisheitsbuch und Johannesevangelium," *Bib* 38
    (1957): 396-418; 39 (1958): 37-60

INDEX OF AUTHORS

Yamauchi, E. M., n.251.
Young, F. W., n.111.

Ziener, G., n.98, n.134.

INDEX OF BIBLICAL REFERENCES